JUNE MICKLE

*One Woman's Life in the Foothills and
Mountains of Western Canada*

by Kathy Calvert

RMB

RMB | Rocky Mountain Books Ltd.
rmbooks.com
@rmbooks
facebook.com/rmbooks

Cataloguing data available from Library and Archives Canada
ISBN 978-1-77160-148-1 (pbk.)
Also available in electronic formats

Printed and bound in Canada by Marquis

Distributed in Canada by Heritage Group Distribution
and in the U.S. by Publishers Group West

For information on purchasing bulk quantities of this book, or to
obtain media excerpts or invite the author to speak at an event,
please visit rmbooks.com and select the "Contact Us" tab.

RMB | Rocky Mountain Books is dedicated to the environment and
committed to reducing the destruction of old-growth forests. Our books are
produced with respect for the future and consideration for the past.

We acknowledge the financial support of the Government of Canada through the Canada
Book Fund and the Canada Council for the Arts, and of the province of British Columbia
through the British Columbia Arts Council and the Book Publishing Tax Credit.

Nous reconnaissons l'aide financière du gouvernement du Canada par
l'entremise du Fonds du livre du Canada et le Conseil des arts du Canada,
et de la province de la Colombie-Britannique par le Conseil des arts de la
Colombie-Britannique et le Crédit d'impôt pour l'édition de livres.

Contents

	ACKNOWLEDGMENTS	ix
Chapter I	GOING HOME	1
Chapter II	THE CITY LIFE	22
Chapter III	BACK TO THE LAND	33
Chapter IV	"I'M GOIN' TO MARRY YOU"	75
Chapter V	EARLY YEARS ON THE MICKLE HOMESTEAD	107
Chapter VI	A SHORT MOVE	143
Chapter VII	MILLARVILLE	160
Chapter VIII	AN IRRESISTIBLE OFFER	175
Chapter IX	EXPANSION AND CHANGES	217
Chapter X	MARRIAGES AND MOVES	253
Chapter XI	THREE DEATHS	289
Chapter XII	JUNE'S STRENGTH	309
	EPILOGUE	335

Acknowledgments

This book would not have been possible without the stories and diaries June kept all her life. But I wish to thank her most of all for all the time she dedicated to personal interviews and constant questions. Her life was truly remarkable.

I also wish to thank Don and Grace Mickle for adding so immensely to the story. In particular, I wish to thank Don for the hours he spent reviewing facts and supplying the information on the family. My thanks also extend to his niece Debbie Smith who helped by providing some of the early history of the Mickles and the Hamiltons.

This book was brought to life with the accounts and insights from family and friends, especially Louie Kohler, Perry Jacobson, Janey Peterson and Billy Monroe. Thanks for the memories.

I especially wish to thank the editors of this book, who managed to make the original prose so much more readable. Their clarity and direction are truly appreciated.

Finally I would like to thank my husband Dale Portman whose help and unwavering support was so necessary to see the project completed. Writing a book is truly a collaborative effort.

Chapter I

GOING HOME

On a dark day a young woman, advanced in pregnancy, wandered precariously close to the slippery tide pools of the Pacific Ocean that defined the western extent of Vancouver. But she was too deep in thought to pay much attention to where she walked, despite the possible danger of a fall. The baby could come any time, but where she would eventually live and raise it was not yet fully decided in her mind.

A year earlier, Clara Hamilton Roughton had married an attractive young soldier with an irresistible smile and an easy laugh. They had met on a double date that her sister Lulu had arranged with Basil Roughton's brother Alan. They were taking in an early evening show and decided to walk to the theatre to allow the two brothers, who had just returned from the war, to absorb the night-life of downtown Calgary, such as it was in 1919. Lulu had originally arranged for Clara to accompany Allan, but Basil impulsively scattered that plan when he ran ahead and grabbed Clara by the arm, determined to sit next to her during the show. Clara was so distracted by this

CLARA HAMILTON (1919)

exciting young soldier that she remembered very little of what was playing. Years later, she realized they had fallen in love that night.

Basil Roughton's family was of English descent and had settled in Calgary in the late 1800s. Basil was one of seven brothers, five of whom enlisted as soldiers in the 10th and 31st Canadian Infantry Battalions, CEF. Clifford and Basil were the youngest and served together in the 10th Battalion. They were exceptionally fit young men, and the recruiters did not look too closely when they both claimed to be eighteen. Clifford just met this qualification, but Basil had lied; he was only seventeen. The Roughton family was exceptionally fortunate in losing only one son during those devastating years, but the ultimate horror was borne by Basil, who saw Clifford blown to pieces while fighting at his side. While Basil choked down the loss of his brother and several close friends, he was awarded the rank of Sergeant Major, along with six medals for bravery. Doubtless Basil had earned these honours, but in that war, the rewards seemed given largely for survival.

Though Basil returned with the Dogs of War snapping at his heels, he found great joy in his immediate marriage to Clara. They enjoyed a rare happiness in their marriage, which deepened at news of her pregnancy. It was only marred by a sadness that would unexpectedly creep over him. It was not something he could talk about with anyone who had not experienced the horrors of the war. A famous British soldier frequently sent dispatches home from the front, trying to describe the appalling conditions soldiers were expected to endure.

BASIL ROUGHTON IN UNIFORM (1919)

Geoffrey Winthrop-Young wrote: "The stories of madness are frequent. This was a monstrous inversion of civilization. To call it war was to imply something of the sun remained … "[1]

The common denominator of these soul-blasted survivors was their inability to convey, even remotely, to those who had not experienced such horrors, what they had lived through. Most buried it deep in their minds and lived with any relief that peace brought.

To all who knew him, Basil succeeded in this, finding the greatest joy in his love for Clara. But their union did not survive even one year. If Basil Roughton had cheated death during a time of war, he was not so lucky under the peaceful skies of western Alberta.

It was a beautiful fall day when Basil joined his brother-in-law Jappy Rogers to go bird hunting near Okotoks. As Basil kissed Clara, who was drowsy with sleep, he whispered a short endearment and promised a pheasant for supper. Clara woke enough to reply, "I know you are a very good hunter and an expert shot, but they need to hang a few days before the pot sees them. I'll whip up something good for supper – keep me busy." She drifted to sleep under the covers, planning his favorite meal of pork chops and applesauce and perhaps a pie for dessert.

The early fall sun was streaming through the window when the phone rang. The call from a close friend in Okotoks was as sudden and unexpected as a fire bolt in the

---

1 Wade Davis, *Into the Silence: The Great War, Mallory, and the Conquest of Everest*, New York: Vintage eBook, 2013.

sky. Basil had been shot in a hunting accident. His death was instantaneous. Clara could not move; paralyzed with grief alternating with disbelief, she slumped to the floor. She could not remember how long it took for people to arrive for support and with sketchy confirmation of the accident.

BASIL BEFORE THE WAR

Newspaper coverage reported that a loaded gun barrel had gone off, shooting Basil through the heart while he was trying to dispatch a wounded bird with the gunstock. It was difficult to imagine how a seasoned soldier could have fatally pointed the barrel at his chest while attempting to knock a bird senseless. One of Basil's jobs had been training other soldiers in gun safety. But alternative explanations were much more difficult to live with. Apart from suicide (not seriously considered by anyone at the time), the only other possible explanation was that he'd been accidentally shot by another member of the party. Testimony and logistics ruled this out, however, and his death was accepted as an accident.

As the dark day near the tide pools grew colder, Clara reluctantly returned to her brother-in-law's house, expecting to be confronted yet again over what she intended to do with the baby. At her sister-in-law's insistence, she had moved out there shortly after Basil's death. Although her own brothers farmed near Calgary, life with them would have been very hard for a young expectant mother. It was difficult enough to deal with her pregnancy, as well as her unshakable grief, without taking on the strenuous housekeeping chores that went with managing a farm for three men. The time spent with her in-laws gave her some respite, but she soon had to decide where she would make her home.

As she entered the spacious foyer, her sister-in-law immediately met her. "Well, Clara, did the walk help?"

She replied, "I know you want an answer, but what you ask is beyond me right now!"

"I don't mean to press, but the baby is coming, and you know you can't provide a home as a single mother. What will you do? You can't work and raise a baby in all fairness to the child. Single parenting is simply not realistic."

"Oh, for heaven's sake, lots of families lose fathers and husbands. The rest of the family just chips in, that's all!"

Her sister-in-law had frequently suggested that she and her husband adopt the child for its own good and have Clara live on as mother/caretaker. Clara was not sure what role they really wanted for her.

"Of course!" the matron replied. "What do you think? It's what we wish to do!"

"You want to adopt the child as your own. You're asking me to relinquish my obligations as a mother!"

Clara was now more agitated than ever. It was unconscionable, though she knew that her baby would probably have a secure future in a well-established family, which was something she could not guarantee at that time. But the thought of giving up her baby, now the dearest link to her lost husband, was intolerable.

Her walks by the ocean had given her much-needed time to reflect on her options. She did have her own family in the Calgary area and had only gone to Vancouver because of the generous offer from her in-laws. She could truly understand the desire they had to be close to her baby (and presumably, her as well), but she missed her siblings.

The Hamiltons were a well-established Alberta family. Along with his brothers, in the late 1880s, Robert Hamilton,

Clara's father, had moved from interior British Columbia to Calgary, where he married and had five children. The three boys and her sister Lulu, now married to Jappy Rogers, still lived there although her parents had passed away.

That night, after the conversation with her sister-in-law, she wrote to her brothers asking for advice. As the child's birth approached, the slowness of the mail service added to her growing anxiety, but she could not give her answer until she had heard from them. The Hamilton boys (John, Bob, and Fred) were loving brothers who were very dear to her, but her proposal of moving out to the farm to keep house with a new baby might not sit well with them. They were bachelors who had been living on their own since before her marriage and had adjusted to their own lifestyle. Adding a woman and baby to the mix would require some modifications.

Despite any apprehension, the unanimous reply came back as the month of June blossomed through the seemingly perpetual gloom of the winter rains. Bob, the oldest, spoke for all of them with no hesitation. They welcomed the idea of her moving home and emphatically refused to entertain the idea she give up the baby. The work would be hard – twice the work of being a wife to one man. It meant taking on the laundry, cleaning, and cooking for two grown men. There would have been three except that Fred, who was crippled from polio, did not actually live on the farm – but he would visit enough for her daughter to feel she had three devoted fathers.

Clara was delirious with excitement and marveled at how much she missed the blue open skies of the prairies after dreary months of rain. Vancouver was beautiful when the sun shone, but that was all too infrequent as far as she was concerned. The day she made her choice, however, the sun was shining, somehow giving consent to the happiness she felt in resolving her issues. Best of all, she knew that Basil had loved the prairies and the mountains of Alberta, and in her heart she knew bringing up young June in the country he loved was right. Clara's daughter was born on June 29, 1920, at Vancouver General Hospital. She was named June, after the month that had brought Clara such joy.

It was difficult to let her sister-in-law know her decision.

"I can't give up my baby no matter what you offer," Clara informed her sister-in-law. "She will have a good home, and I think it will give her a future with freedom she won't see in this city." It was all she could think of in defense of this position, but as she verbalized this thought, she could feel the freedom of the prairies blessed by the strong winds that drove the clouds through the open sky.

Clara's belief that it would be a hard life on the prairie farm was not dispelled. The farm was located in the bleak Balzac country just north and east of the embryonic city of Calgary, an unsophisticated town, which in the 1920s mirrored the essence of western life in all its limited glory.

The work was labor intensive. The laundry was all done by hand. The water for the laundry had to be hauled from a well (often distant) and heated on a wood stove that was fueled by wood chopped by hand. Everything was heated on the wood stove, which was unrelentingly ravenous for an endless supply of wood even in summer when the daytime heat soared. The tasks of keeping food in the belly, clean clothes on everyone's back, and a spotless house never ended. Then there was the garden: planting, watering, hoeing and finally harvesting. Clara often thought she would faint from the heat radiating from the blistering summer sun. But she still preferred the hot skies of home to the cool rains of Vancouver any day of the week.

It was a chore to keep June clean and free of heat rash in the stifling, airless farmhouse. When the suns of July and August seared in the sky, devoid of the smallest breeze, the only cool place was in the icehouse. There was not even a pond nearby to swim in to relieve the daily heat.

Despite the heat, the chores of summer were pleasant compared to the drudgery of winter. Everything was much harder to cope with when the temperature plunged to minus 50°F and the wind blew endlessly across the unhindering plains. Washing was a nightmare when nothing could be hung out to dry. Just melting enough water from ice meant keeping enough of this precious commodity on hand was an endless chore. They were also fairly isolated, and long winter days were passed in close quarters. They all had to learn to coexist and not invade personal spaces or overly tax relationships when boredom became a trial. June got through the winters fairly well as she was too young to be affected by simmering family tensions. Her uncles, particularly Fred, were very good to her, and she did not want for attention.

Clara did not toil alone in her Sisyphean duties. Her brothers worked equally hard in running the farm. They had cows to milk, horses to tend, and acres of land that lay fallow in the spring, rested and ready for a summer of ploughing and planting and reaping. This would supply grain or hay for the following year, depending on the crop. Every step was laborious without the aid of modern farm machinery.

All new fields had to cleared by hand. Trees were felled with an axe, leaving the deep taproot of the stump to be burned and pulled from the bone of the earth. Once the bush was gone, the rocks that had surfaced and kept resurfacing were removed one by one – probably the most backbreaking work of all. The horses were hitched to a stout, barge-like skid, commonly referred to as a stone-boat, which was dragged slowly over the field while the workers tossed the rocks on board. They stopped frequently when a particularly large boulder required several people to haul it onto the boat. Before it got too heavy for the horses to pull, the load was hauled off to the side and dumped where the rocks might be used in further construction projects. This was repeated, over and over, until the land was ready for cultivation.

The biggest change for the family during this period was the move, when June was two, to Midnapore, a small town south of Calgary. An uncle of Clara and her brothers, Johnny Hamilton, bought a farm there and moved the whole family into the new home. Now they were all together under one roof, which brought a significant improvement to their social life. They were nearer to other farmers and ranchers, and Saturday nights were all the livelier. Uncle Johnny had a piano that he'd inherited from his mother, and Clara proved to be an apt player. Friends and family gathered around this rare bit of culture for an evening of song and dance as often as they could. This event was always complemented with good food and home-brewed berry wine. Later the cards would come out to pass the long evening playing poker. As the coal-oil lanterns flickered, the homesteaders proved they had the partying stamina of politicians, and rarely did an evening end much before early morning.

Clara came from hardy, adventurous stock. The Hamilton brothers (Robert, George, and James) were pioneers who had sailed from New Brunswick around Cape Horn with a sense of purpose, hoping to arrive before the gold rush in California was over. They missed the opportunity to stake an early claim there, so they continued on to the next major gold strike in the Cariboo gold fields of British Columbia. Even this formidably remote place was staked out by the time they arrived. It was becoming apparent that the only way to get in on the riches was to find other ways of reaping the benefits of the boom while the gold was being dug out of the ground. Other opportunities to harvest the gold were there if imagination, hard work, and daring were employed.

Johnny Hamilton had not gone with his brothers when they sailed, but later joined them after traveling overland from New Brunswick. He and Jim became drivers for the stagecoach on the infamous Cariboo Road, which ran from the town of Yale to Barkerville. It was a challenging drive full of perils. Precipitous cliffs dotted the route, falling hundreds of feet below to the Fraser Canyon. The road itself was narrow with curves so sharp that often the driver could not see the lead mules. Later, when gold was shipped out by the stage, banditry was added to the list of dangers. In the early days of the gold rush, the stagecoaches only carried in supplies for the camps and often came back empty. But when the gold ore began to surface in alarming quantity, it was converted to ingots, and the value became a magnet for robbers.

This lifestyle was exciting for a young, unattached man but was not conducive to those with families. During his stay in the Cariboos, John acquired both a family and a mine (the Caledonia) from which he saved $20,000, a considerable sum in those days.

After the first flush of the gold rush, prospectors, ever a wandering lot, began to move on. John was also a bit of a wanderer and later moved to Bentinck Arm near Bella Coola where he might have settled for a while had it not been for one of the first First Nations land-claim conflicts in Canada's history. The Waddington Indian Massacre (also known as the Chilcotin War or Bute Inlet Massacre) resulted from a conflict between the Tsilhqot'in (Chilcotin) people and road construction workers. The road had been proposed by Alfred Waddington to run from the Cariboo gold fields to the shipping port at Bella Coola. It would reduce land transportation of the gold and supplies by 174 miles, making travel time fifteen days shorter, which was fairly significant in that country. The Chilcotin Indians were suffering from starvation and smallpox as a direct result of contact with the fur traders. The occupation of their valleys and mountains by the fur traders felt like an invasion to the Chilcotins and their resentment mounted with the construction of the road that they viewed as a threat to their way of life.

Actual road construction had been underway for two years when the Chilcotin, hungry, sick, and just plain fed-up, approached a local ferryman on the Quesnel River for food. When he refused the starving natives even a potato, they killed him, threw him in the river, and confiscated the stores. Emboldened by victory and a half a ton of food, they carried on to the work camp and dispatched a few more laborers. In their minds, they were at war, and so they considered it a reasonable request when they received a subsequent invitation to meet with the New Westminster Gold Commissioner, William Cox (proxy for the governor), to settle their differences. Under Cox's pretense of a "friendly meeting" the natives felt safe, and they attended, only to be thrown in jail and later hanged. There was great controversy over whom to blame, but ultimately, the Attorney General apologized for the hangings and provided funding for the proper burial of the victims.

John and his family had just settled in the area when the conflict drove the settlers from their home, forcing the Hamiltons to relocate in the Cariboos. They bought Beaver Pass House from "Bloody Edwards" (a colloquial term attributed to the man for no real explanation), but it was a small place that did not hold them for long. The next move, in 1868, found them buying the Cottonwood Ranch, which was essentially a rundown roadhouse. They made improvements and even considered establishing a dairy farm with cows brought up from Oregon. Though John's wife was a great cook and they prospered there, his roving days were not over, and after a few years, he moved on to the Nicola Valley, near Merritt, in the heart of British Columbia. His brother Robert and his family settled in the same area not long after. Both families fell in love with the open spaces and established a ranch favored with rich grass that grew abundantly on the hills. They prospered here as well, but Johnny could not shake his restlessness. He was soon on the move again, this time to Calgary, Alberta, where he settled for good. Robert soon followed and also established himself in the Calgary area.

Johnny was quite the entrepreneur in this thriving community, eventually owning several ranches and livery stables. He would visit his ranches frequently but continued living in the city to better run the livery stables. One accomplishment he felt very good about was purchasing the farm near Midnapore that resulted in reuniting the family.

Despite the hard days and the loneliness, June grew up happy and thrived on what the farm had to offer. She particularly loved the horses, and by the time she was three had acquired enough mobility to make it to the barn, where she was a menace. In her desire to get close to the animals, she would untie them, allowing a thunderous escape, in which she miraculously was not trampled. But it was her mother's saddle horse that caused the most grief. June was infatuated with this animal and would repeatedly untie the horse and lead it into the yard. Unfortunately, she was too small to do the leading, and more often than not the horse would drag her through the mud, slough, and manure piles dumped at the end of the yard. Her mother would alternately laugh or spank her for these escapades. If her mother weren't chasing her, then her uncles would be – after they had rounded up the horses wildly running through the fields –

harnesses flapping in all directions and spooking them to even greater flight.

As June became more mobile and more of a babysitting problem for Clara, who was taxed enough with daily chores, her uncles took over some of the care. June was particularly fond of her Uncle Bob, for whom she felt a daughterly affection. He indulged her sense of adventure by taking her with him to the fields when haying or cultivating. More than likely, he just gave in to her precociousness. She would sneak under the seat of the wagon when he left for the fields and hide until they were too far away for him to bother driving her home. At first this was a real nuisance, but Bob did not have the heart to get more than annoyed. He soon tolerated her riding with him in the wagon, pulled by a team of strong draft horses, and enjoyed her delight in the exciting alternative to another day playing alone in the yard.

June never developed a fear of horses, which did lead to trouble on one occasion. Bob, who rarely got ruffled over anything, got upset when she was struck on the head by one of the horses' hooves when she persisted in feeding them handfuls of grass. The injury was not serious, but Bob realized he could not watch her when he was busy elsewhere. He quickly sent her packing back to the house, remonstrating with himself for letting her tag along to begin with.

Child rearing on the farm in those early years was not hampered by over-protective parents. Sending June home alone across the fields with a blow on the head was not a problem for Bob. In his world, children were taught to look after themselves early in life. Though June knew the way home and was more than capable of the walk, the sight of her daughter ambling home with a cut on her head must have alarmed Clara. She'd thought the child was playing in the back yard.

As June grew, Clara realized that her daughter's attraction to horses was probably a result of not having children her own age to play with. This even though June was blessed with three uncles, one of whom was a special companion due to his disability (Fred was still an adult and certainly could not play). The solution to June's horse fixation was cleverly handled when her mother decided that, if she had her own horse, the others would be left in peace. So on a lovely summer morning, June got Topsy, a gentle, midnight-black Shetland pony that soon became a constant companion. She loved her complacent friend and began to resent her obligatory afternoon naps, which interfered with riding.

JUNE ON TOPSY

Hers was a solitary world, and Topsy was her only substitute for friends she did not have. It did not take long before she began to slip out the bedroom window and escape on Topsy to scam cookies from nearby neighbors.

June was ingenious at handling her horse, and how she escaped must have baffled Clara. To reach the neighbors, she had to get through the barbwire fence. This proved easy, for the pony was small enough to get under the wire if she held it up. Mounting proved more of a challenge. A bank or rock was necessary to reach the pony's back but only effective when the horse lowered its head to feed. June climbed over its neck but then had to squirm on her belly on the soft, wide back to turn forward. It was another fight to retrieve the reins that had tangled in the pony's ears. She always managed these Herculean maneuvers without being caught until Annie "tattled on her." Annie was the daughter of a close neighbor who made irresistible cookies, which she happily shared with Topsy.

On more than one occasion, Clara received a call from Annie saying June was in her kitchen scamming cookies. Inevitably Clara would check the bedroom, only to find an open window.

"Alright, thanks Annie. Send her home."

June swallowed the last cookie, knowing she could expect a hiding when she got there.

The early days of June's childhood went by too quickly for her to realize how happy she was until she was older. It was a healthy life that could only have been improved by childhood friends, but that would change soon enough for her when the family moved to Midnapore. This also gave the Hamilton boys greater opportunities to socialize more freely and get on with establishing their own families. Bob was the first to find a bride, having met Edna Carrington "on the streets of Calgary," June would later recall. He approached Clara with his plans to marry, knowing her circumstances would eventually be affected by the coming change.

When Clara saw Bob nursing a coffee at the table, she knew he wanted to discuss his situation with Edna. She sat down quietly, looked directly at him and said, "I suspect you and Edna plan to marry soon." Bob looked over his coffee cup and said, "Yeah, I believe we'll marry in the spring. The old Vader place is up for sale about two miles west of here. Seems like a good prospect for us."

Clara looked down at the old tablecloth and said, "That's great, Bob, and I'm not surprised. John will probably marry soon as well, but until then I will stay here."

Bob suddenly laughed. "I think June is put out. She told me to put Edna back where I found her ... on the streets of Calgary!"

Clara's concern had substance. Bob and Edna did marry in the spring of 1925, when June was five years old. By 1927 John too had found a wife – the pretty neighbor, Annie, who had supplied June with cookies all those years. John and Annie inherited the farm Clara and June had been living on, and Clara knew she could not stay. It would be untenable to keep house now that a new mistress was in charge. Happily, no animosity developed from this change as Clara and Annie were close friends and wished to remain so.

As Clara had said, she had looked into what prospects were available for Fred. This took a while, and for the first year, Fred stayed with Bob and Edna. Soon after, they found him a home for the disabled in Calgary where he remained the rest of his life. Of more concern was where she would go. Clara was one of the war widows who had fallen between the cracks of federal benevolence. Basil had died before he was eligible for death benefits, leaving Clara without a penny for his service to his country. With deep regret over losing a way of life surrounded by family, Clara knew her only option was to move to Calgary and find a job and a place to live. In the end, she did wind up a single parent with a young girl to look after.

Chapter II

THE CITY LIFE

Calgary was a small cow town 50 kilometers east of the mountains when Clara and June moved there in 1926, but it was big enough to feel constricting after the freedom of the farm. The contrast in June and Clara's lifestyle could not have been greater. With its walls that hid the land and horses she had loved, the small apartment they found themselves in now defined June's world. Clara found a lackluster job with the Calgary Seed Bank at minimal income – just enough to afford the rent and living expenses. June's reprisal to this upheaval was to immediately get sick. She announced soon after the move that she had a headache, which would not go away.

"Mom," June complained, "I have a headache, and I don't feel well."

Clara initially thought June was just trying to get out of school, but this was not in her nature. At first she dismissed the headache, thinking it was only an early symptom of a cold or flu virus. This possibility faded as the "flu" worsened until a very disquieting red rash began to appear on

June's face and torso. A quick visit to the doctor resulted in immediate quarantine in the hospital. The rash proved to be smallpox, a disease that killed many young children at that time. If she survived, it would mean a long period of recuperation.

Clara was beside herself. She had just enrolled June in the Calgary Montessori School, which was considered avant-garde for the time, particularly in the backwater of a small western town. Clara was unusually progressive in her understanding and aims for the education of her only child and had looked forward to June's progress. The school emphasized development and learning based on self-directed activity on the part of the child. The learning curve was entirely dependent upon the child, who dictated the level and speed of progression, concentrating on developing practical skills while absorbing abstract concepts. Clara felt June's independent spirit and active mind would meld with this form of teaching better than the conventional, dictatorial approach of regular schooling. The school, despite being progressive, was most likely where June contracted the disease.

June remained in the hospital under close care, wondering what she had done to keep everyone away. Her condition became critical at one point, but slowly she began to respond to treatment. For Clara, who had to keep working, this period seemed interminable.

Once June was able to leave the hospital, she went to live with Bob and Edna who took over the caregiving. It was evident Clara could not keep her job, which required her to be away all day, and look after June at the same time.

Work did not abound for single women of limited education, and she could not afford to give it up. All she could do was visit her sick child on weekends when she could escape the city. What she found brought on increased worry about a relapse.

"Bob, she can barely eat! The lesions in her mouth are terrible. The doctor is hardly encouraging! If this gets much worse, she could be scarred for life or even lose her sight. God, she could even die! I lost my husband after less than a year, and now she may be gone too," wailed Clara as she scanned the rapidly thinning body on the single bed, which was tossing in an almost perpetual state of delirium. At least June did not seem to be aware of how sick she was.

"I know, Clara, I know, but she gets the milk down pretty regularly. It's solid food that's the problem. But she does keep the milk down, and Edna has been able to get some pretty nutritious soup into her as well. It looks bad, but all we can do is let it run its course." He himself was disheartened by this unexpected burden in the early year of his marriage, but Edna was firm in taking on the job. She could not stand to see children suffer. There was also an unvoiced feeling that the country was a much better convalescing environment than even the best accommodation the city could offer.

Clara returned to the dismal apartment and another dreary week of work, often almost in tears. But each week that passed brought survival and hope. As the cold, brilliant weather of winter typical of the prairies set in, it seemed that the accompanying wind blew life slowly back into

June's thin body. It took a long time, but she was a home-
steader's child and heir to a tough body and spirit. The rash
and lesions melted away as spring drew closer, and a clear
skin emerged with a rapidly healing body. She had successfully staved off death, blindness, and scarring.

By the time June returned to school, she was seven years
old. The adjustment was considerable. She not only had
to attend school, she had to adjust to the small apartment
in the dreary city again. No more outdoors playing with
the horses and other farm animals. June missed the volup-
tuous smells that emanated from their old farmhouse, the
promise of fresh milk and new baking that mingled with
the sweet fragrance of split wood piled on the porch. She
missed the moist smell of fresh grass and new buds in the
spring. She missed the pungent odor of fall vegetation as it
diffused into the ground before winter snow promised the
renewal of another spring. It spoke of the life she no longer
had. But most of all she missed the dungy smell of horses
feeding in the barn on fresh hay from the fields. She longed
for the farm and hoped fervently she could return once she
was through school.

Though June had often been lonely as a child, her new
life was lonelier still. Clara put in long hours at work and
could not be home when June returned from school, so June
had to entertain herself. Clara was finding her workload very
much increased, what with her job and looking after both
of them and the apartment. June endured these few long

years away from the farm, partly because she was innately cheerful, and mainly because the tedium was relieved by frequent visits to the farm on weekends and summer holidays. Returning to her former home always brought her intense joy, and she could barely stand to leave at the end of a short weekend. She was still too young to understand the family dynamics of home life or why her mother had to live in Calgary, but she had little choice in the matter.

One problem she did not have to deal with was getting used to a new father. Clara, in the short time she had known her husband, had loved him deeply; she had crammed a lifetime of love into a few short months, almost as if precognizant of his death. She was very young when he died and had lost none of her beauty while caring for June and her brothers on the farm. The increased social life at Midnapore and the opportunity to meet new people while living in Calgary had given her exposure to men interested in pursuing a relationship with her, but she had no impulse to remarry. She had never really recovered from losing Basil, and no one else held any appeal. So it would remain for some time.

As June grew, work became increasingly burdensome for Clara, who constantly felt guilty at having to leave her daughter alone in the apartment for hours. June vividly remembered how tired her mother was – especially on weekends when she would catnap between the cooking and cleaning. By the time June turned ten, Clara felt she could not provide the supervision or support June needed. Fortunately, she was able to enroll her at the Sacred Hearts Convent, which included boarding. It was about this time

JUNE IN UNIFORM

that Clara got a better job at the Alberta Wheat Pool. It paid more, required less physical work, and it even meant being able to afford a larger apartment.

Surprising everyone, June took to the convent with little trouble. For one thing, she knew she was less of a burden. For another, she did not have the long, lonely hours waiting for Clara to get home. With the convent being oriented to skills young housewives would need to keep a home, the nuns kept her busy learning more practical skills than the Montessori school offered. Some skills aimed at a more genteel life may not have been quite as practical considering June's destiny. She was taught very fine embroidery, which she enjoyed but would never employ in the demanding life ahead of her. They also taught her to play the piano, a skill at which her mother was accomplished. She would never be as good as Clara, though, simply because she never had a piano, but before she lost her skill, she enjoyed playing for herself and others. During the long evenings on the prairie farms and ranches of the foothills, entertainment was provided only by what people came up with at home. A piano and a good songfest kept boredom and depression at bay. Emotional and mental ill-health was never really spoken of, but no one was completely immune. During the winter, especially, parties and other social events became very important.

In the meanwhile, visits to the farm were never missed. In fact, they expanded to include visits to Clara's sister Lulu and her uncle, Jappy Rogers. Lulu and Jappy had settled on their own property near Bottrel, just northwest of Cochrane, Alberta.

Jappy was a well-known horseman, having learned his craft from his father, who'd immigrated to Canada from Ireland. Jappy's expertise had made him a valuable addition to the Lord Strathcona's Horse regiment in Calgary, where he looked after horses from Russia which were to be trained for the regiment. This eventually led to a job with the Calgary Stockyards handling horses there. June was never more in her element than when she was absorbing as much knowledge as Jappy was happy to impart about horse care and training. She and Clara would motor out to the small farm on weekends and holidays when they did not go to Midnapore, and June soaked up all that Jappy could teach. It was also during these visits that June became good friends with Kathleen and Patsy Rogers, Jappy and Lulu's daughters (and June's cousins). Patsy would later gain fame as the first Miss Rodeo Calgary. This would take her to Madison Square Garden Rodeo in New York City to represent Canada in various duties and ride with the flag in many events and parades. June was a bit in awe of Patsy, who also benefited from her father's knowledge and mirrored his ability with horses.

Jappy was a generous man and had time for both girls. June would watch him start young colts destined for the polo fields and turn them into well-trained mounts. He instructed her carefully, and she soon became a very accomplished rider – so much so that he allowed her to finish off colts once they were responding well to the training. But there was a price. In return for this incredible opportunity, she had to help with the haying. In the 1920s this was backbreaking work, with a team of horses pulling the hay wagon as the men forked the sweet-smelling dried grass over the rails to be hauled back for stacking. But haying would eventually become a livelihood, so it was time well spent developing muscles that would give her the stamina for the ranching life.

June was at the convent for two years, which gave Clara a chance to get her feet under her, but by then June was old enough to be of real help at home. Also, it was time to enroll in junior high school. On the first day of registering at Connaught Junior High, June met Jacqueline Trusler, a schoolmate who would become a lifelong friend.

Jackie was a lively, impulsive girl given to spontaneity, and on June's first day of school, she introduced herself by running under the umbrella June had open for the rain.

"Wow," said Jackie. "You're new here, aren't you? I live just around the corner – we should be good friends. There aren't too many girls here our age. What do you say?"

June was actually quite shy, having just come from the convent and leading a relatively lonely life with few other children to relate to in her isolated farm life. She stammered, "Well, okay." Jackie took charge, and they were soon inseparable.

They spent all their spare time together, and the only thing to rival this time was a new passion of June's. It was painting. An early introduction to watercolors set the stage for painting the horses, people, and countryside that adorned the walls of her home from then on. This would not stop until later in life when the loss of her eyesight prevented her from seeing the canvases that reflected her world. Though June hated city life, the country summers were, by contrast, a breath of freedom, and she did not realize until later how carefree and simple that time was. The greatest challenge was to ride well enough to meet her uncle's approval.

One year later, June met Vivian Louise Galbraith, who would also become a lifelong friend. Vivian's father also became important to June, as he was a doctor who would eventually tend to all the family needs.

By the time June turned fifteen, she was becoming aware of boys as not just friends or relations, but potential boyfriends. Still, it was hard to think of her mother with another man who might become her stepfather. But Clara was still a young woman, and remarkably pretty at that. She had disabused herself of the notion of remarrying during the trying years of bringing up a young girl on her own, but she was leaving those days behind in a hurry. And she did not lack the attention of men who wanted more than a visit over a cup of coffee at the corner store. It was probably no surprise when one persistent cowboy began to gain real ground.

"June, Tip and I are going to be married!" Clara said by way of announcing that the tall cowboy might be more than a coffee date. Clara had known Tip Johnson for several years, though she had kept the relationship casual up until then. But Johnson was a determined man and was very much in love with her. He also offered a chance at a country life again, which both June and Clara wanted. Neither of them liked Calgary very much, and Tip had a place outside of Turner Valley.

Tip Johnson was a cowboy, born and raised in the foot-hills of Alberta where he'd learned to ride and break horses at an early age. He obtained the nickname of Tip by riding Tipperary, a bronco that had previously never been ridden. Tip was well known to the Hamilton family through association with the horse-breaking work that took him to ranches in the Black Diamond, Bassano and Okotoks regions of the province. He knew his horses well, particularly quarter horses that were bred for herding cattle. He brought some of the finest of these animals to Alberta for stud purposes and was particularly known for introducing the stallion Don Chub to the breeding community. June was thrilled to be moving back to the foothills and a continued association with horses, even though she would not see as much of her friends.

Tip was also range rider for the South Sheep Creek Stock Association, and this took him onto the forest reserve west of the cabin he lived in near Turner Valley. It was a vigorous job that required checking the cattle on the range, ensuring their survival by packing salt and by monitoring the available feed and the presence of predators. Returning to such a simple life was what June wanted more than anything, though it meant leaving school. Tip's place was too far from Turner Valley and high school for her to get to school every day. But in the 1930s, education for young girls was not a huge priority. It was the middle of the Depression and just making a living was a major accomplishment. The fact that Clara had kept her job at the Wheat Pool when so many were out of work spoke well of her abilities.

Chapter III

BACK TO THE LAND

"June, bring in the rest of your clothes later after we clean up a bit."

June was just getting to know Clara's new husband. She would later recall: "Tip Johnson was a cowboy who was a real character. He wore a battered cowboy hat, an old plaid work shirt, blue jeans that looked about a century old, and old, soft leather boots caked in mud. He didn't own a ranch or much of anything … "

Tip must have read her thoughts when he said, "Well, gal, you're goin' to live in a fine place at the tail end of nowhere. There isn't any school, but you'll find friends. We'll get you a fine horse."

The "tail end of nowhere" sounded fine to June.

The road to the ranch wound through deep spruce forests, clinging to the hills, broken by open spaces of golden meadows that led to the distant mountains lurking beyond the skyline. June was getting impatient when Tip finally announced, "It's just up ahead." Both she and Clara squinted in anticipation as they spotted a small, lonely building on an open, bare slope. The closer they got, the rougher the log cabin looked.

June looked around the little house on the Bar T Ranch (Tip's brand) that would be home for the next six years. They entered a dusty kitchen with one door leading to the dirt cellar below, which oozed the musty odor of mold. June could see daylight through the cracks in the walls. Ruefully, she thought, *This place doesn't look one bit like my uncle's farm house,* but she held her tongue. Her gaze turned to Tip, wondering if he was concerned about Clara's reaction to her first glimpse of their new home.

It was not the bachelor pad décor that set Clara's mouth in a rather grim smile, but the lack of any furnishings that made a home comfortable – or at least inhabitable. The first thing that leapt out was the lack of storage or cupboards in the kitchen. There was just nowhere to put anything.

"Tip! We have got to put something together here, or it's just camping out." Clara was a

TIP JOHNSON

34

tough, practical woman and soon had boxes nailed up for cupboards that she livened up with colorful curtains (sewn from flour sacks). But the first task was to clean the place. June remembers "scrubbing the floors with soap and lye water that took the skin off our hands."

With that done, Clara announced, "Time to paint!" They opened small packets of calcimine powder, a cheap paint that cost only ninety-eight cents a box. Mixed with water, it was quite colorful. They saturated the small cabin in color. The bedroom was pink, June's room became bright blue, and the porch beckoned with yellow. They toned it down for the living room, using a more subdued pearly-white.

Shaking her head over the idea that Tip had lived in the house all those years without even basic improvements, Clara and June also covered the walls with cardboard to keep in the heat. It brightened the place considerably when they added several coats of white calcimine to reinforce the cardboard.

That was just the start. They cleaned and painted the privy and tried to find an easier way to haul water from the natural spring half a mile from the house. They turned the soil for the garden Clara hoped would yield more than promised from the rocky ground.

Tip's promise of new friends and a horse did not materialize that quickly. But June barely had time to miss school or socializing. Her days were filled with work, a state that would not really change for the rest of her life. She later recalled: "In the summer I picked Saskatoons and strawberries with Mum and helped her weed the garden. In winter I split firewood and hauled it by toboggan to the house. I had to shovel all the paths to the woodpile, then the privy, then the chicken house, and finally the barn. I milked the cows (they got one the second winter there), then brought the milk into the house and ran it through the separator to skim the cream from the milk. But oh, what cream! It made the sweetest butter in the world once it was churned." Its sweet creaminess was wonderful on the thick, homemade bread Clara made regularly.

They had moved in when the weather was good, but it was inescapable that the winter would be challenging. The late move meant they had no garden produce to provide the staples that most Depression-era families depended on. But neighbors relied on each other, and those with more than they needed (or not) pitched in to help the young family through the first winter. Despite the help, June recalled that beans were more than a staple – beans were the main nourishment for the three of them, and for once Clara was glad she only had one child to feed.

Being one of the driest years during the ten-year drought that had begun in the early 1930s, 1936 was a low point in the Great Depression. There was massive unemployment in rural areas where farm foreclosures were posted daily. No one could make a living off the land whose only produce was the soil that blew away in truckloads. Though Clara wanted June to finish high school, that winter they could not afford the horse needed to make the nine-mile ride to Black Diamond. At June's age, this did not bother her at all. The one horse they did have was required by Tip for the forestry work. June did not expect to finish high school and was happy to work at the homestead with her family. Tip was fortunate in getting work looking after the stockmen's cattle that grazed on the Big Horn Forestry Reserve just a mile west of their home. June was in her glory when he later recruited her to help pack salt to the cattle. She loved the foothill country west of Turner Valley, which she thought was a big improvement over the Midnapore country her uncles had settled in.

Though getting water on Clara's brother's farm had been a never-ending chore, he'd at least had a well not far from the house. Tip's house also had a well not far away, but it only produced rusty water that could not be used for either drinking or washing. Clara sucked up another deep breath when she realized all the water would have to be hauled in barrels from a nearby spring. Fortunately, the spring stayed open during the winter months, but it was an unpleasant, cold task to get water this way.

By the following summer, Clara lost patience with their cramped quarters and announced, "This house is just too small. We barely have room for the three of us, let alone things we have to store. I know this is going to seem like a lot of work, but we've got to have a basement. There's no way we can keep food over the winter without at least a cold storage room." She would even be able to store water in barrels, which could be collected more easily during the summer.

If Tip was a little daunted by the prospect of digging a basement, he kept his griping to a low, inaudible growl. He was doing pretty well at adapting to married life after the simple bachelorhood he had enjoyed prior to meeting Clara.

"I guess," he replied, contemplating just how they – principally he – were going to accomplish this. "It won't be easy, you know. We have to get all that dirt out without a foundation. I guess I better go see some friends and see if they can come up with any ideas." Tip seemed a little subdued.

"Well, I'm strong, and June is getting pretty big, so you have us." Clara was adamant. "We just make a hole at the back and haul out the dirt; maybe it will be good enough to use in the garden."

"Don't count on it. These are the foothills. We don't have prairie soil. We'll be lucky if we don't hit bedrock or some huge boulder you need to dynamite to get out. I just hope the house doesn't fall down!" He was sounding less and less enthusiastic as his mind conjured up every conceivable obstacle he might encounter in this monumental undertaking.

There was a lot to deal with that summer. Tip had his regular job on the forestry reserve, and summer forest fires kept him busy packing supplies to fire-lines that were springing up everywhere. The Depression years were far from over, and money was always short. But they had to have money, so in the end Clara and June did quite a lot of the digging, leaving Tip time to work. Clara was determined to the point of obsession with completing the project. A basement meant she could store vegetables and meat over the winter if she could find time to get in a garden as well. She did not want to face another winter depending on the kindness of neighbors to see them through.

One of the things that slowed the process was not being able to hire any help, though neighbors would lend a hand when they were not too swamped by their own summer work. Tip was well known in the district and was popular with his neighbors, although, with the exception of the Gettigs, not many were nearby. Tip was often away, and though she had a close relationship with Clara, June missed the few friends she had made in Calgary. There had been little opportunity to make new friends around Turner Valley, especially since she did not attend school. She kept in touch with the girls by lobbying to have them come out as often as possible despite the distance.

When they did come, the girls had great picnics in the meadows or down by the stream. They would pack up the horses and ride across the countryside, brimming with confidence in their ability to travel safely through the bush-clogged valleys and open hills. It was usually Jackie and Vivian who came, and June thought her friends were secretly happy she had moved to this wild, remote place so they too could escape the confines of the city. The visits were rarely reciprocal as June had little opportunity to get to Calgary in those first few years.

She scarcely missed the city once she discovered the beauty of the high mountain meadows, which burst with life in early spring, proliferating with a succession of flowers through the summer and fall. The color and variety of flowers abounded, framing the distant mountains that appealed to her developing artistic eye. The impressions laid down in those formative years would radiate through all her paintings as she nurtured her talent.

By fall, the summer projects were coming to completion, and the family, small by comparison with most families of the day, faced another difficult winter. But this year it was eased by the vegetables and canned goods tucked into the warm, new cellar. These were augmented by a rare trip to Turner Valley to get staples for the winter. The precious money that Tip made allowed them to get the canned goods and flour Clara needed for baking. Though the Depression was hard on most people, those it hit hardest lived mainly in large cities where there was no work, no garden, no dairy cows, no chickens or pigs, and no opportunity to hunt for game. By comparison, the farmers who could afford livestock and had reasonable soil for planting got by without the hunger that afflicted the rest of the country. It was hard, cold, and lonely much of the year, especially for June who had no siblings, but this isolation gave her the gift of time and the opportunity to kindle her imagination and develop her drawing skills.

She couldn't remember when she started to draw horses, only that she rode them for years before trying to paint them. She was inspired at a young age by the comics, particularly Dagwood and Blondie, which she would try and copy when in possession of crayons and paper. She was delighted when her mother gave her a set of watercolors, an old gift from a friend.

Although June did not really miss money, because she had no chance to go to town to spend it, the family still needed the currency, and June was encouraged to contribute. When she was not kept busy with her chores, she was out helping Tip pack salt to the reservation. This was a pretty, nine-mile ride up to the reserve, making for a long day after checking the cattle, particularly in winter. It was often made longer when they had to cut firewood. Once the timber was felled, they harnessed a team of horses to skid the wood home through the snow. Winter was the best time for this chore.

June recalled one cold day that had drifted into evening by the time she and Tip got the wood home and had a vivid memory of Clara greeting them at the door, allowing the mouth-watering smells of fresh bread, beef stew, and biscuits to escape. She left her drawing unfinished and drifting off to sleep on the couch, watching Clara mend Tip's long underwear.

By the following summer, Tip felt June had enough experience to make the trip to the forestry reserve on her own. But June's and his confidence was shaken when June decided to go for an afternoon ride to visit neighbors by a route she did not normally take. Tip asked her to take a small horse that handled well but needed more work to settle him down. June decided the ride would give her the opportunity to get to know the surrounding country better. She quickly saddled her horse and was on her way towards the local community center. She rode by the few farms of people she knew but kept going on to the Russell farm where she stopped in for tea and cookies.

It was around two p.m. and getting late before June decided to head home. She did not want to go back the way she came, as it was a longer ride than she wanted, and she had already seen that country. She was young and adventurous and felt she could figure her way back by cutting through the forestry reserve. She had been hauling salt for Tip there and thought she could find that route with little trouble. The only challenge would be negotiating the part of the forest reserve with which she was unfamiliar.

JUNE THE COWGIRL

Knowing she wanted to hit the eastern fence that marked the boundary of the reserve, June began riding in the direction she thought she had come from. She rode for what she considered a long way and then swung east – or so she thought – hoping to find the fence.

After riding for a few miles, she started to get uneasy. As she penetrated deeper into the forest, she became concerned when her route was blocked by deadfall, which she was forced to go around. This continual deviation disoriented her, and soon she lost all sense of direction. Before she knew it, she was hopelessly lost.

By now it was going on four p.m. The late-fall day meant she would soon lose the sun and, to her dismay, it started to snow. June had no warm clothes and was not prepared for this at all. Soon, as a deep chill settled into her bones, she found herself fighting back tears. This was getting serious.

With little recourse other than to push on, she finally found the Forestry fence line. Shaking and sobbing, she saw a little old man by the name of Eddie Bean come up to open the only gate in the fence she saw. Finding the old trapper, who lived nearby in a falling-down shack isolated from a world growing too busy for him, was fortuitous. Eddie had heard her progress as she crashed through the bush, but other than reorienting her, he was of little help. All he could tell her was that she would have to go back the way she came. She was nowhere near the area she hauled salt to.

June was not sure if she could do as he suggested. It was difficult to follow her tracks back because she could not distinguish them from the numerous other horse tracks, which had been left by a herd of wild horses. Fortunately, she had taken her small dog with her that day. Though it was tedious, the dog actually found their original route by scent and followed their tracks back to the road she'd left so much earlier that day.

She finally reached the Russells' just before dark. It was now approaching six p.m. and she was anxious to get home. Mrs. Russell brought her into the warm kitchen and soothed her with a hot drink. They all knew there was no way she could ride back at that hour, despite her anxiety.

"Just set down and warm up. I know you're eager to get home, so I will get Laurie to drive you," announced Mrs. Russell. "Laurie, come here. You don't mind driving June back do you?" Their oldest son Laurie was only two years older than June but had a great sense of responsibility for a young man of that age.

Laurie replied, "No, but we have to get the chores done first, then eat supper." Nothing was going to stand in the way of a hot supper.

June was a bit disappointed, but not overly so when she sat down to an excellent meal. It had been a long day and this was the first food she'd had in hours. She put her horse in the barn, hoping Tip would drive her back to get it the next day. She would be riding back the same way after all.

"So what happened, June?" inquired Laurie's two younger brothers. "Why did you come back so late?"

June tried to explain where she got turned around and was surprised to learn that her intended route was not short at all. She had misjudged the distance from the fence line to the Gettigs' farm by several miles. As the Gettigs' place was only a fifteen-minute walk from home, that had been her destination.

At last the chores were done and Laurie drove her home with the family truck. To her surprise, no one was there. It was past eleven p.m. by then and June felt it was too late for Laurie to drive back, so she convinced him to sleep on the living room couch. She quickly had the sheets and covers out and was relieved to get to bed herself. Though she was still puzzled by Clara and Tip's absence, she was too tired to worry about it. The minute her head hit the pillow, she was asleep.

Her much-needed sleep lasted about an hour. She was startled to wake up to hollering and a bright light shining in her eyes. The missing parents had returned to find Laurie on the couch. The noise was coming from Tip who kept interrupting Laurie while Laurie tried to explain what he was doing there. When she stumbled out of the bedroom, June immediately redirected their attention to herself.

Clara was furious. Of course, she was mad because of the scare June had given her. But there was no way June could have let her mother know where she was, as no one had a phone. She had always been encouraged to be self-sufficient and never thought anyone would be worried about her. She was sadly mistaken. Clara and Tip had been scared silly and they'd spent most of the evening driving around in the sleigh looking for her. As the cold penetrated the light blankets they'd grabbed from the porch, Clara had fought panic, realizing that June could be freezing under some tree with only the dog for warmth and company.

They had first stopped off at the Gettigs', who were by now equally worried. With little more to say, Clara made

June get dressed and run over to the Gettigs' to let them know she was all right. Clara saw no reason why these close friends should have to worry about her all night. In fact, had June not returned, both families had planned to be up before sunrise to keep searching.

The next day, after a good night's sleep and a hot breakfast, everyone calmed down. Laurie was finally able to explain what had happened, and outside of poor judgment on June's part in heading back via the reserve, they could understand why she had been delayed.

Despite this setback, June's solitary excursions gradually left her with a growing confidence in her ability to travel around the country on her own. It also developed in her an emotional connection with the land, which would dominate her life and be fundamental to future pivotal decisions.

That winter, these perceptions and experiences translated onto paper as she started painting seriously. As the winter winds brought the insulating deep snow characteristic of the dark woods of the Turner Valley foothills, she bent over the kitchen table with a coal oil lamp for light and began her creations on every scrap of paper she could scavenge. Her first efforts were painting Christmas cards. But there was more to this endeavor than just the exercise of painting. Her practical side emerged when she decided she would sell them for ten cents apiece. This enterprise awoke another skill that would become invaluable in her adult years. She began to develop a business sense and took her first steps to becoming an astute businesswoman.

CHRISTMAS CARDS

Another enterprise June undertook during the winter was to run a small trapline. Pine martens and rabbits thrived in the deeply wooded hills. She was also fairly progressive in traveling through the deep snow that built up in the forest as winter wore on. Not having the money to buy a set of snowshoes, which were used by most trappers, she managed to cut down two barrel staves and attach a rudimentary binding, creating a crude set of skis. Generally her travel was on the flat valley bottom were she could manage the awkward skis. She had also devised a set of ski poles to help her in more rolling terrain. As often as not, she relied on trees to help her up or slow her down on steeper sections.

She did not wind up with any exceptional skills as a cross-country skier. Though the money for pelts was small compared to the work entailed, it was still an income and gave her another activity to alleviate the loneliness of winter.

There was another accomplishment that would bolster her growing sense of independence and self-reliance, as well. It came in the form of an opportunity to go to the small town of Turner Valley. Occasionally, one of the neighbors would go to town for groceries when they ran low of store-bought staples. The first trip for June was exciting, if for no other reason than it broke the monotony of the winter.

"June, do you think you could go with Dan to get this month's groceries?" Clara asked one morning. Dan Devon was the elderly man who did this trip once a month for the neighbors. It was good of Clara to let June go as they could all have used a break, but there was no call for everyone to go.

"Sure! Just me?" replied June. "Could I take my skis? I bet I could get towed behind the sled if he doesn't go too fast."

"Do what you want. Just don't break your neck. I don't think anyone else will go, though. You and Dan can get the lists of what people need on your way into town. Oh, and take the radio battery in too. It needs to be recharged. I also have a few pounds of butter and some cream for trading. And try to get a good bargain for the groceries. It's nice sweet butter that those folks in town can't get otherwise, so you should do well."

When money was so scarce for everyone, the barter system was a practical way to exchange things in return for other goods or services. Going to town to trade was one of

JUNE WITH BARREL-STAVE SKIS

the most exciting things June had done for a while, mainly because it meant meeting more people. Though all the neighbors were friendly, distance and everyone's heavy workload made it hard to become well acquainted because visits were brief. But once people met and worked together, friends grew fast. Until then, one of the main forms of entertainment was the old radio, though its battery eventually ran down. Consequently, one of the main missions of the trip was to charge the battery in Turner Valley, the closest place where this could be done.

June was up early the next morning but was too excited to eat a big breakfast. The trip would take a while and she would be hungry when she got to town, but it was probably way too much to expect to eat in the local diner. Sure enough, Clara had packed a sizable lunch that would feed both June and Dan, if it didn't freeze before they got to it.

"Okay, my dear. Dan's here and won't want to dally, though he could probably come in and warm up for a bit."

Dan Devon was a slim, happy, friendly old fellow who lived near the Gettigs in his own cabin. As with most people who made a living in the hills, he was good with horses and was an experienced teamster. He was fond of children and always greeted them with a laugh or broad smile, happy to give them buggy rides just for fun.

The elderly man was glad enough to get warm before heading for town, mentioning that it was cold enough to have frozen a wine bottle left on his porch. He had placed hot rocks under the horse blankets on the sleigh and felt June would be warm enough with that. He was surprised, though, when she showed up with the old barrel-stave skis.

"Just what do you plan to do with those things?" he asked.

"Well, once we get down the road a ways, I thought I would tie a rope to the sleigh and let you pull me on my skis," she replied. "That way I can get used to moving on them, like going downhill."

"Why don't you just go to a hill? Never mind. If you think you can stay up on them, we can give it a try."

The experiment worked when the snow was light, but more often than not, she would hit an icy patch or wind-blown, hard crust and down she would go. Dan must have gotten a kick out of it because he never tired of stopping and waiting for her to shuffle back to the rope. The horses were patient too and soon began to stop when they heard her yelling "Whoop!" behind them.

The trip to town was a great success for June. The battery got charged, and the sleigh was loaded with goods for all the neighbors, which Dan would distribute over the next few days. They did not get a town lunch, but they were able to eat their sandwiches in the comparative warmth of the store, so it seemed like going out. The mail also got picked up, and Dan had other errands to run before they began the long trip home.

June did not use her skis any more that day, as she felt too bruised to endure more punishment. Skiing was not destined to be one of her finer achievements. It was also getting too cold to face into the wind, and she was glad of the insulating horse blankets tucked around her for warmth. She was almost asleep by the time she and Dan skidded into her yard to unload the sleigh. Clara was glad to see all the new additions to the pantry that would have to last over the next month. June had been able to get good value for the butter and cream, allowing Clara to purchase a few items they could not usually afford. From now on, June would be the principal "goes to town girl," but not all the trips would be so uneventful.

That summer June turned seventeen. It was a summer she fondly remembered. On several occasions, she brought her friends out to ride through the hills and share picnic lunches in the high meadows or down by the stream. She was happy and did not mind spending long hours in the garden growing vegetables for the coming winter. That summer, Clara added a brood of chickens to the mix, which helped vary the diet with eggs and occasional Sunday chicken dinners.

The garden was put in, and the cattle that had been brought to lower pastures over the winter were returned to the upper meadows of the reserve. Tip and June made the trip regularly to check on them, which never seemed to be a chore for June. She loved the ride to those high alpine pastures with the new growth of flowers that flourished in abundance. She also had a horse that Tip let her ride, which suited her well. Her riding ability was always good, but the constant riding gave her the self-assurance to undertake other commercial adventures.

An elderly neighbor needed help herding his cattle, and June was able to do this for a cash income. She also found work at the local sawmill, hauling large slabs of wood away from the cutting area. She actually skidded the wood away by using her horse as a skid horse. The chain was wrapped around these unwieldy pieces, then attached to the horse's harness and pulled to the side. For this she earned twenty-five cents a day. These were long, draining, poorly paid hours, but they meant a lot to June. She was still a girl, but she had used considerable initiative to carve out her different jobs, and soon it would add up. One of the principal expenses she felt responsible for was painting supplies and paper. She did not want to face the winters without this creative outlet, which made such a difference to her enjoyment of long, cold months short on sunlight.

As June grew, it was apparent she would be tall like her father. Clara wondered what she was eating, but Tip cast a critical eye over June, realizing she was also getting pretty strong. For a cowboy in Alberta during the thirties, he was remarkably non-sexist. He had no problem with June doing all the work a young boy would do. When it came to free help, all that mattered was getting the job done. June was thrilled when he began teaching her all he knew about training horses. Ranchers would pay him ten dollars for every horse he trained to accept riders. He would start the training, and when the horses were ready June would complete it. She told me, "Tip taught me how to ride without falling off, how to calm an unhappy horse, and how to coax a stubborn one to accept a saddle." This was rewarding work for her, but she always had to relinquish the horses to their owners at some point, even though she often became quite attached to them. She never forgot Tip's initial promise that she would have a horse of her own. By now, though, she realized she would have to earn it.

June never shied from any work, no matter how distasteful. She took opportunities when they came her way, so when neighbors told her they were missing a cow, she offered to look for it if she could keep the hide. It had been missing for several days and the neighbors had already written it off as coyote bait. June scoured the area where the cow had gone missing and soon spotted the circling crows. The cow had died of unknown causes in a small field seldom checked.

June dismounted the old grey mare she was riding that day and examined the hide. It was still in good condition and not that hard to skin. She managed to skin the exposed side but now faced the problem of turning the heavy, bloated animal over to complete the job. Her solution was to tie a rope to her saddle horn and have the horse pull it over. Unfortunately the horse was skittish, and the minute the carcass started to move, the mare turned into a bronc. The last June saw of that horse was its tail waving good-bye as it dashed across the field.

June was in tears by the time she limped home, not sure if she was crying more out of pain or anger. Tip commiserated and offered his help to finish the job, which she accepted, even though she *really* wanted to do it by herself. Thoughts of marching home triumphantly with the prized hide had kept her going. Tip said little, he just caught the horse, helped her turn the animal over, and left her in the heat and bugs to complete the skinning. As far as he was concerned, she had done well and deserved her prize.

June traded the hide to Tip's brother, Sam Johnson, who gave her a small pig. She raised the pig that winter and then traded it to Tip for a horse and became the proud owner of a beautiful, black thoroughbred mare she named Marquita. The catch was the mare still had to be broken. The horse was spirited and loved to buck. After several bucking episodes that June failed to win, she finally rode the horse in heavily ploughed fields that slowed the animal down. Marquita soon became one of the best horses June was ever to own.

That summer she also began to meet more people. Her mobility on horseback made it possible to do more visiting, which was a welcome change from the little contact she'd had with other children her age while growing up.

The majority of excursions, though, were still to see the family. Tip did not own a car those first few years, so if Clara and June wanted to see the uncles, they had to ride the lengthy distance to Midnapore. Long miles became standard and toughened up both women. But the visits were reciprocal, and June, Tip and Clara were often doing the entertaining. Someone was always passing by to or from town; many just came for an evening of dinner and visiting. Clara and Tip became known for their hospitality, and June began to feel much less isolated.

The ride to Midnapore was around forty miles, but even when she rode alone, June had no qualms about the distance. It would mean an overnight stay, and with no phones, Clara would have to assume she'd made the journey safely. She would have been alarmed if June did not return when she said she would, but this never happened.

It was early in July when June made an interesting trip that introduced her to an event she would later rarely miss.

"June, the Calgary Stampede is coming up in a few weeks. I think you're a good enough rider to ride in the parade. What do you think?" asked her Uncle Bob. "I can talk to some people – you know they're always looking for good riders, especially if they have some colorful clothing. You must get enough hides from fall hunting to make a good western jacket."

June looked thoughtfully at him. "Oh! Ride in the parade? I don't think I have anything right now, but I could borrow a fringed jacket from Mom. Oh, Uncle Bob, that would be great!"

Another thought came to June suddenly. She had been riding a horse for Tip she had taken a great liking to and felt it was mutual as the horse had responded to her training. He belonged to a nearby farmer who had trouble managing the animal and simply could not ride him. Tip had agreed to train the horse and enlisted June's help. It was a large, powerful gelding that few could stay on if he bucked, and he bucked every time the farmer tried to ride him. Tip made good progress with him and soon had June riding him as well. In a short time it seemed the horse would do anything for her, and she loved him.

Unfortunately, once the horse became tractable, June and Tip had to return it to the farmer. But strangely enough, the training never made any difference and the horse still continued to buck the man off. He would bring it back and go through the whole procedure again. This delighted June, who loved to ride him through the hills. She thought the gelding would be perfect for the parade, but Tip said no. The horse was not hers, and they could not take a chance on anything going wrong with that crowd.

It had to be a personality mismatch with the horse and the farmer, but despite this, June could not afford to buy the gelding and he was eventually sold off elsewhere. If there was ever a horse she wanted, he had been it. Meanwhile, plans for the rodeo went forward. June would ride one of her uncle's horses instead. Though she thought this was second-best, she was assured of a quiet horse that would not be difficult to handle in the parade.

June readily agreed to be in Midnapore on the appointed day so she could ride the remaining distance with the family. Everything came together, and June found herself being waved at by the biggest crowd she had ever seen. It was daunting to set out with fellow riders when they greeted the throng of people that lined both sides of the street. With people standing on bleachers several feet high, the street seemed more like a canyon, and June prayed her horse would not panic. The daunting possibility of having a runaway horse was brought home clearly when one of the wagon drivers struggled to control his team before it ran through the crowd. The driver succeeded in controlling the animals with the help of horsemen close by and no one came to harm. Once the parade was moving, the animals settled down, and the anxiety level dropped for those new to the event though the crowd gave little respite. June finally began to thoroughly enjoy herself, but it was with some relief that she saw the final corrals marking the end of the event. Secretly she was glad she had not ridden the farmer's horse, though she did not say so to Tip.

Clara had come in with the family to witness June's first parade and was relieved to see her ride past, sporting the colorful coat and wearing her glasses. June had to wear glasses at a young age, but as she matured and became more self-conscious of her looks, she began to leave the ugly things behind. In the 1930s, glasses were not flattering. How often had she heard, "Put your glasses on! You know you're blind without them. How can you see if the horse might step in a hole or get too close to a bank?"

But June was afraid to wear glasses, not just for vanity, but because she thought branches could knock them off or do some real damage if the horse bucked and she fell on them. Her stock reply was: "The horse can see just fine, so I don't need to." She did have them on for that first parade, as she really did need to see what was ahead. Besides, she did not want to miss that first impression despite the way she felt about how she looked.

Another highlight for June that summer was the chance to ride to Nanton to pick up a horse. This came about when a woman neighbor asked her if she was free to accompany her on the trip to pick up a horse for the Streeter family, who lived in Turner Valley. The family had bought the horse on a previous visit but had not arranged to pick it up until summer when it was more practical to make the trip. As Nanton was a considerable distance from Turner Valley, this was a long ride requiring two overnight stays with people the neighbor knew along the way.

Because the weather was so brilliant, they took the longer route down to Nanton, giving them plenty of time to enjoy shorter day rides and allow time for an always-welcome visit with friends. June was particularly excited to be asked along as it was a further indication of her worthiness as a riding companion, but more than that, the trip would take them through some of the most beautiful country in the foothills of Alberta. After the spring rains, the gently rolling hills were a brilliant green that contrasted with the deep green of the spruce and pine forests dotting the northern slopes. The country was still fairly open, maintaining a quality of freedom reminiscent of the land that the first settlers saw. June and her neighbor's route would take them past several ranches that ran free-ranging cattle on the hills. Grass was abundant and easily supported both cattle and wildlife.

June rode the lively mare, which was eager for the trip, and her smooth gait made riding a joy. On the way back, June offered to take turns leading the newly acquired horse. To make the journey more interesting, they took an alternative route back, via the Bar U Ranch, run by Bert Sheppard, a friend of Tip's. The trip via the Bar U was shorter and only required a one-night stay, which meant longer days, but both women had obligations at home and did not want to make the semi-vacation any longer than the five days they would be away.

The beautiful weather that materialized for the ride made the journey a delight, but it also brought high water in the rivers when the heat melted the snow high in the mountains. On the way down to Nanton, the women had no large fords. The route on the return home via the Bar U, however, meant they had to cross the Highwood River. They immediately saw that the water had risen alarmingly in the last three days. The river ran through Bert's property, so he was familiar with the terrain and knew where the best crossings were. The following day was still warm, and by the time they reached the ford, the water was so deep it was impossible to avoid swimming. With the swiftly running water, the footing could be treacherous.

"I'll go first, girls," said Bert. "It might be tricky, and you don't want to lose your horses, so watch carefully where I go."

His horse was steady and experienced and found the best footing until the depth forced it to swim. It was only a short distance, but the current was strong. It was important to get across at that point where the bank was shallow enough for the horses to get out of the river. One of the biggest dangers in river crossings was being swept down to a point where the bank was undercut, making it impossible to get out. But Bert had found a good crossing and was out in no time. June's friend went next, with little difficulty in staying close to the line Bert had taken.

June was still leading the new horse, making it more difficult for her as she had to keep one hand on the lead while guiding her own horse. Marquita was not quite as experienced at river crossings, and once the water started to swirl around her belly, she got excited. The high water immediately pulled on the lead rope, sweeping it under her tail. That was too much for the mare, and she started to buck. June was terrified. She knew she had to hang on at all costs and settle the mare before she tipped over in the strong current. Getting thrown from a horse and tangled in thrashing hooves had killed riders before. June immediately let go of the lead to the new horse, letting it fend for itself. Once she let go of the rope it came free of her own horse's tail, and Marquita stopped bucking. The mare could not actually buck that effectively in the deep water, but she could have fallen over. With a lunge of disgust, Marquita made for the far bank, having had enough of the river.

They were out quickly after that and so was the horse June had been leading, but June had experienced a real scare. Bert said with a ring of humor she found a bit disconcerting, "My God, June, your eyes were as big as saucers!"

When June had turned seventeen, she was allowed to go to country-dances. By now she was riding to Turner Valley for various errands on her own. Clara realized, suddenly, that June was growing up. She had been going to the local dances when the family went, but these social events began to outstrip Clara's interest. June was often invited to go along with friends, and Clara had little reason to keep her home if all the chores were done.

In the winter, the neighbors picked up June with a sleigh piled high with horse blankets and warm rocks for the feet. The event of just getting to the dance was almost as much fun as the dance. The most popular dance was at the Kew Community Hall eight miles away. The dances were fuelled by food brought by those attending, and sometimes with locally made beet wine. Though Canada did not go through Prohibition, no one had much money for anything other than homebrewed spirits, of which wine was the most common. It was easy to make and kept the atmosphere lively.

Each dance cost twenty-five cents that June often did not have. This was always overlooked if she brought one of Clara's homemade cakes that everyone loved. In the summer, she would often ride to the dance with the cakes bound up carefully and packed behind her saddle.

A dance often lasted all night and not necessarily because of the long distances traveled to get there. The

Kew dances were held every second week, and few wanted to miss them, for they were social events that kept people in touch when regular communication was not possible. Telephones were only found in the cities, where the lines could be strung economically to provide service to those relatively close by. It would be some time before the lines would reach any of the rural communities in Canada. This was also true of electricity, which would not arrive until after the Second World War. Thus the opportunity to visit was rarely missed.

The lack of telephone service caused other problems, as June would realize on many of her trips to town, especially in winter. Clara often wished they had a phone for more reasons than just the convenience. It would have saved her a great deal of worry, especially on one occasion.

"Okay. You have the battery to pick up and a list of a few things I want you to get. The main thing is to get the mail, though, even if they're out of everything else. Are you going to be warm enough?" she asked June.

"I have enough on. I have so many layers, I can hardly get into the saddle," June commented. "If I get cold, I can always stop at the Middletons' on the way back."

It was a beautiful winter day with the sun gleaming through the hoar frost covering the lower willows. By ten in the morning, June was already halfway to Turner Valley, though the road was drifted in badly where the corners caught the wind-blown snow. In some places, the wind had polished it to a shiny, rock-hard surface that could support the weight of the horse. In other places it was blown completely free, leaving a frozen, slippery surface that challenged the horse's footing. The sections that brought some worry occurred when the drifts were solid on the lee side but just soft enough on the windward side for the drift to collapse under the horse's weight, sending it stumbling forward. Another problem with breaking through slabs was the possibility that the sharp ice edge would cut the horse's legs when they collapsed. As June got closer to town, the track was broken out, making it much easier for her and the horse. The trip home, if she made good time, would be easier as well if they made it before the trail drifted in.

Once in town, the first stop was the garage to check on the cumbersome battery. "Hi there. Can I pick this up after I get Mom's shopping done?" she asked the owner.

"Sure. It's ready to go when you are – as long as you're here before closing. I guess you will be if you want to get home tonight. The forecast is saying a storm might hit tonight. This battery has been pretty good to you. If you ever need a new one, though, the ones they make now don't need to be recharged as often," he proposed.

She laughed and said that would not be likely unless the price of cakes went up. There was nothing to barter on this trip and only a few things to get after the trip to the post office, which meant more visiting time at the store.

"I think all I need on this trip is some baking powder and sugar to get us to Christmas. I have a sack to balance off with the battery, so give me about five pounds of sugar. Thanks, Mrs. Millar."

"No problem, June. Do you have long to wait for the battery?"

"I guess a few hours. I just need to go to the post office. I think I'll see if some of my friends are home so I might not be back for a while."

"Okay. This will be ready for you. Shall I put it on the tab?"

"No, I can pay for it this trip. Tip got paid, and I did okay on my trapline. I'll be back in a while."

June had met some of the local young people at the dances and proceeded to see who was home. She loved coming to town, especially as some of the new friends were potential boyfriends. At seventeen she was as tall as she would get and the active life kept her slim – almost muscular but not overly so. She was an attractive girl with fair hair and a strong face that reflected her father's character. The eyes were her mother's and exuded a kindness that was the core of her personality.

On this clear winter day with mild temperatures she ran into several friends, and before long it was time to collect the mail and the recharged battery. The final stop at the store allowed her to warm up while collecting the sugar and baking powder. At the last minute she added a small supply of salt and thought baking soda would not hurt either. As she was leaving, Mrs. Millar warned her that she might run into a storm and that it would be good not to waste time. "I had the radio on, and they said it was going to start snowing tonight, so best get back straight away."

Mrs. Miller was wrong. It was snowing as June rode past the end of town. She still had a few hours of daylight and hoped the trail would not fill in before she was at least halfway home. The snow came down heavily in the next couple of hours, slowing her progress. The wind was now causing large drifts to develop, and soon the horse began to tire as it struggled through the deepening snow. June became alarmed when she kept stopping and realized she had to break trail for her before she completely played out. *Oh well,* she thought. *At least it will warm me up. Riding in a blizzard is not a good way to stay warm.*

Soon she was ploughing through the drifts with the wretched battery in her arms. It never did ride well on the horse. As dusk enveloped the trees, she felt it might be good to stop at the Middletons' to warm up. Her horse gladly pulled into the yard and headed for the barn, probably hoping this would be it for the night.

June knocked on the door, surprising the Middleton family who did not expect callers at this time of night.

"Why, June! Kind of late for you to be out. Spent too long in town visiting?"

"Not really. I had a lot to do, but I didn't think I would snow so soon."

"Never mind. Come in and get some supper and warm up. Boys, make room for June at the end there. I have a hot stew so just dig in."

The supper was a good country meal, and June was hungry. But before she let herself in, she asked if she could put her horse in the barn with some hay. "I won't unsaddle him, though. I can't stay long."

"I think you'd better, June. You still have over four miles to go and it will be dark. I don't think this storm is going to quit until morning."

"I can't stay. My mom will worry all night if I don't get home."

Mrs. Middleton knew what she meant. Having a child out all night knowing he or she was riding home in a storm would worry anyone to distraction, but there was no way to get a message through other than sending her own kids out. She looked at June and thought the girl was old enough to look after herself. At least she would be warm and well fed and with a rested horse. She should make it home in a couple of hours. The horse certainly knew the way if she could coax it past the barn gate. Still, one thing Mrs. Middleton decided was that her oldest boy Lloyd could ride with June until he was sure she was going to make it home.

With some reluctance, June waved goodbye and headed into the swirling snow. The horse showed little enthusiasm to face the wind, but after a battle of wills he finally quit trying to turn around and settled into a dogged pace. With quiet determination, June and her companion plodded on through deepening drifts into the darkness. The pace was slow, and June felt bad for Lloyd, who still had to make the trip back, but the wind was abating and she hoped that the trail they broke would remain open for him. Finally, they saw the lights of the small house flickering through the trees.

As June rode into the yard she was greeted with a welcome hello from a much-relieved Clara. "Good God, child, I thought you were lost!" Clara laughed.

June had difficulty getting down she was so cold. Clara immediately sent her and Lloyd into the house and took care of the horses herself. With deft hands she unloaded the goods and soon had June's horse settled for the night. He fully deserved the oats and hay she heaped on him.

June could not be peeled away from the stove for some time, even though she was so tired all she wanted to do was crawl into a warm bed. It was not the last time she would face blizzards on her way back from town, but it was a memory that stood out for the rest of her life. She rode many of these trips alone and often had to rely on the horse to find the way when the weather turned. It defined a way of living that she would never take for granted. Though she always made it home, it was not unheard of for people to die in these fierce western storms before they made it to shelter. Lloyd spent the night and found the travel home a lot easier the following day.

The winter that she was eighteen did not seem quite as long as those in the past. At this age her social awareness was growing, and opportunities to meet people were growing as well. People had no other entertainment than what was provided through community events, skating and tobogganing parties, dinner and poker parties with neighbors or just plain visiting for the day. Computers and televisions had not yet driven everyone into social isolation where interaction came largely from a screen. June thought nothing of riding to a friend's house just to visit or stay for dinner. A poker game soon became a regular event after dinner. Again, beet wine was the common drink, and few hands were played for much over five cents – maybe twenty-five cents when times were flush. When money was scarce, matchsticks replaced the coin. The poker parties always lasted well into the night, particularly in the summer, leaving the visiting party to return home as the sun came up and just in time to do the chores ... but not before the hosts provided a good breakfast to travel on.

June took in all the dances and parties she could persuade Clara to let her attend, but she was never spared the morning chores no matter how late she got home. It seemed to her the later she got in, the more there was to do. Curfews were not part of the Turner Valley lifestyle, it seemed. No one gave much thought to her staying out, even though she was now decidedly going out with boys. Boyfriends began showing up on a regular basis, which actually pleased Tip, who would immediately put them to work chopping the fire-hardened wood he brought in from old burns. They would come to visit but stayed to chop, and June was puzzled when they kept coming back.

June was used to riding to all the social events with her friends and was surprised when one early boyfriend named Art showed up with a car to take her to the dance. It turned out to be one particular mode of transportation that didn't impress her at all. Initially the old beater was a curious novelty, but it turned out to be not particularly road-worthy. Art, who could not afford more than a second-hand clunker, was not much of a mechanic either. Most of their excursions to dances or other functions found them walking home more often than not. June quickly decided that horses were much more reliable. She also decided that neither the car nor Art were for her.

When the weather was poor, the days would be set aside for baking, washing hair, doing the laundry, or cleaning house. There was rarely a day that dragged, but when things slowed down it gave June a chance to paint. She was seeing Jack Lowe, a new fellow whom she felt was more of a good friend than a boyfriend, despite his more serious intentions. One of the reasons June was seeing him, though, had to do with her painting. He was quite taken with her creations and thought she had considerable talent. At that point, she had only worked with pastels and water-colors, but he thought she could do more permanent work on canvas with oil paints. He encouraged her work initially by building her an easel, but went further by introducing her to a friend who already worked in oils. Though oil paints were more expensive, June liked the results imme-diately and felt she was accomplishing more by getting her work on canvas, which was much more durable and less susceptible to water damage. She did not conquer this medium immediately as there was a lot to learn through trial and error in mixing the paints. She had no formal training in art and was feeling her way, experimenting with the pigments and mixtures. Oils became a natural medium for her, and she soon began to sell enough early compo-sitions to cover the costs of paint and canvas. It was also a vote of confidence in her natural talent and a source of encouragement to continue painting.

Life on the farm during these years changed little from the daily flow of work dictated by the season. June's rela-tionship with Jack continued, though it became apparent he wanted to be more than just good friends. But June was still quite young and felt a serious relationship was not what she wanted at that time in her life. She was still a young woman enjoying the free life in the foothills, and she wanted the opportunity to attend all the social functions without attachments. Knowing he would soon be going to war, Jack may have wanted a permanent commitment. It was 1938, and within the year, Canada would be swept up in the war in Europe.

Though few followed foreign affairs in much detail, it was impossible to not be aware of the events in Europe, which loomed like a growing storm just above the horizon. Despite the beating of war drums prior to 1939, some people were still caught off-guard when World War II erupted, dragging Canada along as an obligatory part of the British Commonwealth. When Britain declared war on Germany, the Commonwealth countries were considered automatically included. Jack and most of June's friends were of a prime age to enlist, and the general feeling was that not to do so was unacceptably unpatriotic.

Before Jack went into the army, he wanted to know where he stood with June. "Could we go for a ride up to the reserve before I go?" he asked on a late fall day. "I want to see the mountains before I leave, and you make a nice picture on horseback to take with me, June."

"Okay, Jack. But let's go early tomorrow morning. It's too late to get far today, and we should try for some of the higher meadows or you won't see the mountain. I can pack a lunch." She felt like she was trying to avoid this final confrontation over their future relationship and felt guilty putting him off. Why couldn't he keep things light and funny? But nothing could be funny for Jack anymore. He was a serious fellow, and knew what going to war meant.

He looked disappointed but agreed that it was a better plan. He seemed unsure of himself and a bit sad. There was apprehension in his expression as well, though June was often surprised at how many of her young friends professed they could hardly wait to join up and get into the fighting. As one general famously said, "If you go to war, someone is going to get shot." Canada was just beginning to get mobilized, but many families had men who had seen the First World War, and they had no illusions about the death toll of any battle. But this one was a popular war where the lines were clearly drawn. There was no such thing as not participating in the war effort.

The following day, June and Jack rode toward the reserve and up to the higher meadows. It was still warm, and the mountains stood out clearly. As they ate their sandwiches Jack brought out his grandmother's diamond ring and asked June if she would consider marrying him.

"I don't expect you to say yes today, but I want you to think it over at least. I just want to know if you would wait for the war to be over before you say anything. If I could think someone was waiting, it would be easier to go."

June felt bad for him but also a little trapped. No one knew how long the war was going to last, but it did not seem likely it would end any time soon considering the Allied commitment and how much ground had to be fought over. It seemed unfair to be asked for such a promise when she was so young. She just did not feel the way she thought she should for someone who might be her husband and partner for life. All she could do was say she would think about it and would keep the ring for the time being.

"I know that this seems selfish on my part, but it gives me some hope and someone to write to. It's a connection to home – that's not so much to ask is it?"

"No." June looked down at the ring then out toward the mountains. It was not much.

She saw him off on a fittingly cold day, but was concerned about his welfare. He had helped a lot in getting her on track with her painting, which meant so much to her and she was grateful.

"I will write you, June. I sure hope I get some letters from you too."

"You know I will, Jack," she said quietly. She felt bad about not being more certain of wanting him back. Oddly enough, she also felt bad because Clara and Tip liked him so much. Clara had even said she liked him as a son, and that even though June was young most courtships easily took a year or two, after which June would not be much younger than Clara was herself when she first married. Clara was a product of her generation and felt all girls were destined to marry, settle down, and have children. If she had misgivings about June, she kept them to herself. But it seemed to her that June was too independent and her penchant for taking on work like the log mill or trapping could hardly be seen as feminine pursuits. Everything June liked doing was much more suited for men than women. It was a wonder she had so many boys coming around.

It was not long after Jack left that news of the first casualties began to filter down. It came either by word of mouth or from newspapers, friends, and acquaintances, even family members. Many in the community were reported missing in action, dead, or wounded. It soon got to the point where neither Clara nor June wanted to read the newspaper. It was bad enough just to keep in touch with close friends whom they knew had sons, brothers, or husbands in the war. One of the saddest stories came from close neighbors whose son had lied about his age and joined the army when he was only sixteen. He had barely gotten into training when he was drowned in a training exercise. He never even left Canada.

In some part of her heart, June was not surprised when she came home and Clara asked her to sit with her on the porch. "I got news from Jack's family today, June. No point in saying anything but that he was killed last week."

June looked straight ahead but could not do anything. Something sank inside but it brought no immediate tears.

"He was shot down over Belgium," Clara continued. "I guess he got to be a pilot like he wanted. I thought he would wind up in the army, but it seems flying was what he wanted to do. He was flying a bomber, so he must have gone on lots of bombing missions. They didn't have any details. I'm so sorry, June."

June looked at her hands, realizing she still had the ring stowed safely in her room. She had never felt she could wear it.

"I'd best send the ring back to his family. It was an heirloom, you know. They would want it back. I feel bad that I never wanted to marry him. He sent a lot of letters about the war, but he also wrote about home. He wanted me to go back to the meadows and look at the mountains for him whenever I could."

"Well, it's a good thing you get up there as often as you do. He probably knew that," said Clara, but she could hardly keep the sadness away.

Much to June's surprise, the ring was returned to her by Jack's mother with a small note. "Jack can't give this to anyone else now, and I know he wanted you to have it. You gave him hope and a sense that he was fighting for something even if it would not have worked out. June, keep the ring and think about him when you ride to the mountains."

Jack never left June's thoughts, and the events of that day remained clear for the rest of her life.

Chapter IV

"I'M GOIN' TO MARRY YOU"

"Hello," said an attractive young man riding the flashy bay June had noticed as the group set out for the annual Stampede parade from her Uncle Bob's ranch near Calgary. It was July 1940, and June was now twenty years old. "Do you mind if I ride with you into town?"

June began to pay more attention to the cowboy than his horse. He was quite pleasant-looking, but more than that he seemed open and communicative, which was not often the case with men from the farming or ranching communities. They were usually shy on first meeting her. This was a pleasant surprise, and June soon found herself riding along, chatting amiably.

It took a while to get to the parade, giving the pair a chance to get acquainted and for June to realize she was quite attracted to Geoff Parker, a long-time friend of her uncle. She was already seeing Dick Lyall, whom Tip and Clara viewed as a good prospect for marriage. June was starting to get the feeling that they both wanted to see her settle down with someone stable, regardless of how she felt about the man. Having already gone through one devastating marriage proposal, she was not ready for another so quickly. She was still young enough to enjoy a few years of freedom with young men like Geoff, who had already driven the thought of marriage to Dick out of her head.

By the time June got home, her head was spinning with thoughts of Geoff. Uncharacteristically, she excitedly told Clara about her new acquaintance. "Mom! I just met the nicest man. We rode together to the parade, and he talked all the way. His name is Geoff Parker. He's a good friend of Uncle Bob."

For some reason, Clara did not seem too pleased with this development. Clara was not so old she did not remember what it was like to feel the obsession of young love, and she worried that this might be the end of June's relationship with Dick. Dick may not have been as exciting as this new-found friend, but he was reliable, and both Clara and Tip hoped June would marry him.

Clara's concern was warranted. June soon made it apparent that she was happy to be good friends with Dick but nothing more. She immediately began to see Geoff as often as she could. This inevitably led to conflict at home.

"Why aren't you seeing Dick any more, June? I thought you were getting along fine," Clara asked one day.

"Oh, he's nice enough, but Geoff is just more fun. We have a good time together," replied June, now a little wary of where this conversation was going.

"Yes. Well, Tip and I think you are seeing too much of him."

JUNE RIDING IN THE STAMPEDE PARADE

This worried June, who resented Tip's interest in who she saw or didn't see. It seemed inevitable that Tip and Clara's disapproval of her new relationship would not end well. Negative comments about her new boyfriend insinuated themselves into the conversation until she felt the barrage was too much. Though June was not Tip's daughter by birth, they had forged a bond through family ties, commitments, and a common love of horses. But both were stubborn, and neither backed down in a confrontation. When Clara sided with Tip in not supporting her daughter's desire to stay with Geoff, June felt she had no room to maneuver.

June had never thought the day would come when she felt she had to leave, but after a particularly bitter row, she believed there was no option. It was a fledgling flight from the nest, which is necessary at some point for all children on the cusp of adulthood. Often it's triggered by the confidence found in the alliance of a new romantic interest. Geoff was June's escape route, but she also had the support of her Uncle Bob, who agreed to let her live with them until the situation was resolved.

"So you think living with Bob is going to help?" Clara asked angrily when she found June packed and ready to go. "I still don't think Geoff is the grand guy you think he is, but if you must, then find out for yourself – the hard way!"

"I can't see why you hate him so much. He's asked me to marry him, and I'm going to. Just as soon as he gets back on leave from the air force." Protests of not being a child anymore did not seem to carry much weight with Clara.

Although June's words were directed at her mother, it was Tip she felt most alienated from. She thought she had better leave before things were said that would be hard to take back. She knew she would miss her mom, and probably Tip, but at the moment she was too mad to think about it. Leaving the dark hills and high meadows, though, was her biggest regret, for she was not at war with the country that gave her so much sustenance. Subconsciously, she knew the place would always be home, and she wondered if she was as ready as she thought to leave it.

The move to her uncle's was a considerable relief for a while, as the constant bickering was at an end, though she still felt bad about the poor relationship that had developed. She had always been close to Clara; for so many years, despite the support of June's uncles, it had seemed as if it was just the two of them fending off a tough world. They had been through a lot – but now it would seem that Tip had replaced her, and the ease with which Clara let her go did little to dispel that notion. It would be a while before the generosity Tip had displayed in taking in an older child would sink in. It could not have been easy for him to adapt to life with a child almost grown.

June stayed with her Uncle Bob and Edna while Geoff was still in Calgary. They saw each other through December, but by January, he was on his way east for air force training. He seemed to be constantly sick before he left, and was often cranky, but June remained committed to him and promised to write often. After Christmas, her relationship with Tip and Clara improved – probably due to Geoff's absence – and by the middle of January she was ready to move home. Regardless of the reason, June was relieved to be back. She had no doubt that her affair with Geoff would resume despite Clara's hope that distance would cool their ardor, but for the moment, it was not brought up and life resumed its old rhythm.

That rhythm consisted of many visits to the neighbors, dances, skiing, trips to town, daily chores, and considerably more painting opportunities. She had fewer chores in winter and more opportunity to visit friends and relatives as the social calendar whirled with dinners, parties, and dances. June now kept a daily diary and few days passed without mention of her activities. There were even days when she was allowed to sleep in if she had been at an all-night dance. Often the parties at her own home lasted into the early morning hours.

The people June and her parents saw the most were the Gettigs, who lived so close by. Not a week passed by without regular visits, usually for poker games, afternoon visits, and often dinner. Mrs. Gettig was a close friend of Clara's, and June always found her visits a comfort though a certain formality was maintained; June never referred to either of her neighbors by their given names. Her diary always addresses them as Mr. or Mrs. Gettig. Though the Gettigs had no children of their own, they did have one young, long-time boarder named Frank. Frank was not young enough to be mothered, but he was good help and good company on their homestead. Mrs. Gettig's parental instinct went to caring for numerous animals she adopted – even to the extent of bringing up a young coyote. The Gettigs were renowned for their hospitality, and never lacked for company. It therefore came as quite a shock when Mr. Gettig had a serious heart attack in March. He was ill for a few days, then he died. Clara and Tip were over to help throughout, giving what comfort they could, helping with the chores, and of course providing food. At these times, food materialized from everywhere. The Gettigs were popular, and Mrs. Gettig had support from all her neighbors. There was a funeral to arrange as well as just keeping up the farm.

Mrs. Gettig stayed on at the farm where she had been happiest. She was not ready to sell out and relocate when all her friends were nearby, but it was not easy to keep up the work on her own. For some while, friends helped out where they could, and Frank became almost indispensable. June went over as often as she could, but as spring advanced, her thoughts turned to her own affairs. She was good at corresponding, but the same could not be said for Geoff. It was, therefore, another surprise when he suddenly turned up for a short visit in the early part of April. Despite the lack of warning, June was thrilled.

He did not stay long, as he had plans to remain in Calgary during his leave. June told him she would go and stay with Jackie in Calgary to give them more time together. There had been little doubt about how she still felt about him – his return lifted her spirits in a way she had not expected. Whatever doubt she might have had was gone, and she looked forward to a more prolonged reunion.

She arrived at Jackie's full of enthusiasm, chattering on about her future with Geoff, as she waited for him to phone. Three days passed, but no call came from the errant fiancé. When more time passed without a word, a sinking, fearful knot grew in her stomach, but slowly anger overcame her deepening concern. What could be the problem, and why had he not contacted her? Suspicion lurked that her mother might have been right about him. In confusion she went to see his sister who worked at Eaton's, hoping she could shed some light on where he was. At that moment, before anything was said, Geoff strolled in.

His casual response to seeing her upset her more than she expected. She was struck with a sudden anger.

"Geoff, I'm glad you walked in! I've been wondering why you haven't called even though I came in specifically to see you. I think we need to talk about this." June thought she was almost whispering, but the alarmed man, looking furtive as though everyone had overheard her, took her elbow and guided her to a more discreet part of the store.

"Yeah, sorry about that. I've been meaning to call once I got some time ... "

The reason he had not called her was the oldest excuse of all.

"What do you mean? I thought we had an agreement. I told you I would be at Jackie's. I can't stay here indefinitely, you know. Seems like a funny way to treat someone you're supposed to marry!" she said in as controlled a manner as her temper would allow.

"Well sure, but you know … after all, there is a war on and who knows what can happen? I thought we could pick up once I get back for good. Look, there is something you should know. I ran into an old girlfriend of mine – not anyone you know – but I've been going out with her, and she doesn't think I should go out with two people … you know, at the same time."

June stared down at the engagement ring he had given her, wondering what kind of fool he thought she was. Suddenly, she was thinking, *What kind of fool is he?* His moral compass seemed to have gone south. Without hesitation, she drew off the ring and handed it to him. "Here. Give this to her. I'm sure you can't afford two."

"No, no! I don't want it back. Just keep it for now."

This seemed even more incredible. How could he go out with another girl and yet want her to keep an engagement ring? He seemed truly confused. Shaking her head, she grabbed his hand and firmly placed the ring on his palm, folding his fingers around it.

"I don't think we should see each other anymore, even if you stop seeing your other friend. I can't rely on you at all, and I don't want that in a husband. I'm sorry, Geoff, but don't bother to phone or come by again." With that answer, June nodded to his sister, who was discreetly trying not to follow their agitated conversation, and walked out of the store. It was not the last she would hear from Geoff, but nothing would change her mind about where he stood with her. She had never been so disappointed in anyone in her life.

Clara and Tip may have been glad of the split, but they still had sympathy for the pain it caused June. They were supportive and just hoped that she would move on without any lingering regrets. Clara was not too worried, as she knew June well. Once the duplicity was clear, June entertained no remote thoughts of patching things up. She had been jilted, and that was the end of it for her, with no shadow of a doubt. She found as she grew older that there were plenty of men around who found her attractive, and though she knew she would marry eventually, she was not in that big of a hurry to do so. There were still lots of dances to go to and parties to attend without being tied to any one person. She had developed quite an independent spirit that would be one of her greatest strengths, and for the present she enjoyed her freedom.

Life, unfortunately, is not laid out like a map, and the unexpected is often the only thing to expect. The next stage of her life was upon her with alarming swiftness.

On a hot, dusty day in July, she decided she would ride to the rodeo in Bottrel – a good eighty miles to the north of their home. June, who never thought twice about riding forty miles in a day, thought she could break up the ride by staying with the Mickles, whose ranch was conveniently halfway between. Charley Mickle was an old timer from

Cochrane who had inherited a stunning piece of property in the Mission Valley near Jumping Pound Creek. But Charley was a wanderer and left the running of the ranch largely to his two sons, Jack and Bert. No one really thought much about Charley's sporadic visits, but the fact was he rarely got home. Most of the time he wandered from ranch to ranch on his horse or, more recently, in a car he had acquired. No one could say at any given time where he might be, but he usually showed up sooner or later. Tip was particularly fond of him and considered him a good friend. Despite this, both Tip and Clara were wary of the two boys, who had a reputation for being wild.

This was not surprising given the way the boys had been brought up. Jack and Bert were the youngest of a large family consisting mainly of older sisters and one older brother. Charley and Adella had married in 1899 and promptly started having children, spaced evenly every two to four years apart, until Jack – the youngest – was born in 1919. The oldest, Elva, was born in 1902, making a span of seventeen years that saw eight children grace the Mickle household.

But the strain of bearing so many children over a long period took its toll; Adella died in 1930, or possibly earlier depending on who is consulted. Jack and Bert were semi-orphaned when they were eleven and thirteen years old respectively. Adella's death took quite a toll on Charley, who promptly became nomadic. The boys subsequently enjoyed so much freedom that complaints of their unruliness encouraged Charley to leave them on the family ranch in Mission Valley, successfully isolating them from polite society.

JACK AND BERT ON THE HOMESTEAD

BERT, HUNTING FOR SUPPER

They scraped by with farming the land and shooting meat when they needed it – rabbits mostly. Some neighbors used to say they ate so many rabbits they would run for the bushes if a dog showed up.

Charley did not mean to be an errant parent. The older children were pretty much on their own and could look after themselves. Lennie, the oldest boy, was already ranching a piece of property to the north of the Mickle homestead, and Charley may have felt that he would keep an eye out for his younger brothers. Charley periodically dropped by for a visit and left a can of beans or some strawberry jam on the table to help out. The boys seemed to be managing, even if their table manners were a bit neglected. What Charley may not have been aware of was the enmity between Jack and Jack's much older brother Lennie. The two never did get along, making Lennie a poor choice as substitute father. The rumor of Bert and Jack shooting up the countryside floated around, and all Clara would say to June was, "You stay away from them wild Mickle boys!"

But June did not hear that sentiment until she returned from her trip to the rodeo. On that hot day in July, she had little on her mind but the thought of enjoying the rodeo and her prospective stay with the Mickles. She actually knew very little about the younger boys other than they were around her age – which always made things interesting – and that the family had been settled in the area for some time. In fact, as she would learn, the Mickles and the Hamiltons had a lot in common.

The Mickle family's sojourn in western Canada began when Wheeler Mickle decided to make the arduous journey to Quesnel, British Columbia, from his hometown in Essex County, Ontario. He was all of twenty when he became one of the famous "Overlanders" with his brother Florien in June of 1862. It was an unsettled time in Canada's interesting past, epitomized by gold stampedes, renegade Indians, rum runners, and uncertain politics. The Overlanders were a group of deserting colonists consisting mainly of would-be prospectors, who decided to take the overland trail across the prairies and mountains to British Columbia. The goal for most was the Cariboo gold fields in uncharted British Columbia, though many would not make it.

The Overlanders organized an expedition at Fort Gary, Manitoba, from where 220 men and one woman left at the beginning of June in a long procession of a hundred red river carts. It must have been exciting and, to some degree, frightening for the two young Mickle boys, to be leaving for an unknown land so very far from home. They may not have known it then, but it was the last they would see of the east for many years. The difficulties of the trip began shortly after they left Manitoba when the well-known roads deteriorated into a pot-holed track and finally, a meandering path, making for navigational nightmares. By the time the expedition reached Edmonton, one hundred and twenty-five of them had quit. If the plains had been too hard for them, the mountains would be barely manageable with winter hard upon them.

The one woman – a Mrs. Catherine Schubert, who had three children and was pregnant with her fourth – continued with the remaining men, who included the Mickle brothers. But the trip through the mountains proved formidable. They left Edmonton driving the horses and cows until they could take them no farther. The horses were turned loose and the cows became beef jerky. In the race to reach Lytton before winter set in, the luggage was systematically abandoned along the way. But first they had to reach Tête Jaune Cache, where they faced a difficult choice. They could either raft down the Fraser River or go overland to the North Thompson River. Either way would lead to Lytton and thence to Victoria. The route to the North Thompson was considerably shorter, but much more challenging, as it required pushing through deep BC bush to the headwaters of that tempestuous river. But both routes were perilous. The Fraser River swung way to the north and had its own hazards. The Mickle brothers chose the Fraser and reached Lytton in September, only just in advance of winter. Both groups lost people in the dangerous rivers, but miraculously, Mrs. Schubert and her family – who chose the Thompson – survived.

Typically, the brothers arrived after most of the good ground was staked. But like the Hamilton brothers, also there during this period, Wheeler soon realized that money could be made by those daring enough to drive the stage-coaches on the hazardous Cariboo road. Florien was a blacksmith by trade and quickly found work, for it was a much needed service.

Before the road was built, Wheeler packed supplies with horses and mules to the rough mining town of Barkerville. Some enterprising souls actually brought camels in, which were considered to be hardier than horses, but they were a terror on the trail. Both the horses and the mules were trau-matized whenever they encountered these strange animals, causing havoc when they bolted at the sight.

Once the excitement of the Gold Rush days wore off, Wheeler felt it was time to settle down with a family and a home. He had made a promise to marry Julia Thompson, a young lady back in Ontario, once his fortune was made.

Despite the fact that Wheeler preferred the girls from home, he much preferred the West as a place to locate, and shortly after their wedding, the young couple returned to BC. He had exaggerated his circumstances a little, but that would soon change when they established a ranch in the Nicola Valley. This is beautiful country, very conducive to ranching and raising the horses that Wheeler loved. By now he was considered quite a horseman, and the years here passed quickly. All four of the couple's children were born in the Nicola Valley. Florien also moved to the area about the same time, but he never felt the need to move on and is buried there now. Interesting enough, the Hamiltons also settled in the Nicola Valley, but family history does not mention if they knew the Mickles at the time.

Wheeler still had a roving nature, and he took a notion to move to Calgary. Julia may have had some longing for home at this juncture, or felt it was time her children got to know the rest of the family in Ontario. She took the children there for a short visit while Wheeler established himself in the Cochrane area west of Calgary. Julia and the kids joined him thereafter.

Wheeler gained employment hauling freight for the North-West Mounted Police between Calgary and Fort

Walsh in the Cypress Hills. It was lucrative enough for Julia and him to build one of the first dwelling houses in Calgary on the east side of the Elbow River. The house stood out for some time amidst the tent shacks that dominated the town. Not content to drive freight forever, Wheeler soon built a stable and entered the Feed and Dray business, which may have been the first business of its kind in the area. The business was quite a success as the town began to grow, and soon he and his family moved to a larger site on the Bow River. When land came up for sale along the Elbow River, Wheeler was one of the first to purchase riverfront property.

One of the first settlers in the valley was George Livingston. Sam Livingston took over the property from his father and established a trading post in 1872 that became a regular stop on the route from Fort Benton to Morley. Two priests, Father Scollen and Father Doucette, established the first Catholic Mission in southern Alberta there, right next to the trading post. For this reason the trading post soon became known as the Old Mission Post. A cairn, established in 1939, marks the location and stands to this day. This was the property that Wheeler Mickle settled on when he acquired the land from Livingston. It later became the post office, and Wheeler was the first postmaster to provide service for the residents in the area.

Though Wheeler was a successful businessman when he entered his middle years, in May of 1885 he was still young enough, at forty-three, to be called upon for action. When the Riel Rebellion broke out, he was approached by General Strange to work as a teamster for the army when they marched to engage Big Bear's force at Frenchman's Butte in Saskatchewan.

Big Bear, who was arrested for joining the Riel Rebellion, did not actually take part in the battle. Rather, it was several of the young Indian braves who ignored his pleas to avoid the conflict who were responsible for the fighting. The army marched to Fort Pitt, but found it burned to the ground by the rebels who were now dug-in close to Frenchman's Butte. The initial attack was unsuccessful, and to escape capture, the young braves slipped into the hills during the night. The dispersed braves were later caught in individual action, and the rebellion was put down. All the teamsters were praised for valiantly staying with the army, even though they were given the opportunity to return home after delivering supplies to Fort Pitt. In the manner of the day, they all returned as minor heroes in the first real fighting for which Canadians had been called to arms. Though it was an internal rebellion, Riel had close ties with America, which could have led to a larger conflict.

Upon returning to Calgary, Wheeler decided to take up homesteading on the land he had on the Elbow River. He eventually became the first postmaster at the small community of Springbank, which led to further work as mail carrier in the Jumping Pound area. The family moved again farther up the Elbow River, obtaining a substantial amount of land in the Mission Valley where they lived until 1912. This was followed by a brief move to Victoria, BC, but Alberta was their true home now, and they soon moved back to Cochrane where the family remained. Both

Wheeler and Julia died there at the age of eighty-one and are buried in the old Cochrane cemetery.

Though Wheeler had a tendency to wander (which seemed to have been passed on to Charley), the family remained in the Cochrane area and held onto the homestead for some time. The homestead buildings were located high on the open prairie. They had a magnificent view of the Rocky Mountains, which always stunned June when the sky blew violet clouds across the horizon, crimson with the setting sun. How often she would look up to unexpectedly see the horses silhouetted against the White Mountains, manes flickering erratically in the breeze. Unfortunately, the location had a few drawbacks; it was too far from water and the exposure was wicked when the bone-chilling, wind-laced snow blew ceaselessly through the cracks.

On the day June arrived at the Mickle farm, the piercing wind had taken a break, leaving her hot and dusty. She stopped briefly at the Elbow River for a quick wash and let her horse drink his fill before proceeding on to the farmhouse. She was not sure what she would find, but hoped Charley was at the place as he'd promised. She was not prepared to find a very dirty young man with penetrating hazel eyes demanding whose "crow bait" was on the front lawn eating his grass. When Bert Mickle spotted June, he was completely taken off-guard. His upbringing, such as it was, had not included entertaining young women as attractive as June. It took her a while to become acquainted with those eyes, though, as he refused to look at her. But something held her attention; an instant chemistry was ignited, and she found herself very attracted to the bashful cowboy, despite his three-days' growth of whiskers. His lean face shadowed the deep-set eyes that glinted through smoke curling up from a droopy cigarette dangling from his thin lips. He rolled the cigarettes himself, which always left them kind of skinny and bent. It was his trademark, and he continued to roll them all his life, ignoring the ease of simply buying them.

June was not quite sure what she felt — a sudden excitement, or a little fear and puzzlement at the quiet demeanor that belied the stories she had heard. Jack, the younger brother, was far more the center of any half-baked ideas he and Bert came up with to liven up their lives. Tip had chuckled when he'd told June the rumor he'd heard that the boys once tried to rob the Cochrane bank. He had no way of knowing if there was any validity to it, but it made a good story. Tip always covered his tracks adding, "Don't take no stock in what I say!"

Apparently, Jack had thought they could slip into town, rob the bank, and lose any pursuit on well-placed get-away horses. Jack's problem was not having a good watch. Story went that he and Bert got as far as stashing the getaway horses in a corral up the Elbow valley before they lit out for town. But when they got there, the bank was not yet open. Fortunately, the bar was open so they stopped in to have a few beers while waiting for the bank staff to arrive. They lost track of time, and when they left the bar, the bank had closed for the day. With a *c'est la vie* shrug, the would-be bandits rode home. They had lost any incentive to carry out the madcap plan.

To June's relief, Charley finally showed up and introduced her to his son Bert and a few others who had come

JACK, BERT, JUNE & FRIEND

to help with the haying. That evening the family managed to put on a substantial meal for the haying crew, and though Bert would not look at June, he made sure she sat next to him.

The following day, Charley decided to drive to the Bottrel rodeo and offered June a ride with him. The rodeo was worth the trip, but the drive back was more eventful. Charley may have toured around the country fairly safely on his horses, but it was a different story with his driving. It was hard to ignore that his driving was notoriously poor and was not much improved by rain that fell when they left the rodeo. He was also blind in one eye. His depth perception was definitely challenged when it came to deciphering the location of approaching objects. That day, one such object suddenly loomed before them and caused June to shout, "Watch out! You're going to hit the bridge!" Charley made it across the slippery surface but careened into the ditch on the far side. The load of eggs he had picked up from his daughter that morning did not survive the impact.

"My God, what a mess! How will you ever clean up these eggs?"

Charley was nonplused. "These things happen all the time." The rest of the journey was much slower, but June was afraid to move for fear of getting any more eggs on her clothes. She was not sure what bothered Charley more: the mess in the car or the fact that he was out of eggs.

It was still raining when they got back to the Mickle household where they found Bert and his close friend Bill Munro taking a break from haying and keeping dry. Haying is one activity that is put on hold when the rain makes it impossible to harvest. Charley, true to form, did not waste much time at the ranch and immediately left for Cochrane to pick up his youngest son, Jack, who was on leave from the army. It was 1941, and the war was a long way from ending. June may have wondered why Bert had not been called up, but the army still needed food and many young farmers were encouraged to stay home and keep the supplies coming. June was not about to ride back to the Turner Valley homestead in the rain and found herself housebound with two very shy young men. Conversation never really got off the ground, so she decided to make pies instead. Once that activity petered out, she resorted to sketching. She convinced Bill to pose for her as he seemed more comfortable in her presence, but she was determined to get Bert's attention one way or another and soon talked him into posing, despite his objections. He finally had to look at her, and she was suddenly the focus of those hazel eyes that she found so startling. She distracted herself by concentrating on the sketch – but by the time the sketch was finished, she knew he was as attracted to her as she was to him.

That night after the rest of the gang showed up, the usual poker game started up. June had no money and was tempted to go to bed, but Bert was not ready to see the last of her. He kept slipping her nickels just to keep her in the game. He still would not look at her directly but sat close by, passing the nickels under the table. They were intensely aware of one another, both probably a little confused at the unexpected attraction. This was nothing like any other experience June had had with the previous men she had dated. There was an edge to Bert – he was like a wolf: wild, shy, unpredictable, yet strangely gentle.

Finally the game wound down and June headed for bed. As she made her way to the bedroom in the dark, she was astonished to see Bert right behind her. She turned, not knowing what to say when he leaned casually against the wall. He looked right at her and in a slow drawl, with a quiet but determined voice announced, "I'm goin' to marry you." She was thunderstruck.

June could barely reply. She had no idea how to respond and now became shy herself as she stumbled off for bed and sleep that was a long time coming. She only knew one thing – her response to Bert was visceral. He was unlike any other boy she had ever met; they now all seemed like boys to her. He made her blood race with just a glance, leaving her thinking he probably would marry her if she could convince her family to accept the "wild Mickles."

The next day, Bert rode partway back with her to show her a shortcut across the property, giving his shyness a chance to dissipate. They chatted all the way to a final fence where he turned back, not quite ready to "meet the family." If June were in any doubt about how she felt, his farewell kiss would have erased it. Love at first sight? In hindsight it was damn close to that for June, and everything about that was telegraphed to Clara when June got home. If she wasn't talking about the Mickles, she was drifting off in reverie and mooning at the barn or whatever else she was not really seeing. Clara knew the real thing had just swooped up her daughter, and she had to give it some hard thought.

Interestingly enough, after all the disputes she and Tip had with June over not marrying (or trying to marry) the right man, they had fewer qualms about Bert than June might have thought. Charley Mickle, despite his wandering ways, was known to be a steady man with plenty of horse ability. He was also an "old-timer" and a longtime friend of the family. Though they didn't know Bert that well, they were prepared to accept him based on what they knew of his father.

Ironically, while riding the rest of the way back home from the Mickles' place, June had a final encounter with her old flame Geoff. He was driving his truck up the road actually hoping to meet her and renew their affair with yet another undying declaration of love. The old girlfriend had jilted him in turn and whether he was on the rebound or genuinely realized he loved June, he wanted her back. But June wasn't going to take any more chances with Geoff, now that her head was full of Bert. She ended it finally, and though they remained friends, she was able to reassure Clara that Geoff was definitely not in her future.

Distances and pressures of farm work (haying would not wait) meant that Bert did not get down to the Turner Valley ranch to meet Clara and Tip until October. His timing couldn't have been worse for June. Bert rode in just as Clara and June were wrestling with one of the several turkeys that had caught croup – a disease that causes them to choke on phlegm. The only treatment was to hold them down and slit a hole in the throat to drain the vile sludge. Turkeys can be pretty strong when subjected to this treatment and all Clara could do was sit on the bird while June wielded the knife through the layers of feathers. Bert was polite enough not to laugh, but June still wondered if the sight wouldn't be enough to change his mind about their future. She was a mess and hastily ran into the house to clean up, leaving Clara to see if Bert still wanted to come in.

Despite the awkward introduction, a few glasses of cherry wine made the meeting with June's mother quite a success. She was probably captivated by Bert's forthright personality and disarmed by a bashful quality that masked some of the more uncultivated aspects of his personality. Gradually, she stopped thinking about the rumors of stray cattle gone missing near the Mickle Ranch, or some of the tales of shooting up the countryside. Both Jack and Bert were expert shots, which kept them well supplied with meat. The wilder incidents tended to involve Jack rather than Bert. Bert had an innate gentle quality not found in Jack, who was harder and more prone to trouble.

After this meeting, both Tip and Clara accepted the idea that Bert was likely going to be part of the family.

Again it was some time before June saw Bert, but they did keep in touch by mail. The distance between the farms was considerable and not easy to travel once winter set in. But they did manage to finally take in a dance at Kew early in January. The occasion was made more memorable by a funny incident initiated by some of the local boys. The boys did not seem to like the fact that June was being taken away from them by an outsider. Apparently Jumping Pound was just a little too far away to be considered part of the Turner Valley community. Two of the rowdier boys, fortified by a little too much home brew, decided that Bert had no right to take June away to "foreign parts." She was a local girl and they felt she should marry someone from the community, even if wasn't them. June declared it was ridiculous but also found it a bit flattering. Bert was never much of a fighter, however, and always found a way to defuse a conflict situation. He merely asked the boys to step outside for a glass of wine or two to discuss the problem. In no time, the boys declared him to be a good old guy and tipsily agreed he could marry June.

But the difficulty the couple had in seeing each other led June to another decision. Feeling like a young lady about to embark on the adult phase of her life, she felt it was time to leave home and live on her own for brief period before her wedding. Her new status as an engaged woman left her feeling strangely free. She was twenty-one and legally an adult. If she could get past the 'Ladies and Escorts' signs on all proper-minded drinking establishments, she could even drink in the local bars.

She mainly wanted the freedom to see Bert more frequently, independent of her family, so they could enjoy a real courtship. After Christmas, she moved to Calgary to look for a job. She boarded with Jackie and her family, keeping Clara and Tip happy, though neither June nor Bert needed parental supervision. Though the sexual revolution brought about by the advent of the birth control pill was years away, the war had done much to lighten people's attitude to premarital sex. The fact that Bert and June even gave it some thought was measure enough to make that clear – in Clara's day it would never have even been discussed, much less considered. But both young adults knew where they were headed and did not want to jeopardize their life together with any unwanted pregnancy. They both decided to keep that aspect of their life special and wait until after they were married.

It was one of the best periods of her life. Bert and June had the freedom to explore their relationship without being under the constant supervision of either family. The only drawback was the difficulty June had in finding a job that suited her. Jobs were scarce for women with limited education, but she was able to pay for her room and board by keeping house for Jackie's parents, who both worked. The expenditure was not high. They only charged her six dollars per month. The one job she would have loved to pursue was an opportunity to get involved with silversmithing at the Birks diamond shop, but it required a long-term commitment that she could not give if she wished to keep her marriage plans.

The housework left her free to see Bert when he came to town, usually once a week, and gave her an opportunity to meet the rest of Bert's family. They often visited with Bert's older sisters, who lived in and around Cochrane, but it was Rita that June got to know best. It was also Rita who had provided what little parenting Jack and Bert had when Charley was sojourning around the country, and she was especially close to Bert. When not visiting, Bert and June took the opportunity to see shows or go to local dances. Bert also tried again to get into the navy, but the combination of an old ulcer and flat feet kept him effectively out of the war. Neither the navy nor the army missed his recruitment, as the country still needed the ranchers and farmers to keep food and stock in plentiful supply. By New Year's, the couple's intent to marry was formalized when they announced their engagement and set a date to marry in the spring.

The wedding was anything but conventional. June certainly made plans and managed to get her whole trousseau together for just twenty-five dollars. Clara gave June the money that she had scraped together from her baking and dairy products, which was a lot for the times. June found a lovely dress that only cost seven dollars and twenty-one cents. It had a trace of lipstick on the front that she skillfully removed with warm water and toothpaste. She picked up a pair of shoes for three-fifty and a halo of flowers also for three-fifty. With the remaining money, she purchased some nice material for a going-away dress and a raincoat. These last items she made herself. Years later, she would wonder about this meager sum that so poignantly reflected the Depression era. It was all she needed to be happy at her wedding, and she was proud of that accomplishment.

But even the best-laid plans cannot prevent things from going wrong. Clara, who had been heavily involved with her only daughter's wedding, planned the event to take place outside at the Bar T Ranch. It would be the first time many of the Hamilton clan met the Mickles, despite the similarity in family history. It soon became apparent that the Hamiltons were comparatively straight-laced compared to the Mickles. Certainly the Hamiltons were all present and accounted for by one p.m. when the wedding was scheduled to start.

"Mother, aren't they here yet?" wailed June, now confined properly to the bedroom, awaiting the rest of the party.

"Well at least Bert is here," replied Clara, "but I have no idea where the rest of the groom's party is."

The rest of the party consisted of Jack, the best man, and other members of the family, who were expected to arrive from Turner Valley by car. The flowers were also entrusted to Jack, meaning the last-minute bridal bouquet was also missing – along with that of the bridesmaid. June was determined to have her flowers.

She paced nervously back and forth watching in alarm as the clouds scudded closer over the dark hills of the forest reserve.

"My God, it's two thirty! Where can they be?" moaned June, who could only consult her mother and Jackie, her bridesmaid. She could not believe this was happening.

Outside, the Hamiltons were working on losing some of their reserve with the help of a keg of beer brought in for the celebration. By four p.m. June was sure the wedding was not going to happen. It was now raining buckets and the whole party was confined to the small house. She dared not start crying for fear everyone would hear her.

Shortly after that, the wayward best man showed up, clearly having started celebrating early with the rest of the party. Miraculously the flowers survived the journey, and June's Uncle Bob finally got to give his niece away in the crowded little home, to the accompaniment of a radio. Before the ceremony was over, even that source of soothing melody ended abruptly when one of Bert's sisters knocked the radio over before the I do's were said. A startled Clara afterwards observed, "I think she spent too much time making friends with the beer keg."

The crowd began to laugh, causing the minister to start again so that everyone could hear the vows. It did not matter much to Bert, who was so soft-spoken no one could hear him anyway. By then Bert was so weak in the knees, Jack had to prod him to stay upright. The only way Bert managed that was to cling to June's hands with all his strength. This was enough to almost bring tears to her eyes, but out of pain rather than sentiment. In Bert's fear, he had almost clawed her skin away. Tears of pain or happiness at that point seemed justified.

When she finally got a chance to find out what the unanticipated delay was, Jack leeringly passed it off as the trivial oversight of not putting gas in the car. June took this with more than a grain of salt since all they would have had to do was go back for gas. The wedding was over, and it seemed pointless now to create disharmony with newly-met relatives. Keeping the family peace would become a trademark of the new marriage.

The tension of the long wait gradually dissipated as the entire party drove off over the bad roads to the Kew Dance Hall for the dinner and reception. Everyone drank too much, ensuring a memorable occasion most would never forget. Friends reminded June of that party for the rest of her life, for it was considered one of the best the old hall ever saw. Bert and June were the first to leave for the hotel they had booked in Calgary, but all their good intentions of keeping the wedding night special were not rewarded on that occasion. They were so tired they fell asleep the minute they hit the bed.

JUST MARRIED

Chapter V

EARLY YEARS ON THE MICKLE HOMESTEAD

Bert and June began their life together on the old Mickle homestead. This was a contentious issue that would have a fateful influence in the years ahead, but at the time, none of this was evident to June. When they'd announced their engagement officially at Christmas, Bert had told Charley that he and June would be leaving the ranch.

Clem Gardner, who lived close by, had a large operation and had offered Bert a position working for him. This would include accommodation for Bert and his new bride. Both felt it would allow them to live comfortably near the family, but give them the distance they needed to start their new life together. Because Lennie was the oldest son, Bert always assumed Lennie would inherit the homestead. To his surprise, Charley did not see it that way. He knew his sons well and did not think Lennie would look after the place. Jack wasn't even interested in the place. Charley saw a stability and purpose in June that would give Bert the grounding he needed to keep the ranch in the family. Bert, in his quiet way, said little, but he could understand his father's reservations. Jack had no real qualms about this decision, as he was not ready to settle down. Lennie, though, was not happy. As the oldest, he had always assumed he would take over the place and was disappointed when it went to Bert. Bert wanted to keep his father happy and was pleased he would be starting out with his own place, but he knew it might lead to problems. The resentment that festered with Lennie was one of the main reasons for frequent quarrels with his brother. It divided the family and made much of June's early years with Bert a trial, particularly on holidays or at family reunions where old animosities often surfaced.

After the wedding, June thought that they would never have any time alone together. They had barely got out of the hotel, hoping to get some peace at the Mickle place, when they were inundated with relatives. For over a week there was no respite from well-wishers, whom she wished would just go away. She was certainly getting to know the Mickle clan! She had not even been able to get home for a change of clothes before a month of rain set in. It rained so hard they could not travel, and she had to bum a shirt and pants off Bert, but her lack of proper clothing did not bother him. They finally had some solitude and plenty of time to settle into a marriage that would last a lifetime together. No amount of dating had prepared either one of them for this adjustment, but June soon discovered it was all she had hoped for. Bert, despite his colorful upbringing, was a gentle man to whom no other held a candle. He was the love of her life.

NEWLYWED BERT AND JUNE

However, they could barely leave the ranch, for chores still had to be done and the stock tended – which on the Mickle Ranch, meant horses. She found Bert to be an excellent horseman, which endeared him to her even more. They had a shared love for the mountains and horses that forged a bond between them that transcended family tensions. This pillar gave June strength to face the challenges ahead.

Two things June was not too enamored with were the location and the living condition of the Mickle Ranch house. It was a drafty old place that had not been properly cared for in a long while. It was set on high ground, fully exposed to the wind that rattled through the timbers loosely strung together like old bones. She often wondered why the Mickles hadn't built the house down by the Elbow River where water was close and the valley provided shelter.

Once again, hauling water became a constant chore. It was brought up laboriously for everything from drinking water, to wash water, and gardening. It was an even bigger task than at Tip and Clara's home.

Clara had given June more than enough training in running a house and had also taught her the importance of making it cozy. Bert did not stand in her way for any decorating ideas, and he soon began to appreciate the difference between a bachelor pad and a home. The only thing they lacked was a bit of extra money and a chance to get to town.

Shortly after they moved into the drafty old house, Bert tried to get the hay planted for the summer, but the persistent rain made this difficult. He was still using horses to pull the plough, but first they had to ride a mile to the fields each day. More often than not it was a futile endeavor, for as soon as they arrived and hitched the horses the rain came down even harder, making it impossible to lay the furrows. With persistence they managed to slip in one midsummer's crop.

The only relief from work that June remembered was the break they took to go to the Black Diamond Stampede. Though the rodeo was fun, the excitement of getting to the event overshadowed the whole trip. They were faced with crossing the swollen Elbow River, which was laden with washed out trees and debris that hurtled past them at astonishing speed. Being hit by a water-soaked log or rolling boulder could only lead to disaster. June was riding a new horse named Blitz, which Bert had given her as a wedding present. Earlier memories of crossing the Highwood River flashed darkly in her memory. She was also apprehensive to leap into this cauldron on a young horse, as it occurred to her she couldn't swim. Bert gallantly gave her his horse with strict instructions to stay close. She felt a little better on the more seasoned Glassy, a solid horse Bert had ridden for years. They made the crossing and eventually reached her old home at Turner Valley, more than forty miles from the Mission Valley homestead. It was the first time she had been home since she got married.

The rodeo and the time spent visiting old friends was a significant break for the young couple and the only one they would get that summer. They danced all night at the Stampede supper and dance before wearily seeking a bed in Sam Johnston's barn. Rather than wake up the family at four in the morning, they had opted for the hay padded by horse blankets. They stayed on visiting old friends while the hay grew in the fields, and before they knew it, July had arrived and it was time to go back to the Mission Valley to bring in the hay.

Haying became a way of life. This was hard work that June had done before, but at the Mission Valley homestead, it was a full-time job and their only real source of revenue. They hired on a big haying crew consisting mostly of Native Americans and Métis from the reservation, but also a few local men who brought their own horses. It was a good crew, and they had plenty of work ahead of them. After the Stampede, which was a break for everyone, they were able to keep the outfit for the rest of the summer.

June's job was to drive the mower over the wild, tough grass, which dulled the cutting blades at an alarming rate. One old half-breed was kept on just to keep up with the sharpening. It was a skill he excelled at, making him one of the most valuable members of the team. June was also responsible for feeding the crew, which meant large meals every day. The cooking and cleaning alone was daunting and made even more difficult when June realized she was pregnant.

At least this development explained why she felt so sick every day. It became so bad that the sight of food led to a dash for the outhouse, making it almost impossible to cook up the daily meals. Clara would have helped, but the forty miles by horse was too much, and the distance on bad roads was barely possible with their old truck. June was not bothered by this, for hard work was part of the lifestyle of those running a homestead. It was expected that she do her part because it was the only way they could get by. She continued to drive the mower or the rake throughout the summer despite the roughness of the ride. She often felt it was a miracle she never had a miscarriage.

SUMMER HAYING

The harvest was a large operation employing three mowers and two rakes pulled by horses. The hay was gathered by a sweep for a stacker to pick up and toss onto the hay wagon. There were different methods of stacking hay, but the method used by Bert and his crew was to use two horse sweeps, alternately bringing the hay to the stationary stacker. A team at the stacker pulled up the stacker bed and dumped it on the top of the haystack where it was forked and tramped down by one or two persons on the stack. Slowly the large hay-loaf formations grew across the field gleaming in the August sun. They are rarely seen any more, with modern balers making short work of much vaster fields of hay.

This was exceptionally hard work that Bert always looked after himself, finishing off the final stacking at the end of the day. On the hot summer days, the field was alive with men and horses, twenty-eight horses in total, running smoothly in unison, cutting, raking, gathering, and stacking the golden-green blades of prairie wool. June thought it was one of the loveliest sights in the world, all those animals, men and machinery working in harmony, etched against the sky that twinkled with glowing lanterns as they worked the long days into soft, windless evenings. In her mind a quiet symphony welled up from the earth to accompany their movements. She half-expected them to break into song like a scene from a Hollywood movie.

In the early morning darkness before she went to the fields, June would light the old kitchen stove to begin the first meal of the day. The water that was hauled laboriously in barrels from the creek below was set to boiling for the coffee and the cleanup, followed by a large traditional breakfast. Butter was still made by hand from the rich milk provided by two dairy cows. June would wash it in the cold, clear creek below the house, an act that seemed to transform it into the sweetest, cleanest butter she could remember. She usually made enough butter and cream to take to Calgary to trade for groceries and other items they could not produce at home. They were never without chickens, and the surplus from these bountiful providers gave her eggs to trade as well. The value in trade or even coin was twelve to fifteen cents a day for eggs and twenty-five cents for a pound of butter.

After cooking and packing the main meal, which the men ate halfway through the day, she would head out to the hay fields with lunch and the next endless round of driving the horses over the rough ground. Yet it seems impossible to imagine how a pregnant woman accomplished all this work. It was a period of her life that fulfilled her, leaving her tired but content when her head hit the pillow at night.

Once the haying was finished and the produce from the garden stored away, the workload lightened, which in the past had meant more time for socializing. But for June, who was used to being active, the pregnancy was burdensome. She felt restricted and often very uncomfortable. The old house grew draftier and colder with each week as fall crept into winter, which was now dominated by the unrelenting prairie wind that drove the snow through the myriad cracks in the chinking. Too often June and Bert woke up to snowdrifts on the floors and the water in the pail frozen over. As the winter progressed, travel became more and more difficult; the only mode of transportation was by horseback, now impossible, making her confinement complete. In fact, it was becoming a real concern as roads threatened to turn impassable to anything on foot or wheels.

Bert had kept himself busy with trapping and hunting to augment the food and provide some much needed cash for emergencies. He now felt that this was an emergency and decided to buy a car. This was quite foreign to him, as he had managed to keep well isolated from modern progress by using horses for all forms of transportation or work. This mechanical contraption was altogether strange to him and threatened to bring the modern world to his door. Part of his self-image was that of rebel-cowboy/rancher much connected to the Old West. It represented freedom and a claim on the land whether it was his or not.

The old 1929 Chevrolet they bought from his brother-in-law for $125 made Bert face the challenge of the new world abruptly when he was faced with learning how to drive the thing. For this he had to turn to June, who herself had only driven a car a few times with some of her friends. She passed on what she knew, and although she would become a much more competent driver, Bert never did get comfortable behind the wheel. One thing he refused to do was drive in the city. Once they reached the city limits, June took over.

The purchase of the car came none too soon. By March 25, Bert decided the roads would soon be completely impassable as warmer days brought the frost out of the ground, leaving the surface a muddy quagmire. In fact, the only time they could drive with confidence was early morning while the road surface was still frozen. They left for Calgary early in the morning, and despite June's advanced pregnancy, she took over driving at the city limits. She successfully negotiated her way to Jackie's house where she would await the onset of birth.

Bert somehow managed to get the car home where he was able to keep in touch with June by phone, a luxury they finally had when phone lines reached their part of the country. June missed his quiet support during this time, but she had friends in town who made her stay more pleasant than she had expected. But June was on the roller coaster wave of the Baby Boom, and the hospital was jammed to the rafters with women in labor. When her water broke in the middle of the night on April 2, Dr. Galbraith (father of her other close friend, Viviane) could only find her a cot in the hallway as her labor came on in earnest. The only privacy she had was a hastily hung curtain around the cot. It was a bed she began to wonder if she would ever leave.

"Where is the doctor?" she moaned as the hours slipped by, along with her strength. "Where is my husband? Why won't the baby come?" She could never remember if she yelled this or if the thoughts had just roamed through her worn-out mind.

It seemed as if her body was fighting to keep the baby, as though her womb would not let go despite her determination to end this constant agony. She only recalls one clear memory: overhearing Dr. Galbraith mutter, as he resorted to instruments to bring the child past the constricted muscles, "This girl has rode hundreds of miles, and her muscles are so strong they won't let go!" By six o'clock that evening a six-pound baby boy yelled at the world June had thought he would never see. If she fed him, she probably did so barely awake.

Dr. Galbraith was finally able to move her to a case room out of the maternity ward, and soon after to a nursing home where she stayed for a week. She badly missed Bert and was anxious for him to see his new son, but she was concerned about him coming to town with the car — and with good reason.

When he finally did show up, he was as pale as a ghost.

"Bert, have you seen the baby? What's wrong, you look like he has three toes or something."

"No, I haven't seen him yet. I came straight here." He looked downcast out the window.

"Did you drive in?"

"Well, sort of," he mumbled. "June, I sure hope you come home soon! I just can't get that contraption through the city."

"Well, what happened? You should have come in with Mom."

"Yeah, I know, but it's a long drive all the way to her place, then back here. You have to go right past the city and back. I really wanted to see you, and I didn't think it would be that bad ... but it was," he tapered off almost in a mutter.

"What happened?" June was exasperated and now thought he had totaled the car or done something to it they could not afford. "Did you damage the car?"

"No, no, but I almost got killed, that's what." The tale came out in a disgusted blurt. "I got into town all right, but then I came to that intersection on 17th Avenue and

14th Street, you know, where the trolley car comes down the hill? Well I got halfway across and down comes that darned trolley. I got so scared, the car quit. I just froze – I was so scared. I could not get that thing going again, and this trolley just keeps coming. And right behind me all these other cars jammed up and started honking. I couldn't do a thing! Thank God, it stopped before it ploughed into me. But then I couldn't get off the tracks."

He looked up but couldn't tell if June was laughing or just showing concern by hiding her head in her hands and shaking. She was so relieved that she didn't know how to react.

"But you're okay? And the car is in one piece?" She looked up smiling now that no harm had come to either.

"Well, yeah, but I don't want to drive it back. I had to get a bunch of people to push me off the tracks after holding up that trolley so long. Then someone started the car after saying it was 'flooded.' I guess I gave it too much gas or something. Maybe we should phone your mom and see if she can get into town and drive me to the city limits."

June thought this was a good idea. She wanted to see Clara and show off her son, right after Bert calmed down enough to see his son. Together she and Bert decided to call the blond-haired, blue-eyed baby, Donald Robert. Clara and friends soon came to call, though June remained tired from the ordeal and had some problems feeding her son. The baby developed colic, which would plague him through babyhood, giving her little rest until he outgrew it.

She did not leave the nursing home until April 15 and then went to stay with Clara to ease into motherhood. She was anxious to get home and resume her life with Bert, but felt she needed her mother's support before embarking on her own. Once she was at home, she would face all the work she had done before but with the added care of a colicky baby.

By the beginning of May, she returned to the old homestead with Bert, relieved to be finally back. She was much stronger now, but had switched Don to bottle-feeding, as her own milk was not enough for him. Bottle-feeding was a new trend developing as a modern way of raising children – the beginning of emancipation for women, though June did not see it that way. She already felt quite emancipated with all the work she had to do that was often equivalent to that of the men. For her, bottle-feeding was just more practical. And by May, they would soon be into another summer season of haying.

Before the planting started, Bert decided to earn a little more cash by rounding up some of the wild horses running free in the hills west of Bragg Creek. He often went with his brother Jack and sometimes with Lennie. It was becoming apparent to June that the two other brothers did not get along, and Bert always seemed to be in the middle no matter who he went with. It was not a very profitable venture, and they rarely came home with enough horses to make it worth their while. Nevertheless, some of their better horses had come out of this feral stock they called "the wildies."

June may have wondered why they went back so often to catch these unprofitable animals, but after her first adventure chasing them through the open meadows of the high country, she understood. It was more exciting than anything she had ever done. Vince Robinson, one of their neighbors who lived across the river from them, was a close friend of

Bert's, and he loved to accompany him on wild horse chases on the Indian Reserve. Technically, chasing horses on the reserve was not really legal, but the natives didn't interfere. The 'wildies' could be a nuisance to the indigenous people, who felt they competed for graze with their own horses. They were only too glad to get rid of them. But the wildies were cagy and hard to catch. More often than not, the Mickles came home with no horses or only one or two. Not much reward for the effort that went into chasing them.

Rounding up wild horses could be tricky and required great riding skill. Once the horses were spotted, a number of riders tried to push them into holding corrals constructed with large wings to funnel them into the enclosure. When the animals were on the run, the cowboys galloped as fast as their mounts could move through the brush, timber, or open meadows. There was no time to see what was coming, as the rider was too busy keeping an eye on the elusive wildies trying their best to lose their pursuers in the dense bush and dodging haphazardly in all directions. It took wild and rough riding to force the horses into the hidden corrals, which had to be sturdy enough to hold the excited animals. The saddle horses were equally wound up and often hard to control; it was not uncommon for the rider to find himself on a runaway that beat the wildies to the corral. Suddenly horse and rider found they were milling around in the corral with the wildies, hoping someone slammed the gate closed before they all ran back out. Bert often came home with no horses or only a couple of the older, less valuable animals. But the chase was always thrilling, especially when the wildies burst into an open meadow with riders from all sides running flat-out and whooping behind them as they raced to head them off from any avenue of escape. Indeed, as an old friend Jack Fuller used to say, "If horse racing is the sport of kings – then chasing horses is the king of sports!"

One thing that changed in June's life with the arrival of the baby was the opportunity to socialize. Her diary no longer recorded attending the many dinners, parties, dances, or outings the pages were once choked with. Even riding for pleasure was not mentioned as a frequent event. Most of her time was devoted to household chores, childcare, gardening, and summertime haying. She always returned to help with the haying – the lifeline of their financial survival. Despite the added workload, she still felt freer than she had when pregnant. She could get around easily again, and she had never felt better or stronger in her life. Such wellbeing reflected how happy she was in her marriage and her delight in their new son, despite the colic and allergies he seemed to be plagued with.

Both June and Bert were struggling to meet the demands of raising a child and running the ranch with few amenities. To help out, Bert arranged for a young couple from the Sarcee Indian reservation to move into a little bunkhouse that they'd used in the past for guests or part time farmhands. The couple had worked for them in past summers, and June knew that both of them were good, reliable workers. Mary was able to help June with the chores, but more importantly, she looked after young Don, giving

Bert and June the freedom to enjoy an evening out or just to go to town for supplies and visit friends. For June, one of the greatest joys was to have the chance to ride her horse around the ranch or over to the neighbors. Mary was a cheerful young woman who took to her new responsibilities with enthusiasm. She had children of her own who were not much older, and they eventually became playmates for June's children.

By the middle of July, June was back to the strenuous work in the hay fields, helping with driving the teams and delivering the abundant dinners and breakfasts to the haying crew. But the summers were good, and they were pleased with the crop the land produced. By fall, the work abated, giving June a chance to take stock of how her life was going. She knew she could cope with the demands of motherhood and running the farm – and looking after Bert when occasion called. Mary's help made a considerable difference, and June and Bert both began to think about adding to the family.

June really had no doubt that she wanted another child, simply because she remembered often feeling lonely during her own childhood. She always envied her friends who had siblings, and she was determined Don would not have to share her experience. Despite the discomforts of pregnancy, the couple decided to go ahead. Though June was forever grateful she had a second child, she often wondered why pregnancy had to be so hard. She seemed to be constantly sick, especially in the first three months. She wondered if she was working too hard, for she felt weak and suffered through several near-miscarriages. At one point, she had to be hospitalized to save the baby. This was a serious matter, considering the isolation of the Mission Valley ranch and the dubiousness of good roads. Donny was often sick, as well, with asthma and allergies. It was not uncommon for Bert and June to be up most of the night monitoring a steam tent to ease his breathing.

Despite June's illness, the work went on, and whenever possible, she was up working as much as she could, just to keep ahead of daily chores and household duties. That summer, though, she was too weak to do any haying, even though it was important to their livelihood.

Although the social activities were limited both by work and illness, two events were significant for the young couple. Bert's younger brother Jack married his girlfriend Betty, and June's lifelong friend, Jackie, began going out with Vincent Robinson, a nearby neighbor and old friend of Bert. June was quite happy with this latter development as it meant she would see more of Jackie. The Robinsons lived close enough to ride over for supper or the traditional evening poker game.

Like the Mickles, Vincent's family were original homesteaders in the Mission Valley. RG Robinson and his wife Mary originally came from San Francisco, but they moved to the Calgary area in 1888 after listening to RG's brother Isaac rave about the beautiful, open land west of the fledgling city. They took up residence on the Chipman Ranch, (land RG later purchased) on the north bank of what is now the Glenmore Dam. The ranch was a vast holding that included leases from the Sarcee Indian reserve to Bragg Creek. It was nicknamed "Cow Camp" and was famous both for the log fencing to hold the cattle and for its bachelor parties. RG became a successful rancher, who was known for being the first beef entrepreneur to sell cattle to the British.

Large families on homesteads were the norm, and the Robinsons were no different. They had nine children, the oldest sons being Joseph and John. The older brothers stayed on the ranch and kept the homestead going. Joseph was actually eleven when the family moved to Calgary and was one of the few white men to see the last "making of the braves" ceremony at a Sarcee sundance.

Joseph married after a stint in the Boer War and settled on the ranch with his children. Vincent Robinson was the eldest son and married June's friend Jackie after they met on one of the many excursions Jackie made to see June. Charley Mickle had worked for the elder Robinson, and when Bert and Jack moved to the homestead, Vince became a close friend of both brothers. Bert probably knew him better through their early adventures chasing wild horses.

As fall progressed, June grew more concerned about her continuing illness, feeling too often that she might lose the child. Don's unrelenting susceptibility to every cold that came along did not help, nor did the worry of snow-choked roads as the last of the beautiful fall weather morphed into winter. When the wind blew coldly over the prairie, the ditches filled with wind-driven snow, packing drifts so hard horses could dance on it. There were no communal ploughing services, and families were often stranded until the next warm chinook thawed the surface enough for a horse to break a trail through. Even then, they had to wait and hope the chinook lasted long enough to dry out the quagmire left from the melting snow, to make it passable by car.

Christmas and New Year's finally arrived with the usual celebration enlivened by much visiting with friends and family – and occasionally spiked by fights between Bert's brothers. Cleaning, colds, and June's continued sickness measured the days that followed.

Though the baby was not due for another month, Bert remained concerned about getting to town, and he decided to ride to the mail corner with the car battery to be sure it was fully charged. It was always a problem in the winter, and without electricity. The only solution was to ride the four miles to the corner where he could meet the mail truck to get a charge. It was none too soon. Three days later, June felt ill again, but that evening at supper, her water broke and the first labor pains came in a rush. Instinctively she knew there was not much time to get to the hospital, particularly in their old car. Bert, now alarmed, phoned Tom Bateman, a close friend and one of the nearest neighbors, to help out. Tom had a newer car, and they could leave Don with the Bateman family. A mad drive to the Grace Hospital got June to the delivery room only a few hours before her daughter Faye was born.

After the birth of her new baby, June had a few days to recuperate and reflect on how isolated they were, living out on the prairie. She realized what made life there possible was having close friends and neighbors who could be relied on for help at a moment's notice. The Bateman family had lived in the valley as long as most families and were close friends of the Mickles. John Bateman had emigrated from

BERT WITH DON AND HIS NEW SISTER

Ireland and took odd jobs in the West until he settled on what was now the Bateman homestead adjacent to the Mickles. He succeeded Wheeler Mickle as the Elbow Valley Post master in 1905. Tom Bateman, born on the homestead in 1913, was one of Bert's closest friends. Their land being adjacent to the Mickles', it was also situated on the Morley Trail (from Fort Benton) and was a favorite stopping place for travelers or neighbors. Tom was a few years older than Bert, but once Bert and his brothers moved to the Mickle homestead, they became hunting buddies and shared adventures chasing horses with Vince Robinson. June met them when she married Bert and felt much more secure on the ranch knowing they were close by for any emergency.

Faye made up for the discomfort she had caused her mother all those months by presenting an easy delivery for June. It was probably because she was so small, being premature and weighing only five pounds, seven ounces. She had all the characteristics of a premature child, having no eyelashes or eyebrows and purple skin, although she did sport a thick head of very black hair. June, despite her motherly love, had to admit she was not the prettiest baby she had ever seen.

Faye did not stay that way long. She thrived as though her single purpose was to escape the womb and start living with zeal. She bore no resemblance to her brother Don – she was completely the opposite in coloring from her blond haired, blue-eyed sibling and had none of his predisposition to illness. The brown-eyed, black-haired beauty gained weight immediately, throwing off all signs of being born early, and she turned into a round little butterball, bursting out of her skin. Mary, who stayed on in the small bunkhouse with her husband Jim, adopted her immediately claiming, "This one's for me!" But it was Bert's heart that Faye truly stole. He was instinctively protective of her and could deny her nothing. Throughout her life he called her Shorty. June could not remember how the name came about – she thought it started to stick when Faye was old enough to go hunting with Bert. Either way, it subtly underlined the special place in his heart Bert had for Faye; no one else ever called her by that name.

Though Faye was not prone to illness, she did give June quite a scare one cold January morning. Faye was having her usual morning bath, but on this day, with snow still breaching the cracks in the walls, June decided she should bathe her near the wood stove, the only really warm spot in the house. Unthinking, she placed the little tin washtub on the open oven door and soaped the baby thoroughly. But when she picked Faye up, the baby was so slick she almost squirted out of June's hands like an over-greased duck heading for the oven. The thought of dropping the baby in the hot oven stayed with June as a nightmare for the rest of her life.

Though Don never faced a fiery furnace, he was not so lucky with his health. He had now developed hay fever and asthma and was prone to bronchitis. The combination would leave him gasping for breath, often resulting in such severe attacks that only sitting up with him brought any relief. The steam tent almost seemed part of the furniture it was employed so often. The attacks were worse at night, leaving both Bert and June exhausted the following day.

In desperation, they sought medical help, seeing endless rounds of doctors about allergies and diet changes, though nothing helped. But Don was a fighter, and when he was well, his cheerful disposition and bright smile went a long way to ease the misery. Though June often thought she would never get him raised, she was determined to enjoy every day he graced their lives. Years later, much to her relief, shortly after turning twelve, Don began to grow out of all his ailments. As puberty set in, he would gain quickly in weight and height, as if he were in a race with Faye to grow up.

June did not consider their life at Jumping Pound very eventful, mostly because she was so busy with raising the children and running the farm that the days passed by in a blur. The summer was dominated with getting a good hay crop in – so dependent on the weather. It was always a lot of work for June who had the kids to worry about while keeping the household going and coaxing a poor garden into yielding vegetables that were worthy of the table. The cow was more productive, and butter and cream could be sold or traded for items they could not produce themselves. Don clearly remembers taking butter and cream to William's Brothers in Calgary in return for groceries and hardware.

If the summer seasons rushed by in a blur of work, the winter months were eked out tediously while coping with the freezing temperatures that relentlessly pummeled the old ranch house. Efforts to stifle the flow of drifting snow had little effect, probably because the inadequate foundation allowed the building to shift with each change in temperature, constantly reopening cloth-stuffed cracks or just making new ones. June never did like the old rambling house that could never be made cozy. The winter wind was a nightmare simply because the homestead was built on high exposed ground – with not a bush for a windbreak. She often thought, *Whatever possessed old Wheeler Mickle to build where he did?*

The wind also piled the snow in ditches and across the roads making travel sometimes impossible – often for weeks at a time. This was hard for June who was used to company, but she had a young family who needed her time. It was impractical to bundle up the whole family for jaunts to neighbors or a country dance, so entertainment was found at home. June's imagination surprised her with the number of games she could invent to keep everyone amused – considering how little she had been exposed to playmates during her own childhood.

She also tried to wheedle time for her painting, but she usually gave up when the demands from two young children interfered. Every time she turned around they seemed to be getting into something else – Faye often being the instigator, showing diabolical cunning in inventing new levels of mischief.

Though her art was a true passion for her, June had yet to establish any real revenue from it, and income was a serious matter. But June's talents were multiple, and so she turned to making what was too expensive to buy. Clothing and outdoor gear were essential, so when she came across an opportunity to buy a parachute (now war surplus and very cheap) she leapt at it, and in no time the beautiful silk was rendered into colorful blouses, dresses and scarves. The scarves were her inspiration when she realized she could paint western scenes on them and sell them in Bragg Creek. Their novelty was a hit and yet another source of needed income. June was unknowingly developing the skills that would make a major difference in later life.

She had an old Singer sewing machine that turned by hand, and it could penetrate even the toughest leather. Leather hides were abundant in their household from all the game Bert shot or from the butchered cows. She worked the leather into jackets, pants, and riding chaps. It took up much of her time, but she enjoyed the creative challenge it presented while providing revenue.

Bert, it seemed, was immune to the discomforts he had spent his life coping with. Neither the weather, the work, nor the country had changed since he married, and for sure the old house was no different except perhaps a little more worn down. He was adjusting to family life with no complaints; in fact, he quite liked it as it gave him the stability that he had not experienced since his mother had died. The biggest change required of him was toning down the wilder side of his nature. But Bert was basically a laid-back individual, and he knew June was the best thing that had happened to him. Life with her certainly curbed carousing in town with his brother Jack and other friends around Cochrane.

The winter was less of a problem for Bert as he was frequently out hunting or working on his trapline. Where June was housebound with the children, he was able to escape to the land and felt no real curtailing of his freedom. There was no room for June to complain either because they depended on the meat he brought in. The trapline was also essential to their income. June was proud of Bert's hunting prowess, knowing how tough it would be if they did not have this food source.

On one occasion, Bert came home with a pretty little bay and white pinto stallion that he gave to June. She called the horse Flash and had the distinction of being the only one he did not buck off. Bert tried to ride him first and was rewarded with a face plant in the mud. Other hands tried with the same result, but as June commented, "I guess I was lucky because he didn't buck me off." She had a good relationship with her new horse for as long as she owned him. Though they did come up with some good horses on their wildies hunts, most of them were sold to the canneries at bottom dollar. It was the thrill of catching them that Bert could not resist, rather than the money they brought in.

But there was relief from the winter monotony when the weather turned good and blue skies brought the beauty back to their land, honouring them with a vision of shining mountains. When conditions were good, the neighbors often pooled their resources to haul wood. Each household could easily use up eight to ten cords of wood over the winter, which took a considerable amount of work to fell, haul, and cut into usable pieces. These 'sawing bees,' as June called them, were also a great occasion to socialize. While the men hauled and chopped, the women created massive feasts. The families would rotate from farm to farm, bringing sleighs loaded with food, children, and enough homemade berry wine to keep everyone enthusiastic for the work of replenishing the household wood supply. It also reaffirmed people's place in the community as friendships solidified, knowing they could call on each other if the demands of homestead life became too burdensome.

The fabric of these friendships was further strengthened by the dances held at the local school or community hall, and people looked forward to them for weeks. June and Bert were able to attend these events without worrying about the children who were left with Mary and her husband Jim.

It also left June and Bert free to go to Cochrane or Calgary for basic supplies, but more importantly to visit family they had not seen for months. June was particular about this as she was close to her family. Bert's brothers lived on either side of them, and so they saw them frequently, but he kept in touch with his sisters and their children as well. Bert and June never failed to take in a movie regardless what was playing – it scarcely mattered in those days. It was quite a change to drive to the show for June, who used to ride into Calgary to catch epics like *Gone With the Wind*. She recalled that occasion because there was a long intermission halfway through that gave her a chance to give her horse some oats before riding home. It was so common for people to ride into town on horseback that the theatre kept a hitching rail close to the entrance.

During these early years, the kids were brought up like most farm kids, learning to deal with the environment that molded them for the rest of their lives. Of course that meant learning to ride and work with horses at a young age.

Both June and Bert started riding when they were very young, and they saw no reason not to introduce their own children to horses similarly. Don was only two when June began leading him around the yard on a quiet old sorrel mare. Bert would hoist the young boy up on his horse whenever the chance came along for a casual ride, instilling in Don a confidence with horses that he learned from his father. As Don grew older, he would ride whatever horse he could get up on in the long corral behind the barn. Of course there were mishaps. June recalls seeing Don clinging to the neck of an old white horse that suddenly charged down the length of the corral at full gallop. He had never been on a horse by himself when it started to run, but he hung on valiantly until inevitably, the horse stopped abruptly at the end of the corral. Don was thrown off but bounced back up with only a few bruises and a black eye. It did not deter him one bit from his enthusiasm for riding horses. Most farm parents' had a bit of a fatalistic view of survival. Kids had to learn to deal with the riskier elements in a rough environment – there was no over protection in that world.

Faye was similarly introduced to horses at a young age – indeed the kids were always in contact with animals right from the day they were brought home, ensuring they were quite familiar with all four-legged animals. June led the toddler around the yard on a quiet horse or put her in her saddle just behind the pommel when she went riding. The saying "I learned to ride before I could walk" was fairly accurate for most farm kids. When Faye was old enough to ride on her own, June made sure she had a pony that was reliable. They had a wonderful, quiet bay mare that let Faye get away with all sorts of antics. The mare's name was May, and she became a perfect babysitter, constant companion,

DON AND FAYE WITH BABYSITTER

and best friend. June would even find Faye asleep on her broad warm back as May sunned quietly by the stable or grazed around the yard. Much later, Faye would acquire Gypsy, a young mare, which would ultimately be the horse she most fondly remembered.

During their stay at Jumping Pound, Bert and June often had several families from the Sarcee Indian reserve camp on the property to help with the haying. These families had several young children who played with the Mickle children. Faye formed a close friendship in particular with a young boy named Edward. One day she and Edward decided to run away together. June had no idea what prompted this spontaneous act, for it did not seem to spring from any form of discontentment or anger. They just suddenly weren't there when June went looking for them. It took a rather frantic search by Bert and Edward's father before tracks were spotted and the two children were found hiding behind a rock down by the creek. Bert was alarmed when he realized they might have drowned if they had decided to play in the water. He gave Faye a light spanking, but the major punishment came from June who angrily gave Faye a good licking once she got over her relief. Bert never could get very mad at Faye. Some of Faye's future playfulness was beginning to surface in an almost innocent manner, though some of her later pranks seemed to go beyond mere mischief.

The Sarcees were frequently around their place over the summer when help was needed. They often camped down by the creek close to the water supply. Bert had many friends amongst the Sarcee Indians and always felt they were good workers. But Don felt a twinge of sadness in the nomadic wanderings of these people between Eden Valley and the small village of Morley, which he perceptively viewed as a dying way of life. Their colorful caravans left deep ruts along the ancient trail – which can still be found on open hillsides. The women and children often trailed behind on foot, calling to stray dogs as they chased cavorting colts back to the herd. Their slow movements, silhouetted against a setting sun, never gave a hint of hurry or purpose. Don loved to see them pass by on their semi-annual visits to Morley but could not shake the feeling that the freedom they seemed to embody would not last. After the family left the Mission Valley, he never saw this sight again.

One day, Jim, a young Sarcee boy who was the older brother of Faye's friend, showed up calling for help. It was clear that he was scared out of his wits when he roared into the yard hoping someone was home. June calmed him down enough to get to the bottom of the problem, but she was not pleased to find it was related to the death of an older relative. The man had apparently passed away shortly before the workers established their camp at the spring below the Mission cairn. The women who comprised most of the camp must have been spooked over the death and became jittery when they recalled it. One of the women had suddenly thought she'd seen his ghost in the campfire – or some apparition that set them all off. The whole camp was soon wailing and screaming, thinking his spirit had come back to haunt them. The terrified young boy thought that if he rode up to the Mickles someone would come back to calm them down. June was alone with her two kids when he galloped up to the door looking for help.

"For God's sake, slow that horse down before you run over a kid! What's the problem?"

"Oh. Sorry. My mom and the rest saw a ghost down by the river. They're scared crazy. Can you help them?" The boy jumped down and handed the pony to June, who seemed startled at the request.

She called over her shoulder for them all to stay put as she galloped out of the yard on the boy's pony to confront the hysterical women. June was somewhat familiar with the Sarcee culture but was not totally versed in their religious beliefs. She just hoped she could find a logical solution to their fears.

The three young children stayed in the house, but Don remembers becoming quite spooked himself. He figured if the older boy had something to worry about, then there must be something scary out there.

June finally got back just as it was getting dark, so it had taken some doing to diffuse the situation. The young lad was too afraid to ride back until the next morning. It is one of the last clear memories Don has of the old homestead in the Mission Valley.

Though June was not overly fond of the drafty log home, she realized that the land they owned was profitable and gave them a reliable income. It had been in the family for three generations and was part of Bert's heritage. But Bert's and her relationship with Bert's two brothers was becoming more and more untenable as the years went by. Jack and Lennie hated each other. They weren't above taking gun shots at each other if tempers got out of control. Bert was all that came between them, and he often defused potential disputes, which left him unpopular with one or the other of the brothers. As June recalled to me, "If you were friendly with one, the other would get mad and vice versa." Family occasions were fraught with tension and fights when the hard-drinking men celebrated too long. The strain just got worse as time progressed, and Bert's tendency to go to town with one brother or the other to keep the peace began to escalate. The resulting stress had June casting around for a solution.

There were other considerations as well. At this point, Don was getting older, but his allergies and asthma continued to be a problem. By the time he was ready for grade one, the only school he could attend required a long bus ride. They tried him on the bus for a while, but it soon became apparent it was too much for him. The road to the house was so bad by then, he frequently could not get to the bus stop and began missing a lot of school. The only choice was to take him out and put him on correspondence courses – supervised, of course, by June. He did well, and even Faye picked up early schooling that helped her later. But it was just another added strain.

The summer of 1949 started out with wonderful weather, and they decided to take the chance of planting registered oats in a very productive field. It was a gamble, as they had to borrow $9,000 dollars from the bank to buy the seed – a considerable sum in those days. Their careful management of finances in the past and their ownership of valuable land convinced the bank they were worth the risk, so they went ahead. All summer, the oats matured beautifully until it looked like they would harvest a bumper crop in early fall. In fact everything looked so good June and Bert decided to take a vacation. Mountain holidays were a favorite and did not cost a cent. June just had to find out whether Clara minded looking after the kids before she made plans with close friends.

The couple was going on a ten-day fishing trip west of Elbow Falls into country that was still wild. The poor trails that wove transiently through the western valleys ensured the country was infrequently traveled. Old friends, Jackie and Vincent Robinson were eager to go as was long-time school buddy Louise Galbraith. It was the sort of holiday they all loved best. June could not conceive of anything more enjoyable than camping in the mountains with a pack outfit and good friends for company.

They drove as far as the gravel road would allow, to just east of Elbow Falls, after which they headed up the Elbow Valley with their saddle horses and pack outfit. Bert knew of several meadows close to a beautiful stream that would be ideal camping and provide enough grass to hold the horses. Wasting little time, Bert was soon fishing in the quiet pools of the Elbow while the women made camp and set up a cooking station. The horses were belled and hobbled and turned out in grass that was lush and deep from a summer's growth. They would be rounded up only when camp was moved into other side valleys. With the exception of two days shortly after the trip started, they had beautiful, hot weather and they took full advantage of it. If Bert wasn't catching twenty or more fish a day, they were out riding to high mountain meadows. Entertainment at night was seeing how many fish they could eat and singing around the campfire. The sheer number of fish caught on that trip meant they were also doing a lot of filleting and drying. Too soon for all of them, it was time to head home. Though the weather was still good, they needed to get the oat crop in before the fall rains began.

The oats were critical for them. A good crop meant the debt would be paid, leaving a substantial profit. June dared to think they could fix up the old house at last. But farmers will all agree that they are the world's biggest gamblers – they have to be to survive. Unfortunately, gambling does not always pay off. As they were driving home, June could see an ominous bank of clouds gathering relentlessly over the mountains. When they got up the next morning, all they could see was white. A huge storm had smothered the fields in heavy, wet snow. Even rain would not have been so bad.

"Oh Bert! What are we going to do? Is there any way we can get it off before it rots?" As she pondered the grey sky that hid any sign of the sun, June looked out over the white soggy mass covering their beautiful crop with slight hope it could be saved. Bert said little except that he would try to get the hay-binder free of the viscous mud it was stuck in.

He went out and tried to salvage the crop, but it was futile since the ponderous binder bogged down the minute he hit the field. It was so well stuck he knew he would not get it out until spring.

Reluctantly, the young couple reviewed their position. They could not hope to pay off the bank now with no crop. Selling became an option they had to face. June looked around at the old house with dismay, dreading yet another cold winter with a massive debt clinging to them like a proverbial albatross and no money in the bank. Don faced another year of correspondence school, and Bert's brother Lennie did little to assuage June's blacker thoughts when he lost his temper over the idea that they would even think of selling out. But that was what they were doing. When everything was taken into consideration, there did not seem to be much choice. The bank would soon be knocking on the door, and they could not finance another crop the following year. Crop insurance for a bail-out was non-existent in those years.

Bert found leaving the family homestead hardest of all, but he agreed with June that there was little choice. Charley Mickle had been living with them after his eyesight got too poor for him to live on his own. He missed his rambling, and one of the most painful things to do was to find him a home in Calgary during his last years.

Chapter *VI*

A SHORT MOVE

Though difficult, the decision to sell their part of the homestead did not result in a quick move for Bert and June. They decided to sell the land to the Copithornes, who were rapidly establishing themselves as major land-owners throughout Alberta, mostly south and west of Calgary. The Copithornes were successful largely because they worked closely together – something June felt could have been possible for the Mickle brothers if they had managed to get along. Certainly Wheeler Mickle had left them with a considerable amount of prime land that would eventually become some of the best real estate west of Calgary. But a family divided that does not work toward a common goal can't dream big – though becoming a big landowner was never a dream Bert had. He was too easy-going to have any desire to head a dynasty, wield great power, or pursue a future in politics. The Copithornes were a different breed, who would influence many aspects of Alberta's future, from ranching, to the oil fields, and ultimately, politics.

Once the decision was made, June was eager to get resettled and immediately started looking for a place near Black Diamond. The Turner Valley area was closer to Tip and Clara's, but far enough from the Mission Valley to give them some respite from family feuding. She finally found a nice little house south of Black Diamond, in the small town of Royalties. June realized she would have to spend the winter there without Bert, who was burdened with finishing up the winter baling and looking after the livestock. She was not happy about it, but there was little choice. Her priority was to get the children registered before the school year started. Living in the town made this easier as they were within a short walking distance to school. The house was small but warm for once, and June finally had running water, which also meant an indoor toilet.

The winter passed slowly without Bert, but she had the children to look after. Though the town was nice enough, it was still small, with the store, post office, and church being the limited arena for meeting people. The one surprising amenity was the movie theater. The opportunity to see a show in small-town Alberta was uncommon. But the Alberta oil boom was getting into full swing – towns were springing up everywhere like mushrooms and beginning to attract all kinds of businesses. Many of them had lively social scenes that held appeal for families of all sizes. Most of these towns faded into obscurity after the oil ran out – something that June found hard to fathom years later. It was hard to accept that such vibrant places could just disappear in so short a time.

The hamlet of Royalties (also known as Little Chicago) was one of those towns founded on oil. It was at the southern end of the massive Turner Valley oil fields that were turning Alberta into a rich province, launching it irrevocably out of the debilitating poverty of the Depression. The rolling prairie grass crept into the town from the treeless hills, now characterized by stark wooden oil derricks that dotted the skyline. These dark, ugly constructions (beautiful only to oilmen) peppered the valley and hillsides and were only softened by the silhouette of the distant mountains.

Despite living in close proximity to other people, June found it lonely without Bert. Although she had the car, the distance was too far and the roads too bad in winter to make the trip to Jumping Pound for anything but an emergency. She did have friends from her Turner Valley days, and of course the opportunity to meet townspeople arose with her involvement with the school.

Though Donny's health continued to be a concern, he was quite pleased with the opportunity to go to school with other children. The school was only two blocks away, and it gave him the chance to make friends. The school was a makeshift affair, consisting of several small buildings that held different classes. The children would be in one building for certain classes then shifted to other one-room shacks, depending on their ages and what was being taught. The large woman who taught them even had the traditional hand bell that she rang ceremoniously, announcing recess. June was so happy to have the kids in school she even shoveled a path two blocks for them when it snowed so much they could not make it on their own. She ruefully recalled that effort later saying, "Yeah! When I got there, the school was closed!" No one else apparently was as keen to face the blizzard – at least not the schoolteacher.

Faye also went to school even though she was a bit young. Don was not so happy about that, for she always seemed to be blurting out some embarrassing story or just acting out. She was mischievous as always, but she adored her older brother and tried to keep up with him. Despite his occasional resentment, Don was a good older brother and did not mind looking after her when needed. The pair delighted the neighbors when they attended a Halloween skating party dressed as Indians. Faye was just learning to skate and kept falling as she tried to keep up with Don. He spent most of the time picking her up, which seemed to entertain everyone present – probably because their combined clumsy efforts were not only comical but also endearing.

Don, however, was not always so endearing. One event, which he remembers with chagrin, almost ended their stay in that small town. The early spring that year was unusually warm, and the constant wind ate up what little snow there was. The hard-packed winter snowdrifts were long gone, melted by the incessant prairie chinooks, leaving the grass frail and tinder dry. But Don was too young to be aware of this when he and a friend decided to light a string of firecrackers. They were playing near his house in the fields that stretched into the distant hills surrounding the town. He never knew if it was the matches or the exploding firecrackers that started a small fire in the tall, dry grass. All he knew was that a strong wind quickly inflamed the fire, spreading it suddenly in all directions. All he could think of was to get help, but he did not want his mother to find out he had started the fire. He ran instead to the neighbors, who had noticed the fire and were already out the door with wet towels and gunnysacks. Both boys pitched in, swatting the growing flames, frantic that it would consume the whole town.

Early-spring grass fires in the prairies are particularly dangerous as they spread incredibly quickly and have been known to destroy entire farms. Under the right conditions, fires could eat up ground faster than a horse could run. Don was so busy swatting grass that he did not even notice June was not there giving him hell. To his relief, enough people showed up and finally extinguished the inferno before any building was damaged. But Don was not encouraged when he looked around to see most of the surrounding fields were now black. He finally went home to see what had happened to his mom. He had been so consumed with guilt and the effort to put out the fire, he hadn't realized it only burned for a short while. June was busy canning and had not noticed a thing – at least until she looked out her door. Don could not believe no one had asked how the fire started, and he was not about to elaborate on his role.

The stay at Royalties was not intended to be permanent; it was just a convenience to get the children into school and gain a foothold in the community. June and Bert were ranchers first and had no intention of settling in a town.

Once the summer holidays arrived, June and the kids were free to return to the Mission Valley homestead to help with another summer of putting up the hay crop. It was still their major source of income, and they wanted to collect what they could before moving permanently. It was another busy summer for both of them, but June had the added burden of caring for both children, who had contracted bad cases of the red measles. She and Bert were also spending a lot of time looking for a suitable piece of land to buy so they could relocate to the Millarville area. June wanted to put an inconvenient distance between Bert and Black Diamond, where he was inclined to spend more time than she liked in town with old cronies. He had pals everywhere.

Not long after their search started, they got a surprise call from Clara. "June, you won't believe it, but Walter Eriksson is selling a quarter-section west of Millarville! You have to come and take a look at it. It seems to me it is exactly what you want. Tip thinks it's a steal."

"Do you know the people – how they looked after everything?"

"Oh yes, we've known them for some time. They always had good crops – he is a pretty good farmer and he looked after his animals. Tip says his horses were always in good shape, not that you need to worry about that."

"Great," replied June. "We should be able to get there this week."

"Yes, you should," Clara declared. "I doubt if it will be on the market long."

It was a good piece of land far enough north of Black Diamond to keep Bert from spending too much time in town. With the sale of the homestead land and the house in Royalties, they could nicely afford it and not be short for other purchases. But best of all was the snug little house that June could hardly wait to move into. Though it did not have running water in the winter, in the summer they could run a pipe into the house from the clear, sweet spring up the hill. It was the best water June had ever tasted in her life. With the debt gone and the family feuding put aside, she had never felt happier.

But there was a lot to do before they could move in. That fall, June returned to the house in Royalties for school, leaving Bert with most of the moving chores. It took a long time to move all the livestock, machinery, and countless farm tools that kept them in business. Bert had lived at the Jumping Pound homestead from the time he was only twelve years old, and the place had accumulated endless amounts of "stuff" – much of which they probably never used. But it required weeding out and shipping and all they had was one car and a couple of horse-drawn wagons. The roads were again getting poor as winter approached, but June was determined they would have Christmas in the new house.

Bert worked endless, cold hours trying to accomplish this, and at last the day came when they were ready to move the household furniture and other sundry items. The packing again seemed endless, but they decided to hire a truck for this move. The last ties were severed when they sold the house at Royalties and moved in. Typically, Donny had a cold, but that didn't stop them from celebrating Christmas with Clara and Tip. Clara put on the dinner, for which June was grateful. All they had to do that day was enjoy the food and open their presents. The satisfaction

June felt that day was the first of many that June would cherish in the Millarville period of her life. The kids started school in January at Sheep Creek in Millarville, where they would remain until they finished high school.

The rest of the winter did not vary much in routine, except that June had more time to pursue her painting, as well as the sewing, which brought in extra money. She was also making clothing for a growing family. The kids seemed to have put on a growth spurt as though they were absorbing growth hormones from the environment. Don, in particular, looked like he would become quite tall in later life.

Bert was getting to know the country around Millarville and soon had established another trapline. The price for coyote pelts was fairly high if they were in good condition, and this greatly added to their small winter income. As before, he hunted for most of their winter meat, though he had to start later that year because of their time-consuming move. They were now closer to old friends like Mrs. Gettig, whom June had missed. Regular visits with them, her own family, and other old friends once again peppered the pages of her diary.

Despite coming out ahead in the land sale, both June and Bert felt they had to bring in more income. It wasn't just that the kids were growing; June had lived on farms all her life with few amenities. She hankered for running water all year-round and an inside toilet. She could scarcely imagine what it would be like to have a washing machine. Though they did not have as much land now to put into hay or other grain crops, it became apparent they needed a new baler. To pay for this, they had to do a lot of outside work for other people, neighbors mostly, who needed extra help. Bert and June became a team through those years, working side by side during long summer days when the rain did not hinder them. June drove an old Model D John Deer tractor that pulled the new baler while Bert piled the bales. The tractor had no power steering, and it seemed to take an army to get the thing to turn. Soon they both became strong and tanned "as Indians" with the hard work, but June loved it. She could not believe how strong her shoulders got, but she was not concerned as it only defined her arms in an attractive way. She always loved being outside no matter what the circumstance, and she transferred these values to the children who would soon be employed in the family business.

JUNE DRIVING THE TRACTOR

CAMPING TRIP: VOLCANO RIDGE NEAR THREE-
POINT CREEK (FORMERLY NORTH SHEEP CREEK)

June got so adept at running the tractor she even went to
Midnapore on her own to bale hay by herself. She worked
at three farms one year, getting up early to drive the truck to
the fields, work for hours, then rush home to cook supper
and get the lunches made for school the next day. These
fourteen- to sixteen-hour days were hard, but she enjoyed
it and the satisfaction it gave her. In those early mornings,
she always noticed the gentle east wind that blew before the
dawn. When the sun rose above the horizon, the air became
still and laden, ending abruptly the mild whispered breeze
that lasted no longer than a kiss. She would remember
those days of peace whenever the east wind stirred in early
summer mornings before the dawn.

The children picked up lifelong values in these formative years. Their love for the country was heightened in the
summer when the family packed up the horse string and

rode deep into the mountains west of the Forestry Reserve. They took two weeks in the summer for these holidays and went every year during their stay in the Millarville area. These trips were seminal for both Don and Faye, instilling in them a lasting love of the mountains.

In the winters, with both children in school and Bert often away on the trapline or hunting, June filled her days with conjuring fabulous creations that would sustain her in later life. Besides getting back to her canvases depicting their western lifestyle, she created signature western clothing. They had plenty of leather from Bert's hunting exploits that she spun into coats, vests, chaps, and even shirts. If she ran out of hides, people would bring her their own leather for their requests – usually elk or deer hides, tanned to a creamy softness that caressed the skin.

Initially she used her small, hand-cranked sewing machine from earlier years, but soon found it was too slow to get any real production going. It took hours and some frustration to get even the simplest garment finished, making for delivery delays that began to become problematic.

Finally, after a particularly annoying day, she confronted Bert. "I can't do this much longer. It's too slow and tiring with that old machine. I may as well sew everything by hand … it would probably be easier on my back. I want to look for something I can plug in – we have electricity. I need to modernize!" She remembered the exciting moment when they could turn on their first light bulb. The room had lit with unexpected brightness as they all sat and blinked at the luminous globe – it was 1955 after all – and the possibilities seemed endless. It made up for not getting a phone!

Bert looked at her as he always did, a little shyly and with deference to her request. He knew his wife worked hard, and if he looked closely at their life together, he knew she was the rock in their foundation. Common sense told him her request was based on practicality and he rarely denied her.

"Okay, honey. We can make a trip to Calgary next week and you can look around. Haven't seen much of the family there for a while ... might even call up a few friends or my brothers. Have to figure out which brother, though. Maybe we can spend part of the week there ... "

June knew this meant that Bert was looking forward to catching up with his drinking buddies, but he had not been back to town for some while, and she could not keep him at home forever. Knowing there was a wild streak in him she could never tame, she mistrusted his adventures. But it was a quality that had attracted her in the first place, and she did not want to change that. Besides, she needed a new sewing machine. She could live with a few late nights.

Her hunt for the right machine was not as easy as she'd anticipated. Most of what she worked with was leather of varying quality and toughness, and she needed a machine that could handle this difficult material without constantly breaking needles. She made the rounds of various stores, carting along some particularly tough leather to see if the new machine could handle it. It took some time, but she finally found an affordable Bernina that "did the trick." They had to make monthly payments, but it was worth the debt to June, who reasoned it would ultimately pay for itself by allowing her to elevate her creativity and increase productivity. She was delighted with her efforts, making all kinds of inspired garments with her particular stamp, and now daring to tackle even the most difficult outfits. Out flew moccasins, purses, coats and jackets, vests, chaps, shirts, skirts, and the ubiquitous hand-painted ties. And as she had predicted, it brought in much-needed cash.

During the years they spent on the property north of Black Diamond, June and Bert made more friends. At this time, Billy Munro, the young boy June had met on her memorable first trip to the Mickle Ranch, was still staying with them off and on. The bunkhouse on the property served the same purpose it had at the old homestead, and it became a place of residence for many future friends.

Billy had stayed with them through most of his teenage years, but by the time they moved to Black Diamond, he was exploring newfound independence. He began working for Shell Oil as they continued to expand their operations. Soon he became introduced to the D9 Caterpillar bulldozer, and he had found his true calling, dexterously running these large machines with great skill. There were few who could match his ability, and Shell was glad to have him. Eventually, he got the chance to work independently on contracts offered by various companies – the only catch was he needed to have his own machine. When he brought the problem up at dinner one night, Bert very generously offered to back him in his first purchase. As June recalls, "Billy never looked back." He had all the work he could want and soon had the loan paid off in full. Bert never doubted that Billy would pay back the loan and he continued to trust those he dealt with in all of his affairs.

Soon after Bert established his trapline, he felt it would be expedient to have a cabin he could overnight in if the days got long or the weather turned bad. It was a simple precaution against being caught out, but it soon became a place where the family could get away and spend some time exploring the land. June often wrote about packing up the horses and heading to the cabin for a few days. At the same time, they were making improvements to the small house. June loved the coziness of the little house, but that was also the problem – it was just too small and had limited storage space. Inspired by the success Clara had had with Tip's cabin, June soon had Bert digging out the basement. Again, it was a big job that kept them busy all one spring. It seemed the summers were eaten up with all the additional projects piled on top of the regular farm work and daily chores. June had added some winter projects as well, such as painting or rebuilding rooms, cupboards, and bathrooms. Bert kept himself from being run ragged by escaping to his favorite pastimes: hockey in the winter and baseball in the summer.

Bert was actually a very good hockey player. When he was in his teens, he had played so well that an eastern team actually sent out a scout to see if he was up to NHL standard. Unfortunately, he had neither the time nor the money to pursue what could have been an entirely different life. A different life may have also been the problem, though, as Bert had no desire to leave the mountains and the carefree life he was enjoying in those days. He still loved to play hockey,

BERT ON A TRAPLINE

however, and was delighted when he had the chance to play on the Black Diamond team. He was one of the more experienced players, with an aptitude for coaching as well. When he was asked to coach the Okotoks Oilers, June was happy he had found an outlet for his energy, which helped keep him out of trouble.

June always worried about Bert. His rowdier younger brother Jack didn't just keep him out late in the bars; Jack had a penchant for picking up stray cows if they wandered into the yard and easily talked Bert into helping him. (Bert was not always particular about the posted hunting seasons either.) The West at that time still had a flavor of the wilder days before settlement had tamed it down, particularly in the hills west of Black Diamond and Millarville. The Copithornes had gobbled up much of the land, and their cattle roamed freely over the hills with little supervision. When they were rounded up in the fall, there was little to be said if the count was not quite what it had been in the spring when the cows were taken to summer pastures. Cattle were lost for a variety of reasons, from bears, cougars, and other predators, to late spring storms or poor feed. If one or two were missing, and the carcasses were not found, there was often little to indicate exactly what had happened. Bert never felt he was doing any harm to the Copithornes – they had more land and cattle than they could reasonably look after. Donny still rolls his eyes as he ruefully recollects coming across the odd well-hung side of beef stashed in the icehouse from time to time.

Bert did not like to think he was doing anything wrong, and he was a little incensed when Sam Copithorne took him to task at spring branding one year. It was a well-established practice for ranchers to pitch in to help each other out for the big jobs like branding, harvesting, or bringing in winter wood. At the end of the day, the host rancher would put on a big spread to feed everyone. It was often held outside if the weather was good, and it became a much-enjoyed social event. The Copithornes never failed to provide a prime roast beef that had been basted on the barbecue all afternoon. The aromatic wafts of delicious smells, carried across the yard on light spring breezes, tempted everyone's appetite. On this particular day, which was blessed with sunshine, the Copithorne patriarch's puckish sense of humor rose to the occasion. As he began carving the beautiful, perfectly browned roast that oozed rivulets of gleaming fat, he mischievously looked up past the large gathering of friends and neighbors and pasted his eyes on Bert at the far end of the table. He chuckled lightly and in a soft voice that seemed to boom across the laden picnic table, he coyly asked, "Bert! Why don't you come up and do the honours. You've carved more Copithorne beef than I have." June had not known Bert could blush or look so embarrassed. His usual good sense of humor was conspicuously lacking. He waved off the offer with a scowl, which did not diminish the delight everyone expressed at Sam's gutsy witticism. Good thing Bert was such a well-liked man, for it was only taken as an amusing insight by one and all.

To June's chagrin, Bert fumed all the way home, after cutting short the after-dinner visiting – something they never did, usually being the last to leave.

BERT AND JUNE – BEST FRIENDS

Chapter VII

MILLARVILLE

Though June loved the house on the Black Diamond property, it was still too close to town, and eventually Bert began spending more time there than she was happy with. He also seemed to grow restless, as though the work they put in was not enough to keep him occupied. They still had the summer trips to the mountains that they both cherished, but she began to feel they had outgrown the place and needed a new challenge. With typical forethought she began looking around. To her surprise, it was Bert who found the property west of Millarville, which was going for a very good price. It was right next to the forestry reserve and brought back fond memories of the days June had spent with Tip, helping him with the cattle. It was just under Square Butte and was a section and a half of land – more land than she could have hoped for. They paid for it by selling part of the Black Diamond property.

Don recalls, "The land was mainly forest-covered except for about thirty acres of pasture land. We made a living cutting posts and rails and selling them. Dad did get an outfitting license for taking out hunting parties in the fall. We based out of the ranch but also used the trapper cabin as part of it. It all started when we hired out to pack-out game with our horses that people had shot and couldn't get out of remote spots. Dad thought that we might as well take them out to start with, so he applied for a guide and outfitter license. We had enough horses and camping gear to qualify. This may have influenced the later decision to take over Ray's outfit and expand the hunting area. Dad's trapline was also adjacent to our property, and it was part of the family's income."

Initially it meant a lot of driving from home every day to seed and harvest the crop. For the time being, however, it meant Bert spent most of his time there rather than in town.

It was not long before Bert and June both felt they needed to make a permanent move to the new property. But the new property had only a small bunkhouse for living quarters, which was not big enough to remodel into a bigger home. But that is what June wanted, and she felt that this was the place she and her family could really establish themselves.

June had always wanted a log house, and now she saw her way to achieve this. They would build it themselves, using the logs they milled from the property. It was the most exciting thing she could imagine, but it was a big project. Fortunately, there was a crew of log builders currently working in the area. The Dowler brothers were from Pigeon Lake, Alberta, and came with a good reputation. They had done an excellent job on building the Wates-Gibson Hut in the Tonquin Valley (Jasper National Park) for the Alpine

Club of Canada. It seemed almost preordained, and June was quick to make a deal. The price they quoted for building the house was very reasonable, but it would include boarding the crew during the construction.

First they had to get the logs. Before that, they had to pour the basement foundation. Every task that was presented had to be managed by taking into consideration the isolated location. Getting a cement mixer to the property was difficult and also added to the cost. But June was determined her new house would be modern. The world was rapidly moving forward, and it was possible to have modern conveniences in country homes. One of the main things she wanted was running water and the unheard-of luxury of an indoor toilet. A bathtub or shower would be an unimaginable luxury. Of course that meant drilling a well.

Bert went at the task like a Trojan. He had a good skid team and spent the first summer hauling the logs they would need. They lived in the bunkhouse until the basement was built, and then they moved in lock stock and barrel, covering the basement with a plastic and plywood roof. The downside to this was the constant drip of water when it rained or snowed. The water drained through the nail holes like a sieve and the only antidote was to litter the floor with pots, pans, bowls, or any other handy receptacle to catch the drips. On really wet days June thought they might be flooded out, and it took much good humor and a stubborn dream of living in her wonderful new house to withstand the marginal living conditions. The front of the basement faced the driveway, and this became the first entrance to the fledgling house. At June's insistence the first thing they installed was a small bathroom. The luxury of having a hot shower inside – particularly in the winter – was worth the temporary inconvenience of a soggy roof.

The long, hot summer was watered with the sweat from hauling logs that June then peeled. Of the 160 large logs Bert brought in, June felt she must have peeled one hundred of them. This could only be done manually with a hand-held peeler that balked at every knothole. Her arms gained strength she had not thought possible, until she felt she had arms like a boxer in his prime. Again, the thought of the completed home that would shelter them for years to come made the work seem to go quicker. She found comfort knowing they would look with satisfaction on the walls they built through hard work, which would keep them warm in the winter and cool in the summer.

The construction work began in earnest when the log men arrived the following summer. June was very glad to see them, and she was pleased when they used her house plan with only minor suggestions critical to building restrictions. They were professional and quite particular with the fit of the logs. There would be no cracks for the wind-driven snow to penetrate this house. June anticipated a spacious but very warm home, and she could hardly contain her impatience to see it finished. They would have running water (which meant a washing machine) and elec-tricity – but still no phone. She silently wondered if there was some underlying conspiracy to keep the last vestige of modernization from her door.

While Bert was somewhat freer to get back to the busi-ness of running the ranch, June continued to work on her house. The kids were now old enough to be a real help with the chores, and June made sure they did their fair share of work. As the logs went up, she bleached them with concentrated Javex, a very strong solution that gave off caustic vapors. It was not so bad working on the outside of the house, but the confined interior left June weeping from the fumes. It was also harmful to her lungs, despite her using a scarf to filter what vapors she could. She was certainly dedicated to the task, but the prolonged exposure left her with a bad cough for several months. At one point, she thought it might lead to pneumonia. But the bleach left the logs white and bright, hiding all the marks and defects left from peeling. Not satisfied with this, she then sanded them down by hand to eliminate all knots and scrapes, leaving them finally smooth and gleaming. The final touch was to soften the effect by applying a mixture of turpentine, linseed oil, and varnish. This cured for a month before a final coat of urethane brought back a soft gleam that was easy to clean. She worked long hours to finish this onerous job just so she could sit quietly and contemplate her beautiful walls.

No matter what the weather brought, the logs had to be protected during the process, so it was a happy day for her when the roof was finally finished. She watched impatiently while the final ceiling boards were nailed to the long, massive roof beams, blocking the last of the daylight that streamed in from above. The windows had been strategically placed to allow in the maximum light, so the effect was not one of darkness, but of bright corners of light, which framed the awesome views that favored the front porch.

During the whole process, the men were boarded in the bunkhouse while June cooked the meals in the makeshift home in the basement. It had been hard, but like all births, it was worth the pain. Indeed, she had put as much effort into this project as anything she had done in her life. The day they moved into the main building, she felt most of the challenges of life were behind her – but she was young and had no reason not to nourish this youthful idea of a bright future that looked so promising.

The house had the essential appliances and furniture that belonged in the kitchen, living room, or bedrooms, but as yet they had no partitions. Except for the small toilet and shower in the basement, she still did not have the bathroom on the main floor she had so carefully imagined in her mind. For the time being, clothes hung up on racks served as room dividers. It was not a problem as the kids had their bedroom in the basement. Bert and June had a bedroom upstairs with only a blanket for privacy, leaving the rest of the main floor for the living room and kitchen. But it seemed like they had all the space in the world. It was 1960 when the Mickles moved into their twentieth century home, complete with electricity and running water.

Shortly after they moved to the Millarville property, the children switched to the Sheep Creek School in Millarville, but they spent the last two years of high school at Turner Valley. During their teen years, June had her hands full dealing with all the friends they began to bring home.

With this many kids to work with, Bert dove right into organizing the Millarville Jack Pine Savages baseball team. It was aptly named.

Don adds, "Mom learned how to dye cloth and made us all T-shirts with "Jack-Pine Savages" printed on them. This was our uniform. We had a multi-cultural team including Roy Adams (Smoky) and Leo (a black fellow) and a few others that came and went from the not so reputable part of Calgary."

By 1961, Donny and Faye were just finishing high school. Faye had made up the extra year from when Don had been forced to start school one year older than the normal six-year-old. To June, it made them seem closer in age than they really were. Every day, more children would show up, especially on the weekends when the whole house turned into an endless party. One old friend from those days recalled that, as parents, the Mickles seemed to be very lenient. It was during this period that different boys came to stay with them, mostly because they were not happy in their own homes. One boy stayed for over two years.

Shortly after they moved into the main building, Bert got an opportunity to work on some seismic line construction, and he jumped at it. A regular paycheck beat the uncertainty of making money from the weather-dependent crops. June was just beginning to feel a bit more secure when Bert managed to deliver a nasty blow to his foot while chopping wood. The accident put him in the hospital just before he was about to start the seismic work.

Unfortunately it was some time before he was mobile again. Ever resourceful, June soon found another way to make up the deficiency. Soon she was renting space on their property to the families of men working on the oil rigs who had their own house trailers. She also found up to four boarders to rent the basement. Don tried working on the oil rigs, himself, for a few months but was soon convinced it was not his line of work.

The workers were quite happy about this development, but went the extra length of asking for full board. This meant cooking, cleaning, and laundry as well. As June later reflected, "It was a lot of work, but we really needed the money." In addition to this, the family managed to put down a beautiful white poplar floor and finally put the partitions in. It was a considerable workload with Bert laid up, but the kids were old enough to help out, and in some ways it just seemed like an extension of what she had been doing all her life.

It was understood that Don would work on the ranch after finishing high school, which he was more than happy to do. Taking over a ranch was not considered a future for young girls at the time, however. In the rural community, they were still expected to marry and settle down to have a family. June did not necessarily agree with that, though. One of the things June wished she had done when she was younger was to work on her own for a while.

Though times were changing, with young girls wanting more freedom to choose independent careers, Faye was not comfortable with these choices. She did not want the opportunities of the city life when she had all she wanted at home. Nonetheless, she felt it was expected that she find independent work after she graduated. She pursued this by taking a business course in Calgary.

FAYE AT GRADUATION

To make it affordable, Faye was able to stay with Bert's sister and her family, and this also made it less lonely. Faye was turning into quite a beautiful young woman with dark eyes and a clear rosy skin. Her eyes danced with mischief when with friends, but she was quite shy and did not mix easily in a foreign environment. And Calgary, for her, was a decidedly unknown world. Though it was scarcely the modern, cosmopolitan city it would become, it was still a city growing in that direction. It was the business hub of Southern Alberta with all the accoutrements of a large center. Faye hated it. This did not surprise June, but it was a commitment she felt Faye should stick with, though she grew concerned at her daughter's obvious unhappiness.

"Faye sure seems to cry a lot when she gets home these days," Bert observed.

Faye's only relief was getting home on the weekends, but after a while it did not help at all. She dreaded going back to the city when those precious days at home were over.

"I can't help it, Bert. She enrolled in that course which will help her get a job. She sure won't get one without some kind of training," replied June.

"It won't do her much good out here," he retorted. "She doesn't belong in the city any more than I do. You can see she'll never be happy there. If she stuck around she might meet someone her own age with the same interests. She needs to find a home back here. God knows there are enough kids around here."

Bert was right. The place, particularly on the weekends, seemed like "Party Central." As the kids grew up, they became increasingly connected to the community through school and related activities. Both of them were popular, but Don, in particular, had a lot of friends, many of whom would eventually work for the Mickles. Bert's casual and carefree nature made everyone feel welcome, and not too many rules were laid down when the party got started. June too was easygoing, though she often thought some rules should apply.

Bert's hillbilly baseball team turned out to be surprisingly good and soon qualified to play in the topnotch leagues. They were a serious threat to top-rated teams and cleaned up at many tournaments. Being winners, it always seemed that the party after the game wound up at the Mickles'. Perhaps June let Bert relax the supervision when she saw how much all the fun helped Faye. It was impossible for her to remain sad when everyone was having such a good time. June could see it was a really good life for them and knew this period of her children's young lives, so worry-free and exciting, would give them the strength to face life's eventual challenges. At the time, she often thought she would go crazy with the endless hectic days, not knowing how precious or short they would seem years later.

She recalls now with nostalgia how the kids would bring the party home and immediately turn on the record player to choreograph the gymnastics of the newest dances – testing the foundation of the house. The kids were inclusive with their partying, often waking June and Bert up and insisting they join the fun. June ruefully recalls how sleepy she would be, but that she danced anyway, often until daybreak, when the party finally wound down. It had seemed like a "piece of cake" when she was their age, though she

A TYPICAL PARTY AT THE MICKLES'

can't quite fathom how they found the stamina to stick it out that late. Both she and Bert were turning forty and were beginning to feel the effects of these rowdy nights. She was thankful it was only a couple of days a week.

When June had a spare moment, she continued to fill her canvases with lively scenes of ranching life. She was becoming well known for her ability as an artist and continued to sell paintings at every opportunity. A bit to her surprise, she was commissioned by the owners of the Black Diamond Hotel to paint a series of murals on the walls of the bar. This delighted her, and she took on the task enthusiastically, knowing she could not get better exposure for her craft than in this lively watering hole. She presented a series of sketches to the proprietor, who then agreed she should complete the murals on individual panels. It took a while to complete all the scenes, but by the end of the year, the walls told all who came about life in the foothills. Years later, with many layers of smoke to add to the character of the murals, they were in danger of being destroyed when new owners decided to renovate. But they were too much a part of the history of the Black Diamond settlement to destroy, so a decision was made to try to preserve them. Reconstruction soon found a new home for them on the ceiling of the bar. Patrons looking up in curiosity – or in drunken stupors – can now admire them from the small tables that still dominate the interior.

The lively weekends did not deter Faye from graduating from business school, and soon she was looking for a job to justify her training for a career she did not really want. A friend of Bert's knew a lawyer in Calgary who was looking for an office girl to run errands and eventually work into a more demanding secretarial position. He agreed to give Faye a try. Hoping it would suit her, Faye timidly showed up for work soon after school was out.

Faye's stay in Calgary while attending school had not been pleasant, and she never adapted to the city like other girls from rural settings. She did not like the place and consequently never ventured farther than Bert's sister's house and the school. She had no interest in exploring the town and got easily lost when she had to navigate unfamiliar streets. She never mastered the rudimentary transportation system and had no idea where to find such basic institutions as banks, post offices, or government buildings. This was not helped by her shyness, which kept her from getting advice from family or friends. As a result she floundered at work. The job entailed getting mail, delivering messages, doing the banking, and other prosaic daily routines. When she was sent out to deliver or pick something up, she would get lost – sometimes for hours. She often returned without accomplishing her task, but was too shy to say why.

June became increasingly alarmed when Faye would return home in tears, mumbling about the impossibility of doing the job. Bert's heart would melt every time she gamely struggled with returning to this tormenting job. Eventually, it became apparent this was not meant for her. With as much kindness as possible, her employer told her to find something more suitable to her temperament and abilities. Though hard to hear, it was good advice. Some flowers just transplant badly and do not thrive out of their element. It was with great relief that Faye went home to stay. Her future was bound up with her heritage. Her love of the land and horses superseded any glamorous career in the city or the prospect of a pampered life there.

FAYE AT THE MILLARVILLE HOME

Chapter VIII

AN IRRESISTIBLE OFFER

It was not long after Faye returned home that the family decided to visit Bert's brother, who was now living south of Golden, BC. It was a propitious trip that changed the course of their lives. Though it seemed exciting at the time, June often wondered at how different things might have turned out had they not stopped for coffee and gas at Lake Louise. Though she never regretted the eventful years that followed, she knew their path had been irrevocably altered.

Since they had to stop for gas in any event, Bert thought they might as well take the time to visit an old friend before pushing on to Golden. Bert knew Ray Legace from the time he had spent working on the Banff–Jasper Highway years before. Ray had the outfitting concession for Lake Louise, and he often pastured some of his horses at the Mickle Ranch for the winter. Bert and Jack broke some of his horses for him in winter months, and Jack had worked as a hunting guide for Ray years ago.

Another reason for the visit was concern for the health of Ray and his wife. Ray was recovering from a heart attack, possibly brought on by the stress of his wife Alpha's battle with cancer. When the Mickles arrived, she was recovering from a major operation that had left her quite debilitated. Ray's heart problems were not helped by the concern he had for the future of his guiding business. He had operated in the Lake Louise area for over twenty years, running the pony stand near Chateau Lake Louise and an outfitting business in the park. On top of this, he managed Skoki Lodge for the Lake Louise ski hill in the winter and summer months. The lodge was twelve miles north-east of Lake Louise, deep in the backcountry. The pony stand ran daily rides to the end of Lake Louise, but the more exciting part of the outfit was running hunting and fishing trips, as well as dude camps in the summer. It meant packing-in large camps for fall hunts and supplying Skoki Lodge all year round. It was a lot of work that never ended and was clearly becoming more than the older couple could manage. But the business had been an integral part of Ray's life, which he had built up over fifty years, and he did not want to hand it over to anyone he did not trust to run it as he had all of his life. Without hesitation, he decided to offer it to Bert.

June was stunned. The very possibility of assuming such an undertaking went contrary to anything she expected for her family. But the year was 1962, and the kids were now young adults with definite opinions. They had always been a close family, and decisions were democratic. They tried to make choices based on what was best for all in the family.

Bert listened politely to Ray's offer, but typically did not say much. He knew it would not happen without June's backing. June, just as politely, said they still had to get to Jack's place that night and that they had a lot to consider before making a commitment.

Back in the car, June explained the offer to her two children. With a mixture of excitement and trepidation she listened to the rest of the family. Bert was keen to help out an old friend and was clearly excited about the offer. But the swaying vote went to the kids – and in particular, Faye. Don was more than happy to move to the mountains and the certainty of embarking on a big adventure. They had always gone to the mountains for holidays, and he loved the wildness of the high country. The Lake Louise country epitomized everything the front ranges had to offer on a much grander scale. It was vast, high, and beautiful. But Don was as easygoing as Bert, and he knew he had years ahead of him to get back to the mountains in some capacity if he wanted to. Still, a chance to take over an outfit like Ray's comes but once in a lifetime and was too good to pass up without serious consideration.

But it was Faye who viewed the offer as the opportunity of a lifetime. She hated the city and knew she would not go back, but neither could she just sit around home. The outfitting business was perfect. The mountains beckoned to her with the promise of limitless freedom in a land that was incomparably beautiful. It was wild and exciting and offered a way of life she knew she was meant for. She would not let up on June, asking daily if they were going to move. Bert could never refuse Faye anything, and soon his voice was added to hers. Youth and enthusiasm were infectious, and June could not hold out against all of them.

Though everyone had a role, June was the organizer in the family. It was her business sense that kept them solvent and even successful. She also knew she held the family together and provided the direction they needed. Her organizational skills were exceptional, and of course she was a hard worker. Bert had the knowledge of the country, and the hunting and horse skills to run the outfit. But he needed her abilities if they were to make a go of it. Faye and Don also were hard workers, but they were young, and Don was now old enough to be interested in girls, wild parties, and good times. He had no lack of equal-minded cohorts to party with. Aside from that, Don brought youth, enthusiasm, and all the skills he had learned from Bert. The deal Ray was offering was hard to turn down. They had to raise $5,000 in cash for a down payment, but the terms for paying it off were more than reasonable. June knew they could handle it financially, but it was a difficult decision for her.

All her life, June had wanted a place of her own that she could be comfortable in and be proud of. Building the log house of her dreams had not only been a financial investment – paid for in large part with sweat equity – but it was very much an emotional investment as well. She loved that house and the land with a passion. She knew they could have had a good life there with most of the hard years behind them. Now they were faced with launching a whole new business (with a steep learning curve) that was certainly not risk free. It also meant going back to primitive living at the pony barn at Lake Louise or Skoki Lodge. She had finally achieved the luxury of running water and indoor plumbing! Skoki meant hauling wood and water all over again. Forget flush toilets, showers, or washing machines. On top of this, she was back to cooking huge meals on a wood stove. She blanched at the thought of it. She would have to learn new skills such as skiing and running a snowmobile. She and Bert were not that young anymore and did not have the endless stamina they'd had in their early years. But with trepidation and courage, she finally nodded in assent.

It was too late to take over that summer as they had a lot of work left on the ranch. As soon as things slowed down and June had a chance to adjust to the idea of outfitting in the mountains, she began assessing what had to be done to be ready for the following spring. The first thing they did as a family was make an inventory. Even though Ray had the basic equipment they needed, he had slowed down in recent years, and many things needed mending or replacing. They also hoped to expand, which was very realistic with the huge increase in tourism that assaulted the mountain parks in the sixties and showed no sign of slowing down.

After the war ended, the economy in North America took off like a rocket, and the average family now had the means to own cars and take holidays. It was also the era of the Baby Boomers. Young kids were gaining their freedom, and they flocked to the mountains on a wave of outdoor mania.

Charlie Reigner, who was Ray's top hand, helped them out. Bert kept on many of the people who had worked for Ray, as they knew the horses and the country. Bert had been to the mountains before when he'd worked with Ray on building part of the Banff–Jasper Highway, but he had a lot to learn about the country, which included the Siffleur

Wilderness on the northeastern boundary of Banff National Park. It was remote and most easily accessed from Lake Louise via the Pipestone and Siffleur Rivers in the park.

Though Ray described the area and mapped out the location of all the camps, Bert still had to familiarize himself with it first-hand. Game had to be located, camps set up, and feed for the horses assessed. Cooking for the clients in camp meant organizing menus and ordering the food. And that was only for the moving trips. Skoki Lodge was a much bigger operation, with a more sophisticated clientele. It was daunting enough that the Mickles would have to master winter skills such skiing and snowmobiling to cater to both sets of outdoor enthusiasts. June was used to cooking for large numbers of people and she was a good cook, but it was her management skills they needed to make a success of the place.

LOADING THE STOVE FOR SKOKI

Don was eager to get started, and he thought the best way to get some experience with the country and the operation of the business was to spend the summer of 1962 in Skoki. He recalls:

"Bob Barker was working for Ray that year, and I spent some time with him in Skoki – mostly chopping firewood. We had an interesting trip packing a heavy cook stove into Skoki. Charlie Reigner, Keith Foster, and I tandem-packed the stove in, and it is still there. In the fall, Bert, Charlie and I spent some time in the Kootenay Plains, scouting out probable hunting areas. I looked after about eighteen horses [at Two O'Clock Creek] for a few days, while Dad and Charlie went to Rocky Mountain House – I can't remember why – but they got caught up in the bar for a few extra days while I ran out of food at the Kootenay Plains and was eating at a hunters' camp where they used our horses (good trade off). Charlie and I then trailed the horses up the White Rabbit to Indianhead and the Ya Ha Tinda (my first visit to the ranch). That is the time that our horses had a runaway when they saw a milk cow.

"I remember that Andy Anderson was at Indianhead and Mickey Gilmar was at the Ya Ha Tinda Ranch at the time. When we got to the Red Deer River, Ray Legace drove over the Cascade Road with Faye to meet us. They stopped at Windy, and Ray and Hal Shepherd (resident warden) got into a bottle of whisky. Hal was starting to chase Faye around the kitchen so Ray and her took off. Ray decided that Faye should drive because he was under the influence. The problem was that Faye had not driven much and almost stalled Ray's old truck on one of the cliffs near Snow Creek

Summit. They made it to the YHT somehow. Charlie had taken off meanwhile, and I was alone at the Red Deer with a couple of horses; we turned the rest loose. Ray was mad at Charlie for taking off, so he left Faye with me and headed out to Sundre to find Charlie. We never saw either of them again, but they somehow got word to Mom and Dad that Faye and I were stranded at the Red Deer River. We ran out of food, of course, and were too shy to visit the ranch, but we did a lot of riding, and I caught a couple of fish. Mom and Dad arrived and starvation was put aside again."

Running out of food was a recurrent theme for the wranglers on many trips. Dale Portman, who later worked for the Mickles, remembers running out of food while at the hunting camp on the Siffleur River. They were down to the ubiquitous beans but little else. When they spotted a couple of spruce grouse, they decided to add to the larder. Mutually inspired, they each picked up a rock and hurled it at the birds. Unbelievably, they both hit their marks and feasted that night on the slightly stringy game. As Dale would say later, "You could never do that again in a million years!"

That fall, Charlie Reigner moved in with the Mickles at Millarville to help put the equipment together. To Bert and June's alarm, they realized that Faye was attracted to him, and it soon came out that they were "going together." Both parents felt she was too young for this, particularly when it got as far as being a formal engagement. She was seventeen at the time. Faye quickly pointed out that it was not many years ago that an unmarried girl was thought of as an old maid if not married by twenty. Bert and June did the wise thing at the time and decided not to interfere. As it turned out, the close proximity of their living quarters gave Faye a chance to see what it would be like to live with Charlie full-time, and as the winter drew on, this prospect didn't seem so exciting. By spring, she called it off, to everyone but Charlie's relief. He accepted her decision with grace and continued to work on the winter projects. This was also a relief, as the Mickles badly needed the help. They mended halters, built pack boxes, and repaired saddles while June worked on creating new saddle pads and outdoor clothing. Charlie remained long enough to launch them into their first season, but he wanted a home and family, and later, he drifted off.

That winter, June took another child under her wing. Sometimes she felt like the mother of a halfway home. The girl's name was Patty Cooper, and she was a slight, dark girl with a sharp wit. June remembers that Patty came home with the kids from a dance one night like a stray calf that came to stay. She was only seventeen, had coal-black hair, and could hold her own in any fight. It seemed she just did not get along with her parents – possibly because she had been adopted – and one day she announced she would stay with the Mickles, which she did for many years. That winter, they got her a job at the Post Hotel with Alpha Legace in Lake Louise, and she worked for the family in the summer. She and Faye became close friends and would collaborate on many a nasty trick directed at the boys if they got out of hand. June sighed and thought to herself, *Another one to raise!*

During the winter, Faye spent most of her time with Bert on the trapline. She had become a crack shot and never failed to come home without a load of squirrels stuffed in her coat. She was such a good shot that she won the annual turkey shoot at the Square Butte Hall. A real Annie Oakley, she beat all the men, to their consternation, with just an old gun of Bert's that had the sights taped on. Her competition was embarrassed that she beat them despite their new guns with powerful scopes.

It was time-consuming to skin the squirrels, but fur was in demand, and she felt she was contributing to her keep. She had an interesting way of attaching them to the lining of her jacket, which was a bit dramatic when she took it off. Standing in the doorway, she would open her long coat to reveal the now dead rodents attached to the inside lining, like a hustler showcasing his collection of watches in a dark alley. Some of them landed on the floor, as they broke loose. Amongst the hoard, an occasional grouse would appear to help with the next night's dinner. The family was used to this, but on one particular night, Bert had some hockey friends over planning the next week's game when Faye came in with her catch. The young men's jaws dropped when they saw this teenager reveal her bounty. She certainly seemed eccentric for a girl who, under the bulky clothing, might even be pretty. Little did they know. A few weeks later, wondering what kind of a chance he was taking, one of the boys invited Faye out to a dance. To his astonishment, Faye cleaned up real well. The girl greeting him at the door was dressed to kill, with a flattering dress and high heels. The scruffy huntress had morphed into a very pretty young woman. Even June was impressed and suddenly realized her little girl had grown up. Bert wasn't surprised. He'd known all along what a prize she was.

After they spent considerable time in the late fall and early winter working on gear, the time came to open up Skoki for winter customers. The horse aspect of the outfit did not faze June, but winter in Skoki was another matter. They took their first trip into the remote lodge on February 13, 1963. The party consisted of June and Bert, Don and Charlie. Bert had never used skis in his life and was not about to start at his age. He plodded in on snowshoes, but June recalled the days she'd spent on her old wooden ski staves and thought she could manage on more modern equipment, so she chose to ski in. Don and Charlie also used skis and did fairly well with them, considering they wore rubber boots with bands around the toes to keep them in place – possibly the most inelegant outfit to brave the slopes of Boulder and Deception pass, though fashion was not a great priority for them. Don gained a great deal of experience skiing the following winter when he started working in avalanche control in Rogers Pass.

What June had not counted on was the terrain she was tackling. She had spent her youth skiing on the prairies, or at best the gentle foothills near their home. She had never skied in the mountains before, and the result was not encouraging. She had never heard of skins or wax that would enable her to climb the steep slopes, and with no help, she spent most of her time sliding back. She did not know how to side-step, and even if she did, it would be exhausting to scale those passes without knowing how to climb efficiently. The skis were long and not cut for tracking or turning. Bert had to stay with her to help when she fell or slipped back, which occurred frequently. The unwieldy pack she was carrying seemed to be falling over her shoulders or swinging sideways, taking her with it in constant downward momentum. She was terrified of going up the steep slopes of Deception Pass, but there was no choice. After being pulled out of numerous holes and aided by Bert, she finally stood on top of the pass only to realize she now had to ski down. Thinking she had conquered the ultimate by reaching the aptly named "Deception" Pass, she had no idea of how to manage the descent.

With newfound fortitude gained through necessity, she bravely pointed the wooden albatrosses downhill and pushed off. Sitting down followed immediately. This maneuver did not stop her downward plunge, and she descended several meters before the deep snow accumulating between her legs forced a halt. She struggled with her poles to stand up and was alarmed by the snow that seemed unfathomably deep, suggesting the ground was a long way down. The effort to get up was wearing her out so much that she was afraid her body would give out before she was anywhere near the lodge. In desperation, she decided to gingerly side-step down the rest of the way. She was exhausted well before the lodge loomed into sight in the dimming day. Don, who had gone on ahead to get the fire going and hot water on, returned up the trail to take her pack and give much-needed encouragement (lying when he said the lodge was just around the corner). No fire was ever more welcome.

JUNE AT DECEPTION PASS ON SKIS

JUNE AT SKOKI THAT FIRST WINTER

Wrapped in warm blankets and sipping hot tea, June turned to Bert and exclaimed, "What are us old people doing in these mountains? I'm over forty years old and should be in my own home like any sensible woman my age. I swear, I'm not leaving here until I can either walk or ride out – preferably ride! I'm sure glad Faye didn't come with us; she wouldn't have made it with her cold."

When she recovered enough to check her pack, she was dismayed to find the dozen eggs she'd been carrying had been scrambled beyond belief in the many falls she had taken. The sticky remnants coated everything from her clothing to the cheerful little guest book she had found in a stationary store. She didn't even have a nightgown for bed that night

Faye had stayed behind very reluctantly. June promised that she could join them as soon as her strep throat was better. Fortunately for Faye that meant getting a much easier trip in on the double-track skidoo that they bought when they acquired the lodge. It was the first one in the area; the warden service bought one soon after, and it was used by Gerry Lister, who was the district warden at the time.

But Faye's eagerness to join the family was almost her undoing. She was not fully recovered when she arrived after a cold journey on the sled. By the following day she had developed a high fever with a throat so sore she could not even swallow water. Fearing the worst, June had never felt so isolated in her life. Her main fear was that Faye had developed diphtheria. In the early sixties, mountain rescue was in its infancy, and helicopters were not yet used in rescue work. The best they could do was to send Charlie out to consult with a doctor in Banff. He came back with antibiotics that probably saved Faye's life. In the meantime, all June could do was collect long, frozen icicles from the porch to wrap in towels for Faye's head.

It took a long time for Faye to recover, and in the process, her skin began to peel off. If June had any doubts about the choice they'd made to take over the outfit, that winter gave her many occasions to question their decision.

She would often think: *We may as well be in that old farmhouse of your dad's. Here I am right back to hauling water, chopping wood, and washing clothes and bedding by hand again. There isn't even a wringer washer – just that old scrub board and wringing things out by hand. Everything freezing on the line again. The snow is so deep in here I have to wear snowshoes just to step outside.* She did not say this aloud, wanting to keep harmony in the family, and kept the "pity me" thoughts to herself. The kids and Bert were clearly very happy with the arrangement despite the hard work.

Shortly after the Mickles arrived the first guests came in. June had no time to think about the drastic change in her life, or indeed of little else but baking cookies, pies, bread, cakes, and cooking stews, roasts, steaks, and hearty breakfasts. All the lunches were laid out once breakfast was done, leaving the cleaning and washing for the main part of the day. But the evenings were cozy in the old place, with a warm fireplace crackling as the endless snow fell outside.

It took June a while to get used to the snow. The prairies had snow but nothing like the depthless layers that piled up over the buildings until it seemed they would cave in. At times she thought it would bury her long before spring came. And spring along the Great Divide certainly never came early.

The work that never ended saw the time slip by quickly, leaving her wondering if everything got done. As she adjusted to the routine and became more efficient, she was eventually able to absorb the beauty of the valley, especially when the sun finally shone and the snow became a playground. June was quick to take advantage of the willingness of guests to help teach her to ski. She was a practical woman who enjoyed life, and she soon realized the best way to get the most out of this new environment was to embrace it. She never became a great skier, as it is a hard activity to learn well without starting at a young age. But she became competent and relished the freedom that came with this new skill. She soon learned all the trails and, in turn, was able to help the clients, telling them where the best day trips were.

Driving the skidoo was another skill June wanted to master. Unfortunately, it was an unwieldy machine and hard to drive without getting stuck. Once it was stuck, it was almost impossible to get unstuck. But she persisted and soon was zooming over the sparkling meadows and trails around the valley. In fact, she became a little over-confident. Returning from Banff on a supply trip, she found herself going too fast on the downhill run to the lodge. Suddenly she bounced unexpectedly over a hidden log that launched her skidoo into the creek bed. She was thrown over the top when the skidoo came to a sudden halt after being driven into the steep bank on the far side of the creek. June sported quite a few bruises and a black eye for some time to come, but she was relieved nothing was broken. Bert gave her a hard time over the misadven-ture, and she wasn't sure if he was joking when he hid the skidoo keys. It turned out the reason she had not seen the log was the fault of a turkey. She had not been able to find room for it behind the seat so she'd stashed it between her and the handlebars. The turkey survived with aplomb and helped ease embarrassment over the mishap when it became dinner a few days later.

After surviving the first winter in Skoki, the family had a couple of months to finalize the work for the summer season. Finally, in the spring of 1963, they formally started running all aspects of the outfit. June established herself at the pony barns near Chateau Lake Louise. She sighed inwardly as she moved her belongings into the small cabin, which would act as office and residence. Although there was cold running water, there was only the wood stove for cooking, and of course no electricity. She wondered why, as she grew older, she had even dreamed of enjoying the amenities of civilization, which the ranch had provided for so few years. Now the pony barn would be principally her domain as long as they ran the outfit. In time, most of the managing of the stable would fall to Faye – a job she was eminently happy with.

FAYE AT THE PONY STAND

As Don writes: "It was also our central staging area. The stable or "pony stand," as we called it was located behind Deer Lodge in Upper Lake Louise, and you can still see it there today (2015). A small dirt road winds through the trees then opens up to the stable area. It had that folksy, hillbilly settlement look to it. A small, two-storey building served as an office, kitchen, and bunkhouse. Another small one-room cabin was where Mom and Dad stayed. The stable was a long, open building with a tack room on the far end. A large double corral that could hold around thirty horses, and was almost always muddy, was accessed with rubber boots, a necessity in getting feed to the mangers or catching horses. A stack of hay was located conveniently at the edge of the tack room. A shoeing stand and a water trough were across from the stable and more to the middle of things. The shoeing stand doubled as a hose-down area to make the horses presentable after being led out of the muddy corrals. Hydro was not available, and gas lanterns were used extensively at night. Two outhouses served both staff and guests. Black bears and grizzlies frequently walked through the yard en route to the big government dump located below us, a couple of kilometers away. Flashlights and a wary eye were necessary in completing a trip to the outhouse at night."

June was astounded at how rapidly the family took on additional commitments. Now that they had the outfit, there seemed no end to the expansion that was possible. That year they also established a pony stand at Wapta Lake in Yoho National Park. In 1968 they took over the Emerald Lake stables at Emerald Lake, a spectacular location on the shores of that emerald jewel. They actually started running a concession at Shuswap Lake for the summer of 1965, which Patty ran for them, but June was glad when it proved not financially worth pursuing. In the heady excitement of such big changes, June was not sure if she was on a roller coaster or drugs – and wondered who was on the brakes.

The following winter, Don went to work for Noel Gardner at Rogers Pass in Glacier National Park, where he had his own special challenges. Working in the world of avalanche control and research was as foreign to him as flying to the moon. Skiing was almost as new to him as it was to June, though it was a major part of the job. His first day was a nightmare.

Bert knew Noel Gardner from Bragg Creek and managed to get Don a job working for Noel at Rogers Pass. Upon receiving the offer, Don wrote back to say he would take the job – it was good money in those days. Noel told him to buy his own ski boots and that they would supply the skis and skins. (At the time, Don wondered what skins were.) He bought the boots at the Hudson Bay Co. store in Banff for ten dollars and showed up at Flat Creek to be met by Noel and the Sno-Cat. The trip from the highway up to Mt. Fidelity Station was uneventful. Here Don was run quickly through his duties, which included maintenance, snow measurements, and weather readings. On the first day of work, he had to put his skis on and follow Noel up to the top of the mountain inappropriately called Roundhill. His bafflement over the skins was soon resolved when Noel produced a long strip of sealskin, which attached to the bottom of the skis to prevent slipping back when they walked up the hill. Copying Noel, Don soon had his skins on, then up they went.

When they got to the top, Noel off-handedly pointed to a tall, skinny, thirty-foot-high pole that had some revolving cups sitting on top, and he told Don to climb up and clean the rime out. Don reluctantly slithered up the shaky thing, using all available appendages for questionable grip. To his dismay, he suddenly realized he had a great view all the way down to Schuss Lake, a thousand feet below. Now terrified, he realized he had to let go with one hand to clear the hoary cups. He used the side of his face to stop the twirling things and stabilize them, while he cleaned them with his free hand.

Thinking he had survived the worst when he at last reached firm ground, he was now confronted with the ski down. Mt. Fidelity is not a good place to learn to ski. Noel was busy taking the skins off his skis when Don asked if he should do the same. Noel replied sardonically, "It's up to you." So Don took them off. By now the fog had rolled in, and all Don could do was follow in Noel's tracks. He fell a lot on the way down. Actually he fell a lot that winter. This was Don's second time ever on skis, and Gladys (Noel's wife) decided she would teach him how to ski.

Don continued with his main job of shoveling snow, checking the light plant, and on occasion taking some readings. The job gave him good insight into the duties of the avalanche observer and assistant observer in the control program back then. Observers were there to train staff in safe travel procedures, take all the critical readings, and help out with avalanche control. They also did snow profiles and managed the data. Assistants did mostly grunt work, shoveling snow, running around and occasionally helping with observations on avalanche shoots. As Don settled into the routine duties, he came to know the people he was working with. Unlike many others, he candidly remembers Noel as a "really charming guy – really interesting to talk to." To Don's happy surprise, he also discovered Noel loved to teach, and soon he learned a lot about the avalanche program and some of technical side of avalanche behavior. Don also recalls, "He had a temper. He was tough. He learned by the school of hard knocks. He certainly didn't pamper you." Despite this, Don adds, "He was fair, and I really liked him, but when you earned his wrath you wanted to hide.

"Noel's nickname was Old Snowflake, but he had a lot of power on what was going on in Rogers Pass. People jumped when he said jump."

Don also felt that Noel was good to Fred and Walter Schleiss, who would eventually take over from Noel on his retirement. "Noel was spending a lot of his time sorting out where to shoot with the artillery, and so was doing a lot of testing. He was also doing more observations and trying to perfect the art and science of avalanche forecasting. He had a lot of visitors, and this is where he first met Hans Gmoser. Hans was just getting his heli-ski business going in the Bugaboos and was a good friend of Noel's."

Gmoser, in later years, praised the control work of Gardner and his team as he states here: "The best example is what has been done at Rogers Pass, starting with Noel Gardner who identified the avalanche paths – trigger zones – and set up the program with the armed forces to shoot them down with artillery. Under Freddy Schleiss I think it was developed to perfection, or as close as it came to perfection."

Don would continue to work in the avalanche field until he joined the warden service several years later.

The arrival of spring after their second winter at Skoki seemed to take forever, but by April the days were getting longer, and the sun seemed that much stronger and brighter. In a flurry of activity brought on by the nicer weather, June varnished all the logs in the main building and painted the kitchen logs white. They did not have any guests later in the month, which gave her the opportunity to get this task done – a task she felt was definitely needed. Again the days raced by, and by May they closed the place for the spring.

That spring, June realized just how much work their new lifestyle entailed. The spring was given over to house cleaning and preparing for the summer. This meant spring roundup at the Ya Ha Tinda for the boys, while June headed for Lake Louise to clean and prepare the pony barn. Even Faye and Patty went to the roundup, leaving June to cope with the cleaning and organizing by herself. In a way, she was not unhappy with this as it meant no distractions and she could concentrate on dealing with the problems ahead with a certain amount of peace. One of the things on her list was to qualify both Faye and herself for their guide's license. Without it, they could not take people on day rides, either to the end of the lake or the trails beyond.

When Bert took on the outfit, he knew he would need a competent staff to run it, which meant finding men capable of handling horses, packing, and guiding clients. In the hunting camps, this would also mean cooking and tracking game. During their years at Millarville, they always had lots of young people hanging around – most of whom came from farms and ranches in the area and knew their way around a horse. They were also a pretty wild bunch. Many of them worked for Bert then went on to rewarding positions in the warden service, which caused those who had known them in those days to shake their heads in wonder.

Perry Jacobson, Bob Haney, and Keith Foster all became Chief Park Wardens toward the end of their careers. Dale Portman became a dog master and area manager in the Lake Louise district, while Dave Wildman became a successful rancher in the Millarville area. John Nylund was the government barn boss in Banff before he took over the management of the Ya Ha Tinda. Don flourished in the warden service, which gave him so much freedom to travel the backcountry on horseback. Eventually, he succeeded to the position of Cultural and Heritage Manager for Banff, which was the highlight of his career. The young men's early days partying at the Mickle Ranch in Millarville had held no hint of such future respectability.

Perry Jacobson recalled one party in particular that summed up many. As usual, a party that had begun in the bar after a ball game, wound up at the Mickles'. The house was jammed with the local kids, when a party of horse guides from Lake Louise showed up. For some reason, the two groups did not mix well, though no one knew quite why. Perry chalked it up to some misconstrued idea of rivalry. They just did not get along. By the early hours of the morning, the cheap wine kicked in and a fight broke out. Perry clearly remembers Bert sitting in a corner, nursing a jug of wine, when one of the offenders staggered by. Without much of an upward glance, Bert delivered a wallop that sent the guy flying across the room. For some reason, Faye, who was really quite shy, got the impression that Bert had been hit. Without a thought and with a yell, she delivered another blow to the unfortunate cowboy, saying, "You can't hit my father!"

Perry laughs at these old memories, saying, "We were always getting in trouble, but in those days there didn't seem to be any cops around. If we got rowdy in the bar, they just kicked us out. No real harm was ever done, though we probably shouldn't have been driving on many of those occasions." Perry does not remember where June was through all of this but suspects she discreetly retired to let the party take its course, knowing they would be on pretty serious cleanup detail the next morning. Perry adds, "June was a great gal, but it always surprised me how much she put up with."

Don was pretty wild himself in those days. He was an easy-going, good looking young man with a streak of recklessness in him that would take a few years to burn out. Having discovered girls, he was pretty democratic in who he picked up. One night Perry was sitting with Bert, sharing the usual jug of wine, when Don drifted by accompanied by three young women who looked fairly rough around the edges. No beauties by any standard. Don didn't care. With his squinty stare, Bert followed them through the smoke curling from his fingers, then said casually, "I don't know where he finds them!"

Sometimes the boys' sense of fun got a bit carried away. Don, on one occasion, had reason to regret what, at the time, had seemed like just a fun way to pass a lazy spring afternoon in the back yard. He and Johnny Nylund found themselves drinking beer on the back porch after a hard few days chasing wild horses. Johnny was one of the Millarville Mafia crowd, who would later find his way to working for the warden service as barn boss in Banff, and then as boss at the Ya Ha Tinda. June and Bert were at Lake Louise getting ready for another hectic summer, so Don and Johnny were fending for themselves. A couple of slapped-together sandwiches had not put much of a dent in their hunger, and for once, there was not much else in the house for a meal. The beer filled the empty spots nicely.

The boys sat taking in the sun when Johnny spotted several coyote carcasses hanging from an old poplar tree across the yard. "Say Don? What are those old, beat-up pelts doing still hanging on that tree over there?" he asked.

Don lazily looked over at the moth-eaten, ragged ends of the pelts, which were left-over rejects from a winter of trapping. "Oh, those. Curly Sands shot them last winter. I guess he never got around to cleaning them up."

Curly Sands was a colorful old bachelor who never seemed to have a permanent home. He mostly lived west of Millarville, making liberal use of people's tolerance for

"Squatter Rights." He would take up residence in abandoned trailers, forgotten bush cabins, and when things were good, at fire lookouts and forestry stations. Don first met him when he was working for the Rangers, checking game hunters on the Forestry Reserve.

Curly's lifestyle may have been forged in the battlefields of the Second World War where (according to him) he single-handedly defeated the German Army. There was little doubt, however, that he'd seen a lot of action. Seven years of hard battle left many veterans unable to readjust to the placid, repetitive job of settled society in the fifties. Curly found his solace in telling stories and living mostly by himself in the bush of Alberta's foothill country.

Like many of his ilk, he was a talented man. He'd been a noted bronc rider in his younger days, and he was a natural mimic. He could faithfully whistle all the bird songs that inhabited his world. He was also a deadly shot. Don would never forget that first meeting with Curly. He and Bert had ridden up to the North Sheep Forestry Station for a visit with the Ranger Bill Palmer and his wife.

"I was about ten or eleven years old and was quite fascinated watching Curly with his gun. Suddenly he pointed it out the door and fired a shot in the small cabin. Betty almost landed on the stove. Dad and Bill were startled into sudden silence as they peered at a post outside sprouting a few grey feathers. Curly drawled through the cloud of smoke 'That whiskey jack has been stealing my bacon all winter.'"

On the afternoon that Don and Johnny were eying the carcasses, Curly was living in the small bunkhouse on the

Mickle property, where he'd been for the last few years. He kept an eye on the place when the Mickles were off at Lake Louise in the summer. He had spent the winter hunting coyotes, making a meager living from the hides he sold in town. These poor remnants were the last of the lot and well past having any commercial value.

Since Curly wasn't around that day, the boys could not resist taking a few potshots at the pelts, watching them twist lazily in the sun with each well-placed shot. That got to be a bit repetitive until Johnny spotted a new target. He took aim at the old steel-wheeled tractor that Curly had for odd jobs. The mirror mounted on the fender erupted nicely into flinty shards that shot rainbow colors through the air. Don was particularly pleased when he sent the tobacco can covering the smoke stack flying heavenward into the air. The next target did more damage when they placed a few shot into the radiator. Nothing of note materialized from this, and they lost interest in the game, which they soon forgot.

The fruit of their labor that day soon had unforeseen repercussions. A few months later, Don and Johnny were sent home from Lake Louise to pick up a load of horses needed at the pony stand. It was raining heavily (and had been for a week) turning the yard into quagmire, but they managed to back the stock truck up to the loading ramp. Scurrying as fast as they could to avoid getting totally soaked, they soon had the horses loaded and ready for the road. But the added weight sank the truck down into the soggy ground and they could not pull away. They churned the tires until the truck was hopelessly stuck. In the process, they also managed to get a flat tire. Their efforts took on a malevolent quality when they realized they had only succeeded in pulling the truck forward about a foot from the ramp, making it impossible to unload the horses. It was a Sunday when nothing was open, and with the rain coming down even harder Don wondered what else could go wrong. They didn't even have a spare tire.

Curly was home that day and offered to take them to town to get the flat fixed. By the afternoon, in the now torrential downpour, they got the repaired tire back on the truck. With a new tire, they hoped against impossible odds that they would be able to drive away. Further spinning put an end to that idea.

Curly looked on with concern; they were all getting worried about the horses that had patiently been confined to the small enclosure in the rain for some time by then. The animals were getting cold and restless trying to keep their balance on the slippery floorboards.

Suddenly Curly said, "Well, boys, I'll start the old McCormick (his pet name for his tractor) and pull you fellas outta there." Memories of a hot afternoon slowly emerged, but Don thought it better to say nothing. Curly fired up the old beast that had not been run for some time and they filled the radiator from the horse trough. Curly happily chugged over to the imprisoned truck, backing up and ordering Johnny to hook the heavy chain to the bumper. He could not see the merry arches of water springing from the bullet-damaged radiator at the front of the tractor.

With gusto he floored the tractor, telling Johnny to gun the truck at the same time. Curly lurched across the field, hitting the end of the chain with all the power the old machine had. The chain snapped in half and flew forward, landing a solid blow to the back of Curly's head. Don could scarcely believe his eyes when Curly jumped down swearing profanely then stopped in his tracks when he saw the bright arches of water streaming from the radiator.

He was still yelling, "Someone shot my tractor!" when a logging truck drove up the road. It was the only good fortune they had that day. They quickly hailed the driver and convinced him to pull them out with his much bigger machine. The last the boys saw of Curly, he was gesticulating wildly, sending baleful glares in their direction. When Don returned in the fall, Curly had moved on — tractor and all. He must have convinced Bert to help repair the old beast.

Poaching was another misdemeanor that was taken fairly lightly in the community as a whole. The Depression days were not long gone and feeding your family from the avails of the land was not considered an offence. As the sixties progressed, this attitude would change, particularly in more settled parts of the country. But in the late fifties, in the wilder part of the foothills, a rancher taking the odd elk did not spark much alarm.

Perry Jacobson knew of Bert by reputation when his family first moved to Millarville, but he gained a much clearer insight into his character one night in the Black Diamond bar. Perry was astonished when Bert leaned casually over and quietly said, "Saw that elk you got last week." Bert's habit of smoking his cigarette through a clenched hand close to his mouth, bringing a squint from the smoke to an intense stare, unnerved Perry. Bert peered at Perry, with a slight smile that revealed a sense of humor brought on by his discomfort.

Perry stammered, "Why, what do you mean, Bert?"

"Yeah, I saw you and your friend over there with that six-point elk." Bert was pointing at a small man across the bar Perry had been hunting with that week. "Saw your white horse too. Believe it was in that small valley off the upper Elbow drainage."

Perry knew he was caught but could not understand how Bert could have seen them. As far as he was concerned, no one else had been in the country. There'd been no sign of anyone else camping or traveling in that remote area, and he could not believe Bert had seen them without them knowing he was there. "Were you there?" he asked in disbelief.

Bert laughed. "I was on the ridge just to the north of you. Nice elk."

Many years later, Perry would observe, "Yeah, Bert was like that. You never knew where he was. He would just pop out of nowhere. He was a real bushman."

These were the kind of young men Bert took on their first spring round-up after buying the outfit. Spirits were high, as were expectations, and despite some tension and hijinks, everyone was anticipating some hard riding. Knowing they had to find all the horses to have a successful summer, Bert was a bit more circumspect. It was a very serious form of play that had both rewards and dangers.

The immediate challenge was to find the horses. The horses knew the country much better than the cowboys. Many of the horses were unknown to the men, as they all came from Ray Legace's string rather than their own. Some of the older mares that led the herd had the advantage of having spent many winters on this range and they knew all the escape routes. Bert's big advantage was years of experience chasing wildies in the bush west of Millarville. He knew how to outsmart a horse by reading the land, finding the telltale tracks, and being familiar with the animal's habits.

Don and Faye could hardly contain their enthusiasm as the pickup truck roared out of the dark spruce forest onto the open grass meadows of the Ya Ha Tinda. This large ranch belonged to Parks Canada and was used as winter range for the horses that went to the different mountain parks in the summer. It was a special place, blessed by open meadows sheltered from the worse of the weather, providing ideal conditions for horses to over-winter with little loss. The name Ya Ha Tinda was Stoney/Nakoda for "Prairie in the Mountains." But there was a lot of area surrounding the ranch that had the same open meadows, and for years, several outfitters had used the area for the same purpose.

The pickup truck loaded with camp gear, food, beer, and horse tack (and a few hidden bottles of rum) was followed by the stock truck carrying the horses the riders would need to collect a herd of over eighty head of horses. Among them was Ben, Don's favorite horse, which would be with him throughout the outfitting years. Don would eventually write about those special years in a written tribute to his horse called, "My Friend Ben." A good horse was invaluable in the outfitting business, but that first year Ben was still a young horse and Don would have his hands full ironing out the kinks.

There were eight of them that first spring: Bert, Don, Keith Foster, Dave Wildman, Roy (Smoky) Adams, Ron Echlin, and the two girls (Faye and the adopted Patty Cooper).

Dale Portman, who would later join the team, described the boys in his book *Riding on the Wild Side*:[2]

"Keith was a skinny, bow-legged little cowboy from Millarville who could rattle off a staccato torrent of cusses and insults in record time. He usually wore a wide-brimmed hat, but because he didn't want to lose his new black Stetson, he wore an English style derby for the roundup.

"Dave Wildman was the tall, dark, good-looking member of the crew. He was also one of the Millarville boys, raised west of town. He managed most of the work on the family ranch after the untimely death of his father. Dave had worked with Bert in the mountains the previous summer, and he was helping out on the roundup this year before resuming his busy ranch life. It was a break for him and he loved the sport of chasing wild horses for all of its excitement, risk, and hard riding.

"Roy (Smokey) Adams was a young Cree man who had spent a lot of time over the years with the Mickle family. Smokey, Bert, and Donny had spent the last couple of years making a living cutting posts and rails in the area on our land. Faye and Smokey were also the best of friends. In many ways he was like another brother to her. For one thing, she had long, dark hair, soft, dark eyes, and a dark

---

2   Dale Portman, *Riding on the Wild Side: Tales of Adventure in the Canadian West*. Victoria, BC: Heritage House Publishing, 2009.

complexion. Smokey, in fact looked more like Faye's brother than did the blond, blue-eyed Donny.

"Ron Echlin was fresh out of high school, but was already a seasoned horseman and an excellent rider. His parents ran a horse-training business at Elkana Ranches near Bragg Creek, west of Calgary. Ron wanted some experience working with horses in the mountains, so he had signed on with Bert for the summer."

The girls were quite different from one another though they were the best of friends. Pat's edgy, forthright personality contrasted with the more reserved, painfully shy Faye. But they both harbored the same wicked sense of humor, which they aimed at the boys with frightening success if given cause. And that summer they were often given cause. When June agreed to the arrangement it was with a suppressed worry that she was overlooking her role as mother. But she was busy and realized that sometimes it was best just to let things sort themselves out.

That first night when the girls were setting up their tent, Keith inadvertently tripped over the guy lines, bringing their tent down around their ears. Incensed at the perceived slight (though it was a simple accident), Patty and Faye plotted revenge that would escalate to something just short of a feud over the summer (and many years to come). This was particularly true for Faye, who did not get along with Keith at all. In fact, you could say oil and water stood a better chance of mixing. Faye's sensitivity made her especially prone to Keith's sharp tongue, but she did not have the verbal skills to retaliate and resorted to inspired practical jokes for revenge. She was cagy enough to plot the unexpected joke to emerge when they were well down the trail and retaliation was unavoidably deterred. June was not sure if Keith was insensitive or just plain obtuse when he did not appear to link his insults to some of Faye's sneakier tricks. It certainly did not curtail his venal verbosity.

The biggest problem facing the group was the Red Deer River. In May, the river was in spate, making the daily crossing a perilous affair. Drowning in flooded rivers was always a risk for ranchers, cowboys, or outfitters forced to cross under these conditions. Unfortunately, the horses they were looking for roamed the hills on the other side of the river from their camp, and most days they had to cross to bring them back. For the first few days, the river was relatively low, not yet swollen by rain. It was still low enough to avoid swimming if they followed the shoals and avoided deeper holes.

They began the roundup successfully, bringing in several horses from the flats west of the river. Bert's scouting was dead-on, and the horses were soon bunched up. A couple of riders would start the horses running across the flats, driving them in the direction of a winged corral deeper in the bush where the rails were not easily detected. Other riders galloped as hard as they could to cut off any horses trying to escape back into the bush.

Dave Wildman had valid reason to anticipate the great adventure of chasing horses across high alpine meadows and deep timber. But a lot of the excitement came from surviving the ride. Everyone faced the perils of the ride, regardless of gender, as demonstrated by Faye when her big black gelding tripped spectacularly, taking them both down in a heap of flying hooves and crushed bush. Donny saw her go down out of the corner of his eye and rode back to pick up the remains. From what he saw he did not think Faye would be around to bless June with grandchildren. Despite the amazing acrobatics, Faye and Snuffy were sound and unhurt – just temporarily out of the chase. Faye remounted quickly and they both rode hard to take up their positions. They caught up in time to wing the far side of the herd down the rail lines into the corral. Everyone was jubilant and on a high that only comes from the thrill of a successful chase. That night the energy soared around the campfire as beer and good food oiled the memories of individual achievements. Their exploits soon achieved tall-tale status, bringing promises of even greater deeds to come as the evening light deepened into early morning.

Some of those future deeds turned into semi-disasters as the good weather failed and the horses – now aware they were being hunted – became wily opponents. They had inherited some crafty lead mares that were notorious for escaping, usually taking their companions with them. Two Bits was a small black mare that gave Don the slip on a hot sunny day when he dozed off on his grazing patrol. It was their custom to let the horses graze on the lush meadows of the Ya Ha Tinda during the day then corral them at night on a large island close to camp. Two Bits had an uncanny way of knowing when surveillance was at a minimum and took every opportunity to slip away with a few good friends. On this day, she slid off with three other horses back to her home turf on the Panther River. Don was alerted to her absence by the distinct absence of her bell. It was a long ride for him and Ben that day to recover the strays.

Another lead mare known for Houdini-like escapes was White Lady. She had to be caught with a snare that year. Annabelle was a favorite of many of the cowboys for her fierce stamina on a horse chase, though she was famously known for having a mouth of steel. A chase on Annabelle usually resulted in a pell-mell charge right into the corrals. Nothing less stopped her.

Once the outlaw mares were caught, they were belled, hobbled, tied up and fed hay, the group hoping to end their freedom once and for all. Bert could not afford to be hunting horses all summer; he needed to get them to Lake Louise as early as possible or risk losing potential business. Summer is too short in the Rockies to waste time at the Ya Ha Tinda looking for horses.

One dark night, their plans to get an early start on trailing the horses back to Lake Louise was almost thwarted by an unexpected and potentially dangerous event. The clouds had rolled in dark and ominous, throwing lightning bolts around like pennies, but with little rain. The downpour had already been expended high in the mountains, swelling all the tributaries of the Red Deer River. By suppertime, the water was breaching the banks and was still rising. The cowboys sat nervously around the campfire as Bert patrolled the shore hoping for some relief. They turned uneasily into their soggy sleeping bags but the long days spent chasing horses were catching up with them, and sleep came quickly despite the discomfort and worries. They had good reason to be concerned. Most of the horses were corralled on the island, and they would have no escape if the river swallowed the shallow gravel bars. But the prospect of herding them to higher ground in the middle of the night was fraught with danger. Still, no one was surprised when Bert woke them up shortly after midnight.

Don had faith in Ben to handle the challenge, and before he could take a deep breath, he and Dave, riding Annabelle, were up to their waists in freezing, swimming-deep water. They finally reached the rapidly disappearing island where the horses were stomping in water over their hocks. Don opened the gates, but the panicky horses just milled around, more afraid of leaping into the raging torrent than staying on solid ground – no matter how fast it was disappearing. The boys finally pushed the seventy head of horses into the river, praying that they would not be swept past the shallow exit where the rest of the riders waited to push them to safer pastures. He did not want them scattered as they emerged from the river; it would take all the manpower they had to keep the horses bunched and not stampeding. Don was just hoping they would not lose any; if the current was strong enough there was a real danger the horses would be carried down to the steep, overhung river banks below their camp where they could not climb out.

Suddenly shouts rang out in the misty dark, indicating the leaders had made the crossing. With luck, the rest would follow. Miraculously, all seventy head – even a yearling colt – survived the swim and rested, exhausted, on the far bank. They nervously began feeding, and showed no sign of pulling out. But it was a long night for all the riders, who dared not leave the herd in the persistent storm which continued to spew out lightning and deafening thunder.

SWIMMING HORSES IN THE RED DEER RIVER

June had long worried about the problem they might have with high spring floodwater, and with ingenuity she had sewn together inflatable vests that she insisted they wear. After giving them a whirl for a few days, most of the cowboys had abandoned them as too cumbersome. Faye was certainly not wearing one when she had a serious mishap on one of the crossings while riding a small black gelding. It was a nightmare situation all the wranglers feared when crossing deep, fast-running water. To plan for the horse to get good footing on the opposite bank, it is imperative to know how fast the water is running. Faye's horse was small and could not get across fast enough to make the ford. She and the gelding were swept around a steep bend into a deep hole and could not get out. Don remembers Faye getting swept off Blackie and when she went down, being struck on the head by the horse's frantically flailing hooves. Dazed, she was swept farther down the river, but it actually left her on a gravel bar where she could get her footing. She struggled to shore, hoping the horse had had the same luck. She found him shaking and cold but safe, nervously munching the sparse grass in a stand of trees farther down.

As is common, a beautiful day beamed on the weary crew the next morning but brought no relief from the work ahead. A fellow outfitter who worked in the area rode into camp with news of where the remaining horses were. He had spotted them near the West Lakes, which was good news as it meant only a short ride with no river crossing. These were the last of the horses to be brought in. With luck the expedition would be ready to trail back in the next couple of days.

The holdouts acted as though the jig was up; it was time to go back to work for the summer and they came in quietly. That night, everyone relaxed, except for the girls, who headed to the small town of Sundre with the truck for trail supplies. No one paid attention to last-minute sly looks and suppressed giggling behind curled hands as the girls drove off. If anyone noticed, they put it down to the prospect of a hot bath and a good night's sleep in the local hotel. They would not have the same luxury by a long shot.

Keith was the first to slip into his damp bedding, wondering why it had not dried more thoroughly. The girls had certainly had enough time to lay out all the bedding to soak up the sun – at the boy's request. Just as a desperate curse was forming in his brain, he heard a wild shout from the next tent, followed by more curses from the rest of the camp. As he leapt from his bed, he knew suddenly why the girls had volunteered to go to town. His sleeping bag was packed with wet manure. To make things worse, it had started to rain again. He was not alone. Immediately, the rest of the boys began shaking out sodden bedding followed by half-hearted efforts to dry the bags around the fire. Only Bert was exempt. He roused himself briefly to laugh at their antics, then rolled over into a peaceful sleep. Keith's eloquence rose to new heights as he dreamt up one diabolical revenge after another. But he would never be in Faye's league at that game.

The only thing that kept the girls from a harrowing payback was the urgency for the cowboys to get the camp packed up and the horses trail-ready. Bert's good humor persuaded them to defer any retaliation, as did a plentiful supply of beer and the truly fine steaks the girls brought from town.

That night, June finally joined them in camp, bringing yet more beer, (which was totally uncharacteristic of her). She also brought home-cooked meals, apple pies, cinnamon buns, and clean clothes for all. She was actually picking Bert up to drive him to Lake Louise. She needed his help there, and the crew was more than capable of driving the horses over the passes, now mostly free of snow, to the pony stand up at the lake.

The following day, Bert and June left for the lake, and in anticipation of the summer to come, the riders took leave of the beautiful Ya Ha Tinda without regret. Faye had found her home. She poignantly expressed her happiness in poetry that would always be a solace for her.

> "And I know the answer's here
> Amongst the wilderness so free;
> A million different sights and sounds
> I know this world was made for me."

Chapter IX

EXPANSION AND CHANGES

When the Mickles went into the outfitting business, June's talents as an organizer and businesswoman became vital. Don soon realized that she was the heart of their success. He knew that Bert was well loved and provided the experience to keep things running, but he would have been adrift without June. Don later wrote:

"Mom was the organizer of the family and the one who kept everything going, the glue that held everything together. She was the spirit of it all. While we were rounding up horses, she had been kept busy taking the bookings for the summer, hiring staff, house cleaning at the pony stand, and trucking up supplies. Any spare time was filled with making leather clothing and chaps – or maybe completing her latest oil painting of wildlife, along with its customary backdrop of mountains."

One stipulation June insisted on was hiring more help. June realized they needed reliable staff to keep the growing business rolling and was relieved when Rita and her husband Norm Smith offered to help. Rita was Bert's closest sister, and her experience and energy made all the difference in the summer when they agreed to run Skoki. Norm was an old cowboy from the American Mid-West and had come up to Canada in the 1930s. Some thought he was looking over his shoulder when he crossed the border, which made him popular with Bert. Bert always thought that having a colorful past made people much more trustworthy. As he would later say, "Sometimes you just have to break the rules – keeps life interesting." Norm Smith harbored a similar philosophy, and the two got along like long-lost friends.

Though the working conditions were primitive and the days were long, the early years were good. After the spring round-up, the family settled into the routine of running the pony barn and Skoki, along with other recently acquired concessions. The horses were successfully trailed to Lake Louise via Red Deer lakes and the Pipestone, arriving in good shape for the summer. Most of the horses to be used at Skoki now enjoyed the deep-green grass and the freedom of Point Camp, while the rest were taken to the pony barn where they earned their keep more pedantically. The Skoki horses were kept at Point Camp – a beautiful, open meadow on the Pipestone River, a day's ride from the lodge – until Deception Pass lost the last of the winter snow that kept the first clients from reaching the lodge. For Don, the thrill of the first ride over this stunning pass never faded. He would later write:

"It is always a pleasure to reach the top of Deception Pass for me. The view back down the valley toward Lake Louise is spectacular while overlooking Ptarmigan and Redoubt Lakes. Mount Temple and the Valley of the Ten

Peaks, stretching farther back, are the center of a magnificent panorama located above and beyond Boulder Pass, which in itself acts like a gunsight toward these peaks. Skoki Lodge, in the opposite direction, is nestled in a forested area at the base of Skoki Mountain, straight down the valley from the pass."

On the first trip of the year, Don was accompanied by Rita and her family, which would be their first visit to the place. He reminisces in his memoirs:

"Aunt Rita was a pioneer in her own right. She raised six children, often under primitive and trying conditions, in a rural setting. Norm had a background as a horseman, who had spent many years on the trail packing, wrangling, and cooking. Their youngest two children, Dona Lee and Ricky, were also coming to Skoki for the summer to lend a hand. Dona Lee was an attractive blonde girl in her early teens. Ricky was about ten years old and already capable of taking care of himself in the mountains. He had brought his own horse this year that he was quite proud of. A long-haired German shepherd named King was the last member of their family."

Bert was along, as usual, sharing a pint of rum with Norm at the back of the pack. Rita could only roll her eyes and concentrate on what lay ahead. This year she was in for an unpleasant surprise.

As they approached the lodge, Rita felt a moment of satisfaction. The trip in had been uneventful despite the steady disappearance of the rum down the throats of the two renegades who fell farther and farther behind. This quickly changed when Don spotted fresh grizzly tracks "the size of dinner plates with claws," which circled the lodge. They had arrived none too soon. The back end of a very large bear was all they saw of what appeared to be a large, male grizzly. Judging from the claw marks on the front door, they had obviously interrupted the bear's attempt to gain entry into the lodge. Rita gasped and hurriedly ushered the kids inside. The whole outer screen door had been demolished and the main door badly scraped. Bert was worried that their presence, even with the dog, would not keep the bear from making further visits to the easily accessible food supply. It was too tempting for a bear hungry from a long winter's hibernation.

After unloading the packhorses, Bert and Don saddled up the horses and rode down the valley, following the distinctive tracks to see where the bear had gone. They stopped at Merlin Meadows when the tracks headed for the bush. Unfortunately, the bear's trail was not far enough from the lodge to be of much comfort. Feeling that it would be back, Bert decided to spend the night on a cot in the kitchen. Rita was a woman who had grown up with all the vicissitudes of ranching life, but that had not entailed facing grizzly bears. She was not impressed with the start of a long summer season.

Knowing that this could be a serious threat to their operation, Don decided to ride over to the Cyclone Warden cabin to see if the resident district warden had arrived for the summer. The warden was long-time Banff resident Andy Anderson, who ran the Cyclone district with his wife Barb, whom they knew well. Don wanted to get permission to have a gun on hand should the bear turn nasty. He bribed Andy with promises of fresh cinnamon buns, which Rita was famous for, enticing him to ride over and inspect the damage. It was a bombproof bribe, which had Andy saddling his horse within minutes. It was also in Andy's own interest to see how determined the bear was to get at the food, as he had a large oat cache at the warden station. If the bear had no success at Skoki, it could easily turn its attention to raiding the oat bin.

"Yup, that's a big bear," pronounced Andy. "Maybe you should bring in a gun. I'd feel better if Norm had a rifle, 'specially since you have the kids here." The cinnamon buns had a better effect than Don had hoped for. But Norm did not have to bring in a gun. Old hunters like the Mickles always had one stashed close at hand despite park regulations. Rita gratefully sent Andy back with more buns for Barb, ruefully wondering if they would survive the ride back.

After Andy left, Bert settled on the makeshift cot for the night. His instincts were well founded. Just after midnight, Don was woken by a yell and loud crashes coming from the kitchen area. As he leapt out of bed, he saw a large, black shadow disappear behind his cabin. He rushed to the kitchen and was greeted by the sight of Norm brandishing the no-longer-hidden rifle and Bert swinging a broken lantern. As expected, the bear had returned. Bert and Norm had been enjoying a nightcap from the not-yet empty rum bottle, when they heard a tearing sound coming from the pantry. Bert opened the door to observe a large paw ripping out the pantry window. A massive head with bright, beady eyes peering at the goodies on the shelves accounted for the happy grunting. With a wild yell, Bert smashed the hot lantern across the bear's twitching nose. The animal roared, backing out hastily, undoubtedly more scared than Bert. That was the hope anyway. Only time would tell how successful the rout had been. It made for some uneasy days following the incident, but the bear did not return to the lodge that summer.

The first summer that the Mickles ran the outfit, Tip and Clara agreed to stay at the ranch while they were gone. June rested easier knowing the place was in good hands and would not appear abandoned. One of the best things to come out of having the pony barn at Lake Louise was seeing the happiness it brought Faye. June and Faye looked after the daily rides while Bert and the boys ran the trips into Skoki. June later wrote, "I got my guide's license and did the guiding from the pony stand. Faye was in her element and was so good with the horses and the people. She loved everyone and the faithful dude horses, and they loved her. We were at the pony stand most of the time as the boys did the outside trips. They were no good at the pony stand."

In fact, June was glad to see the boys in the backcountry rather than hanging around Lake Louise. They could get into too much trouble there. At twenty-one, Don was of legal drinking age and quite capable of getting into trouble if his energy wasn't drained by long, hard, working days. June kept him as busy as she could, but even then he would find time, with pal Keith, to give her reason to send them packing. Don recalls one incident when Alpha Legace phoned up June with a warning that it was time the boys "take a trip to Skoki." Alpha was managing the Post Hotel in those days and was inclined to look the other way when the cowboys got a bit rowdy. As Don recalled:

"Alpha Legace was the manager of the Post Hotel. She was a very organized woman and ran the place like a Swiss clock, but she also managed to remain close to her staff. She was a very popular and well-respected person in the small community back then. Fortunately, she had a soft spot for trail guides after putting up with years of shenanigans from the boys who worked for her husband, Ray. She would often look the other way when she found our jeans and shirts hanging from the rafters near the staff quarters."

So when June got Alpha's call, she knew they had gone a bit too far even by the lax standards of the Lake Louise community. As it turned out, the boys had been enticed up to one of the rooms at the hotel by a pair of comely young women calling from a window, "Come on, boys! We're having a party!" Don and a friend, Bill, were quite happy to accommodate the ladies. Unfortunately, the women already had a couple of boyfriends prowling somewhere around the hotel. The men showed up just as Don and Bill were getting nicely settled in, enjoying a glass of wine with the fickle girls.

Don laughs in hindsight: "We wisely slipped out the window in 'Keystone Cops' manner, clambering down the outside lattice, hoping not to break our necks." A major feat considering they were less than sober.

The evening might have passed by with no further incident had Bill not remembered he'd left his jacket in the room. Keith, who had been previously sidelined by one of the girls who worked for Alpha, volunteered to go back with him, gallantly offering to ask for the coat. The ensuing encounter led to the inevitable scuffle that resulted in another hasty retreat after Alpha came on the scene to tell the "boyfriends" that the cops were coming. She then advised Don, Bill, and Keith to "Get out of sight."

It turned out that the two girls were prostitutes from Edmonton. The "boyfriends" had come with them from Edmonton, but were quite a bit more unruly than Don and friends and continued to bust the place up. The cops did arrive and, with little ceremony, invited them to spend the remains of the night in jail. The next day they were last seen hitching out of town with promises of revenge. Don chuckles when he remembers, "They had to hitchhike back to Edmonton the next day, but not before they threatened to bring back half of Edmonton to Lake Louise and beat up anybody they found wearing a cowboy hat. It is safe to say that an early start to Skoki Lodge was orchestrated on our behalf the next day by Mom and Dad."

Though the boys enjoyed a spirited life in town when they could, there was plenty of work to keep them busy. They had seventy head of horses spread out between Lake Louise, Skoki, Temple, and Point Camp up the Pipestone River.

Point Camp was "a place Heaven would look like if cowboys got their wish." It was in the Upper Pipestone Valley where the trail broke out of the trees into an open meadow surrounded by mountain scenery of unparalleled beauty. It was perfect for holding horses and was used as a base for most of the herd. It was a place where tired horses could rejuvenate, feeding on the nutritious mountain grass before being rotated out for another trip. There was always lots of shoeing to be done, and of course someone always needed to be there to watch over the herd. Don loved the place and found it was a good place to rejuvenate his own spirit as well. They were also a bit short-handed as both Dave Wildman and Ron Echlin had returned home for the summer. With the packing, moving horses around, and shoeing, neither Keith nor Don had much opportunity to get carried away with parties at Lake Louise.

· Don did not particularly like the boring routine at the pony barn, though he did show up to shoe horses when needed. But June inadvertently livened the place up when she brought along a small donkey called Jose. June had acquired Jose in a trade the previous winter with a local rancher, who Bert felt got the better of the deal. June had given the rancher a beautiful leather jacket in trade for the small donkey who had been "foundered in his youth." As a result of an over-rich diet, Jose tottered around rather stiffly on his little turned-up hooves. No doubt June felt sorry for the little creature, and she would bring him in when the winter weather proved too much for him. He would ramble about the ranch house basement until the weather warmed up, giving the place a manger-like ambience.

She could not leave him at home, so she brought him up to the pony stand where he became quite notorious. He was a 'Jack' donkey, resulting from a half-hearted attempt to geld him, and he would get excited if any of the mares came into heat. He had a singular bray that was so loud it could be heard clear across the lake, sounding like the foghorn of a lost ocean liner. When this clarion call sounded, it meant Jose was hunting down the mares again.

He also had a penchant for flowers. When things got busy around the pony stand, he would slip off through the trees to a cornucopia of flowerbeds planted every year by the Chateau Lake Louise and Deer Lodge. It would not be long before June would get a desperate phone call from the proprietors suggesting she come and get her donkey. It was a good year for landscapers in the area, who were constantly on call to replant the beds.

CLARA ON JOSE

Jose was also anathema to the dude horses. When he was first put in the corral with them, they were so terrified that they threatened to break the corral down. Jose often gained his freedom just for this reason. He could not be kept in the corral and tying him up was a major inconvenience – thus he wandered unhampered around the yard. He had the same scary effect on black bears, which was a good thing. It was one of the few benefits he brought to the pony stand besides his dubious personality. Black bears and grizzlies were a constant menace, not to mention a serious danger if they were habituated to humans. In those days, garbage control was minimal and it was usually left in open dumps. Running across a bear at night was a real concern. But Jose kept the pony barn safe. The bears were terrified of him and kept their wanderings to other parts of the community – except for one very unusual exception.

Early in the spring, Jose was wandering around as usual when a young black bear cub showed up. It was small and seemed undernourished. When June looked out the window she was shocked to see Jose lying on the ground behind the bunkhouse with the little bear curled up between his legs. Jose had adopted the lonesome cub, whose mother had disappeared. He took a possessive attitude toward the small animal, but he could not provide nourishment nor teach the cub how to survive. It was a short-lived affair and one day the cub was no longer there. Jose wandered around looking for him and seemed a bit despondent, but the elements were beyond the cub's chances for survival. June took comfort that the little fellow had had some warmth and companionship before disappearing.

Jose also provided entertainment for the children who came with their parents and were slated to take one of the hourly rides. Faye had a sombrero that she would let the kids wear and took pictures of them riding around on Jose. Later, it became a small source of income when they took the odd little donkey down to the lakeshore and had him pose for pictures with the tourists, who happily parted with small change for the privilege.

Though the Mickle horses became used to the donkey, the nearby Brewster stable horses did not. On one memorable occasion, Jose escaped and ran down to the water just in time to meet a string of Brewster horses carrying several dude riders back from the end of the lake. One loud bray from Jose and the whole string was stampeding in panic. Fortunately, the cowboys got everything under control before anyone was hurt (riders or bystanders). Jose was very unceremoniously packed back to the pony stand, but this last encounter was to prove his undoing. The resident warden was obliged to tell June she either find a permanent way of keeping Jose under control or remove him from the park. It was the end of the season anyway, so he remained until taken back to the home ranch. That winter Jose suffered from kidney failure and died shortly after Christmas. June no doubt had extended his stay on the planet and made it a pleasant one at that. Nevertheless, she did not pick up any more donkeys. Jose was just too good an act to follow.

June was kept busy at the pony barn with Faye as her main source of help. Bert returned to the ranch periodically throughout the summer, and June would often go with him to ensure the place did not fall apart. She was so consumed with keeping the business going, it seemed as though she lived her life vicariously through her children. Don was definitely sowing wild oats with his buddies, and she did not necessarily want to know what he was up to. Neither Faye nor Don seemed about to settle down in marriage, but June was happy with that. It seemed she had her hands full just keeping everyone organized and working – even when it meant being a bit tyrannical.

June could not be faulted for trying to keep a lid on her young employees, as even slow days could unexpectedly turn more exciting than even the boys wanted. Don recalls a rainy day at the pony barn when things couldn't have gotten much slower. He and the guys took the opportunity to shoe some horses and catch up on chores around the place. Don had just bought a new lariat and decided to practice catching a few sedentary stumps while Lee Edwards, another old friend/employee took a turn at shoeing. When they traded off, Don left his lariat for Lee to fool around with. He was getting nowhere with the stubborn stump when a young black bear wandered into the yard. Jose was no longer with them, and they were back to fending off bears as best they could. Being a polite young man, Lee asked Don if he minded if he tried to rope the bear. Don saw little future in this other than scaring the bruin back to the bush – hopefully with enough respect to stay away. He casually consented. "Sure. Go ahead! Good Luck."

Lee clamped his teeth together and threw a perfect loop over the bear's head. The squalls that erupted from the small bear cub as the rope tightened around its skinny neck abruptly caught Don's attention. Bob Haney was working for the Mickles that summer and happened to be at the pony barn that day. The frantic commotion brought him running as Don and Lee tried to wrestle the creature to the ground to liberate the lariat. Don was more concerned about the fate of his rope than the welfare of the bear. Faye joined the fray when she came running out of the office with a butcher knife to cut the rope. She definitely had more sympathy for the bear than the rope. Don, now bemoaning the destruction of his prize lariat, agreed to let the bear and rope go in hopes it would fall off. With a holler, they all ran after the terrified animal as it dashed through the trees behind the bunkhouse. The chase was abruptly halted when the cub's mother stood up just a few yards from the stables. All the boys could do was run back to the safety of the cabin. Don made one last attempt to find his rope by jumping in the truck and driving down the road to see if he could spot the bears below the barns. All he saw was mother and cub running madly away down the hill. He never saw either of the bears again, nor did he find his brand new, expensive lariat.

That was not the last of their bear trouble. The summer was progressing with fewer rough edges to the trips when an old nemesis returned to liven their days. Predictably, they had not seen the last of the bear that had broken into Skoki. In fact, the bear, a boar as males are called, was proving to be a menace to everyone camped in the area, including a group of researchers studying glacial movements on the Drummond Glacier.

One of the principle sources of the Mickles' summer income came from the University of Calgary. Several years before, Ray Legace had contracted out to pack-in supplies and equipment for glaciologists studying the Drummond Glacier a few miles east of Cyclone warden cabin. The Mickles picked up this steady, lucrative work when they inherited the contract. Not long after the boar's visit to Skoki, they learned that he had also paid an unwanted visit to the Drummond camp while the geologists were away. Unfortunately, he had looted a poorly hidden food cache – a success that was guaranteed to keep him in the valley. Boars tend to forage in the valley bottoms, leaving the high country, with its rich resources, to sows and their cubs. Though no one had actually seen the boar, the camp was in his territory, leaving little doubt it was the same bear.

The damage was enough to cut short the researcher's summer season, meaning less work for the Mickles. The only work for them that summer was to pack out the demolished camp. Knowing little about packing horses, the geologists assumed the cowboys would only need a couple of horses. Most likely, they were just trying to get by on the minimal budget common to most university projects, and they hoped they would not have to pay for any extra horses. But past experience had left Don skeptical, warning him that if two horses were requested, they probably needed four. They also had a fair distance to take the equipment, as they had to pack it out to Scotch Camp warden station, nineteen miles down the Red Deer River.

On this occasion, Don recruited Ricky Smith, who was happy to escape the routine at Skoki and the strict eye of his mother, Rita. Sure enough, Don recalls:

"I conscripted young Ricky from Skoki and assured Aunt Rita that we would be back sometime that evening. Ricky and I arrived at the Drummond camp to find a huge pile of lumber, iron hoops, tents, various other assorted camping gear, and a louvered instrument box that was about the size of a small doghouse. Ricky was only ten years old but was astute enough to say, 'I think that we should have brought more horses.'"

With much struggling, they finally managed to pack the whole lot on three packhorses, which kept looking at them as if to say, *Are you kidding?* The six-foot timber and instrument box were especially troublesome. At ten years old, Ricky was just barely strong enough to help pull slack. Most of the grunt work was left to Don. And he had plenty of that as they labored down the valley, repacking (it seemed) every few miles.

The trip was turning into an epic of survival, soon to turn worse. The sun was setting by the time they reached Scotch Camp, but Don was not too concerned as the cabin was well stocked, and he looked forward to a good night's sleep with a roaring stove to keep them warm. With any luck, he might also unearth a bottle of rum, often kept on hand for visitors, whom the district warden was always glad to entertain.

The first shock was finding the cabin locked – a situation unheard of in those early days. *Times they are a changing,* he ruefully thought. To their further dismay, a small trailer kept there for the researchers was also locked. Now disgusted at such a show of inhospitality, Don boosted the wiry Ricky through a small window in the trailer and they got the door open.

Unfortunately, the ravenous pair only found a package of peanuts for supper. Don looked with longing at the warden cabin, which would have supplied a very filling dinner – not to mention a sip of rum – and wondered at this new policy of locking doors.

Their misfortune carried on the next day. They passed a small tent camp about ten kilometers up the trail, which held a slight chance of providing food. But in their haste to raid any cached supplies, they neglected to tie up the horses. They found only an inedible piece of moldy bread, but what they did not find was their horses when they emerged from the tent. Like them, the horses were apparently fed up with this trip after lugging the inhumane load down the valley, and they had decided to head for home.

Don reassured Ricky, now very tired and hungry, that the horses wouldn't go far. "Don't worry, Ricky," he said with as much determination to sound cheerful as he could muster. "They should be hungry and won't go far once they find a nice meadow."

He couldn't have been more wrong. He and Ricky hoofed it for twelve kilometers back up to the Red Deer lakes before they finally found the horses. Not even the drift fence at Sandhill's warden cabin had stopped them. Much to Ricky's dismay, the beautiful new hackamore[3] Patty had lent him for the trip was gone. It had been handmade by

---

3   A bitless bridle

Patty herself, and Ricky had promised on everything he held sacred, (all the cinnamon buns he could eat), that he would take care of it. Now it was gone. Don could do little to assuage his grief – and fear of the inevitable reprisal. But both were too tired and hungry to do more than get back to the lodge as soon as possible. An hour later, they were wolfing down Rita's chili and trying to explain what had happened, through mouths stuffed with food. Rita had not been overly concerned when the boys did not show up the night before, as she had greater faith in Don's survival abilities than he probably had himself. One thing that was to follow sure as rain in a thunderstorm was Patty's wrath. But predictably, most of it was vented on Don.

One adventure that scared June silly happened to Faye on a normal, deceptively peaceful day during one of her infrequent excursions to Skoki. It reinforced June's awareness that their way of life exposed them to more than average risk.

Faye had had a busy summer at the pony barn, and the repetitive trips to the end of the lake and back were becoming nauseatingly redundant. She longed to see some new country – or at least some places she had not seen in ages – like Skoki. Happily, an excuse to make the trip to the lodge arose when a new client made an unexpected booking for a night there. The man was a regular visitor to Chateau Lake Louise, but in the past had done little more than stroll around the summer trails near the hotel. On this trip, he impulsively decided to book a night at Skoki and get out on mountain trails he had not hiked since he was a child. His companion for the trip was the hotel pianist. With no one else available, Faye quickly volunteered to guide them in.

They certainly needed a guide. Marshall, the client, who had spent his youth exploring the mountains, was getting old and fat. Faye looked askance at him when he mentioned in his boisterous voice, "We'll have a lovely trip, sweetheart, but I must warn you, I have a medical complication we will just have to put up with!" She stared worriedly at him when he announced he had bladder problems and would probably have to dismount frequently to urinate. She wondered how that was going to happen when it appeared he would have enough trouble just getting on the horse at the barn. The pianist was not much better. His tentative approach to horses only spooked them. With help from Don and Keith, Faye managed to get Marshall on his horse. It would be a long trip, but Faye was still happy. She was on her favorite horse, Gypsy, and it was a beautiful day.

Despite his timidity, the pianist could still lend a hand with his friend's frequent dismounts. Fortunately, Marshall had a very patient horse. Despite the irritating distractions, the pleasure Faye had as they took in the spectacular view from Deception Pass was not diminished.

The next morning, Faye was surprised to see Keith arrive with a packload of food. It turned out that Bert had some fishermen scheduled to ride out the next day, and he had sent Keith in to pick them up. Keith was put out by this change of plans as he had a date that night with an old girlfriend, who would not appreciate being stood up. Slyly, he coerced Faye into swapping jobs – he would ride out that day with Marshal and his friend if Faye would stay over and pick up the fishermen the next day. He promised to take her to the movies and pay, as well, if she agreed. Though she feigned irritation, Faye was happy with this arrangement as she did not relish another day with Marshall's incontinence, and it would give her an extra day of visiting and riding in the area.

The next day, she and Norm rode over and brought the fishermen back to the lodge. On the ride back, she noticed storm clouds brewing in the west, but such weather was common in the high Rockies, and it just meant they would be riding out in the rain. Norm was a bit more apprehensive and suggested they put off the trip until the worst of the storm dissipated. Faye was happy with that, but the fishermen had their own agenda. They had to catch the late-afternoon train to Banff and did not want to wait.

With no real reason to refrain, outside of discomfort, the party set out. But the huge thunderheads gathered ominously as they approached the summit of Deception Pass. It is one of the highest and most exposed passes in Banff, and is not a good place to be in a thunderstorm. As they rode to the summit, the wind picked up with a vengeance, driving rain and sleet in ferocious gusts into the face of the oncoming party. Just as they passed the exposed summit, there was a flash of lightning, closely followed by an ear-splitting thunderclap. The men were struggling to control the frantic horses when to their horror, Faye and Gypsy collapsed in front of them.

They looked on as Faye struggled to her feet, giving them a dazed look. She mumbled, "We better get out of here," confusedly looking for her hat. A puff of steam rising from the ground was all the evidence left from the bolt of lightning that miraculously had not hit horse and rider directly. It would not have been the first time lightning had killed a horse and its rider.

To their relief, the squall passed over as Faye weakly remounted and led the party down the far side of the pass to Ptarmigan Lake. They had only Boulder Pass to cross, which would leave them exposed, but the main storm body was now heading east to menace other outdoor enthusiasts.

Though the sun peered out as they reached Temple, Faye and her horse were still visibly weak and shaken. They met Keith riding up the road for another trip into Skoki. He looked at her queerly, noticing how pale she was but only asked, "What's wrong with your horse? Seems a bit shaky." She grudgingly told him of her close call at the pass. One of the reasons she was still shaken was the realization that in a fraction of a second, her life had almost come to an end. She never again tempted fate when storms blew in.

After a bit, she asked how his hot date was. Not worth the ride out with Marshall, according to Keith, when the girl he'd been buying copious amounts of beer for disappeared out the door with a man on a motorcycle. One good thing came out of the adventure. Faye and Keith put aside their differences long enough to take in the movie he had promised. Even more unusual, he did not gripe about horseshit on her boots and paid for the tickets on top of that.

Faye's brush with death heralded the fall hunting season. It was near the end of August, and June had booked enough hunting trips to carry them from the beginning of September to the end of October. Since they had taken over the outfit, she had managed to keep them busy every fall. Some were new clients, but many were returnees from the days when Ray Legace ran the business. This was an especially busy time for June, who had to keep it all together even though everyone was now spread out all over the country. Their hunting camp was based on the Kootenay Plains on the Saskatchewan River. It was a beautiful location of low, open montane meadows and pine forest, but it was about a three-hour drive from Lake Louise.

June was still running the front country concessions (the pony stands at Lake Louise and Wapta Lodge), but without much help from family or staff, who had all but disappeared into the backcountry. Both of the girls (Patty and Faye) were recruited to help run the camps with the principal job of bringing in the hunters and supplies. Bert, Don, and Keith spent most of their time at camp as guides. This was a mainstay of the business as hunting big game in Canada was quite lucrative for outfitters. It was also Bert's forte. He was a considerable support for June in the summer, but his skills as a hunter made a big difference to the success of the business. Later, June also helped bring the clients to the camp and on occasion became the camp cook. Everyone was happier when she was there, not only for her stellar ability as a cook, but for the warm and harmonious way she ran the camp.

This year they had new clients from the United States. Don had been corresponding with a young man from

Arkansas. The man was a farmer there, and this was a big trip for him. He had demonstrated his commitment to the hunt by running five miles a day in the months prior to heading for Canada. Don reflected ruefully that "Arkansas George," as he called him, would be in better shape than he would. All Don had done for exercise was jingle horses in the morning at Skoki. He managed to beef up by packing-in fly camps up the headwaters of some of the creeks they would be hunting in. Arkansas George turned out to be fit for the trip, as promised, and a good companion as well. He was also an excellent shot.

Despite being plagued by bad weather at the beginning of the trip, the young man managed to get all the animals he had a ticket for. The first animal was a fine billy goat with horns that measured ten inches. For a while it looked as though George would miss what he really wanted, which was a trophy big horn sheep. He also had a ticket for black bear. With uncanny luck, he got both just one day before he had to leave. It was one of the better trips Don had with a companionable client.

Unfortunately, they were not all like that. The next three hunters were overweight and in bad shape, and they turned out to be poor riders. They were also loud and bragged a lot about their hunting prowess. Though they all managed to get an elk, it was only due to Bert's ability as a hunter. He had to keep a firm hand on how they behaved, for they were prone to scaring the game off before they could get in shooting range.

Bert was glad when the hunt was over and all they had to do was get the hunters out safely with their trophies. But as Robert Burns famously wrote, "the best laid plans of mice and men oft go awry." When they packed up their personal gear before returning to the main camp, the clients had overlooked a bottle of scotch. Bert sent Faye with the hunters, while he remained behind to pack up the trophies, meat, and the rest of the camp. Don and Keith grudgingly agreed to stay and help, despite wanting to rekindle any wayward romance left behind in the bright lights of Lake Louise.

The rediscovered bottle of scotch quickly helped return their good spirits. But it did not help their prowess as packers. There is a saying for horse packers: "Pack light, bind tight, and ride like hell!" As Don recalls, they had too big a load to pack light, and they certainly found out they did not bind tight. But the well-lubricated packers had no qualms about riding like hell! They did not get far. Spooked by an overzealous yell from Keith as he hazed them down the trail, the pack horses tore off through the bush in one of the most spectacular wrecks Don or Bert had ever seen. The meat, packed so assiduously by the hunters in bolts of cheesecloth, bounced gloriously off deadfall and pine branches, leaving a blaze of white cotton strips gleaming in the sun, and egging the packhorses into a renewed frenzy of running. It took a long time to round up all the animals, gear, meat, and antlers and repack the outfit. The bedraggled pack train did not get to the Kootenay Plains camp until well after midnight.

Along the way, they dreamt up an excuse for bringing back what was left of the bruised meat. At least they had all the trophy heads and only a few tines missing from the once impressive racks. The reason they gave for the spectacular wreck was a surprise encounter with a grizzly bear. Don was hard pressed to not laugh as he outdid himself describing the fictitious calamity.

"Well that bear just appeared out of nowhere – came charging out of the bush like he was waiting for us. Must have smelt the fresh meat."

"Yeah," chimed in Keith who could invent cover-ups like no one Don had ever met. He'd certainly had enough occasions to practice this surreptitious art. "Them horses never saw that bear till he was trying to tear-em apart! Betcha it was the same bear that tore up the Drummond camp. And Skoki too!"

Fortunately, one of the hunters was convinced that he had a nose for bears. He quickly (and most unexpectedly) agreed with them immediately when they pinpointed the location of the encounter. "Yeah," said Fred, the loudest and most obnoxious of the threesome of hunters, "I remember smelling that bear just where you said!"

Bert replied, "Sure wish you were there. It would have saved us a lot of trouble!"

The men packed up what remained of their meat and headed back to California, convinced they were great hunters and just a bit sad they had not seen the grizzly, which they no doubt would have shot with or without a tag. They were happy and would probably recommend the outfitters to friends. Bert, on the other hand, was pretty sure he would be booked up if those three had any idea of coming back. Faye took one look at Don and snorted, "Sure was something, you coming across that bear. I wonder if it had a scotch label on its tongue!"

After the hunting season was over, the pony stands had to be cleaned and shut down for the winter. Preparing Skoki for the winter season followed that. June really looked forward to the late fall and getting back to the ranch. They would stay there until they were ready to return to Skoki in February. It meant June could have Christmas in her house with her family, and that was important. Nonetheless, it was a lot of balancing and juggling of time and people.

June was very happy to be back in her home but felt a foreboding it was only temporary. They had labored hard to turn it into her dream house, with amenities like electricity and running hot and cold water. The bathroom and indoor toilets were a special luxury. She could hardly believe that in a few short months she would be back to enduring the primitive conditions that she had lived with most of her life.

Everyone seemed to have different plans for the fall and winter. The young men who had worked for the Mickles off and on that summer needed to find work for the winter as they were not needed at Lake Louise.

Bob Haney was another young man who'd grown up in Millarville and become good friends with Don and the family. His father was a school bus driver in town, so Bob's experience with horses was obtained by osmosis. He would usually visit with the Mickles after school and was given the opportunity to ride with Don or Faye.

June was quite fond of him, as he seemed more settled and mature than some of the other men who worked for them. Don, who had more occasion to party with Bob, saw a wilder side of his personality, but in general Bob exerted a stabilizing influence. Both Bob and Keith decided to head north that winter for work on ice road construction and oil rigs, where the money was good.

Don was temporarily at a loss for plans. He could go back to Rogers Pass and work for Noel Gardner, but close calls with avalanches had him thinking twice about that line of work.

Bert was soon asking, "Well what do think you'll do this year? Going back to the Pass?"

Don snorted, "No! I don't plan to be buried up to my neck again. The snow-flakers can have it and the fun dodging avalanches all winter. I like the idea of living a little longer."

Bert gave him a skeptical look, thinking that some of the scrapes Don got himself into didn't guarantee that. But he did need help with his trapline and running Skoki. He asked, "Well, why don't you stay here this winter? Your mom would like that. I think we could maybe catch us a few wildies while the weather holds."

Don liked the idea of going after wild horses. It was exciting work, though not much safer than out-skiing avalanches. "That sounds pretty good to me. Be nice to see more of this country. I can ride Ben and really get him into shape."

Bert had anticipated Don's help and already had the permit for taking horses from the forest reserve. The government was anxious to reduce the number of feral horses now roaming the hills, justifying the cull by claiming the horses placed a burden on the wildlife population. At one point, wild horses had been part of a natural ecosystem, but that was long ago. Now they mostly came from the farming communities and were considered a nuisance by most of the ranchers.

June was happy with this arrangement, as Faye was planning on staying in Banff and working at the Sunshine ski resort until they opened Skoki for the winter. Because this was still new to the Mickles, they only ran the lodge from the end of February through March and possibly into April, depending on the snow and the bookings. June was happy to have the time at home with only Bert and Don to cook for.

They also had help from an unexpected source. Don had been out hunting on the reserve when he noticed the lights on in a neighboring ranch house. It turned out Johnny Nylund, a local cowboy who had also grown up in the Millarville area, was managing the place. Don stopped in on the way home, and over coffee Johnny offered him a few days' work cutting rails. The talk led to Don's plans to chase horses, and this got Johnny excited. The men drove back to the Mickles' home, where Johnny pursued the matter with Bert. Bert was more than happy to have Johnny's help, and soon Don and Johnny were teamed up for many miles of riding in the dense bush, flushing out the ever-elusive wild horses.

The fall and winter months passed by more quickly than June would have liked. The men worked steadily on trapping and other contracts they'd picked up during the winter, while June was kept busy with updating the tack and preparing food for Skoki. She also found time to pursue her passion for painting. The horse-chasing punctuated the early season with lots of thrills, but it did not add much to their own stock. It may have been fun, but it was not a particularly good way to make a living.

February was soon over, and it was time to open up Skoki for the winter season. June was happy enough to return to the beauty of the high Rockies, as it was a delightful time of year with the deep snow and longer days. She had not seen much of Faye that winter and was looking forward to working with her again. Also, she could catch up on what developments were happening in her daughter's life. At least Faye would be easier to keep track of than Don, though at nineteen she was old enough to lead an independent life – despite June's reservations. Banff was a resort town and was well known for its party scene, and the Baby Boomers were certainly testing the limits of their newfound freedom. At Skoki, Faye would be relatively isolated from the party scene. June felt the break would be good for her.

Though Don and Bert were originally only going to come up on weekends, June felt there was a lot to tackle in opening up the lodge, and she wanted more help in getting it up and running. Most of the logging contracts were fulfilled, and the men were certainly not packing the corrals with horses – though Bert would need to return to his trapline for the spring. It was soon decided the whole family would go to Skoki, at least for a couple of weeks. They all felt happy at being reunited again under one roof. Though they did not know it, it was the last time they would live together as a family.

One of the main reasons June wanted the extra help was the need to replace the old light plant that had always given them trouble. They picked up a much newer one at a good price from a neighbor who had gone to another source for power. They also had a lot of food that needed to be brought in.

A helicopter flown by Jim Davies brought in all the supplies, along with batteries for the light plant. Jim had recently obtained his license to fly helicopters and was setting up business in Banff. Prior to this, he had flown fixed-wing airplanes, which the family had used in the past. The plane was limited to landing on lakes in the backcountry, and the closest lake to Skoki was Ptarmigan Lake, which was well on the other side of Deception Pass. That meant a lot of hauling to get everything to the lodge. This year, Jim could drop everything off at their doorstep.

The task of preparing the shed for the light plant was given to Don. He skied in earlier with a friend, who happened to be an electrician. Before Bert and June arrived, the boys shoveled out the trails, removed the snow from the roofs, got the fires going, and warmed up the lodge. They just had time to clean up the shed in preparation for the new light plant. A few days later, Faye and June arrived by skidoo with an amazing amount of gear, including the dog. They were nicely unloaded when Bert arrived by helicopter with the bulk of the food and eclectic supplies. With a foreshadow of things to come for Jim, he offered the boys a

LAST REUNION AT SKOKI

lift to the pass so they could enjoy skiing back to the lodge. It would not be long before Jim did this for a living, initiating heli-skiing in the Bugaboos with Hans Gmoser. It was Don's first ride in a helicopter, but it was far from his last. He would later do a lot of flying both in and under a helicopter as a park warden.

The next big task was to get the new light plant installed. When Don skied out to Temple, he was surprised to see a Tucker Sno-Cat parked in front of the lodge, which looked suspiciously like the one he used to drive at Rogers Pass. Sure enough, it was the same machine. Noel Gardner had purchased a new one and had retired this familiar beast to the Banff warden service. Old pal Andy Anderson was planning to drive it into Cyclone with winter supplies.

"Say, Andy, I bet that thing could haul in our new power plant. What do you think?" enthused Don. This was one large piece of machinery the helicopter could not handle.

"Well now, I guess I could make a patrol your way," mused Andy. "I don't suppose June would be set up for making cinnamon buns this week." Andy's weakness for these famous goodies never faltered.

"Oh sure! Oh and on the way out, maybe we could send a pink rock out with you?"

There was no reply to this odd request. Don was referring to a huge pink rock collected by one of their eccentric clients, who wished to have it shipped back to Manitoba for his rock garden. Don thought ruefully of what lengths they would go to placate their guests.

The client's name was Arnold O.B., a "shriveled-up, old eccentric mountaineer," as described by Don. He was also a member of the Alpine Club of Canada, though any climbing he may have accomplished was well in the past. His itinerary never varied from year to year. He had the cowboys pack him into Merlin Lake for two weeks each summer. He always had the same guide as well, in this case, Keith Foster. Unfortunately, Keith was not happy being the chosen one and complained bitterly every time the old man showed up. It was not surprising that Keith soon earned the nickname "the Merlin's Apprentice."

Arnold's main mission on these outings was collecting distinctive rocks for his alpine garden back in Winnipeg, (a showpiece for all of Canada, according to Arnold). He also collected native plants (both activities highly against the National Parks Act), which he nurtured in his hotel room until they were safely exported to his garden. Don was obligated to point out that no natural objects could be removed from a national park without a permit. Arnold said he had one, though Don doubted that. Still, it would be Arnold who had to pay the consequence if caught. Don, though, vaguely wondered about "aiding and abetting" this potentially criminal conduct.

The summer before, Arnold's greatest find had been a large, pink boulder that was way too heavy to pack out with a horse. Don was not even sure if they could skid it out with their skidoo, so there it sat on the porch reminding everyone of Arnold. The appearance of the Sno-Cat seemed a God-given solution to this persistent problem.

June was more than pleased when Don told her about solving the problem of getting the power plant in and the rock out. She happily baked copious numbers of cinnamon buns for Andy, who so frequently came to their aid. The spring season was shaping up very well. From postings at various warden stations, Andy was also experienced in operating light plants, and he soon had it up and running at Skoki.

With everything stored away, cleaned and overhauled, it was time to open up the lodge for their first guests of the season. June had left the ranch house in mint condition for Don and Bert to return for the spring trapping. She repeatedly reviewed her instructions on how to care for the house and look after things while she was away. To Don's chagrin, she would then look away, rolling her eyes as if these instructions were just a waste of time. Nothing was ever done quite to her standards when she was not around to organize anyone.

The following summer, Bert and June were offered the chance to run Temple Lodge at the Lake Louise ski hill. With some concern on June's part, they took it on. Temple was strictly a winter operation and did not involve any horse use, though they did have a corral located there as a staging point for Skoki in the summer.

But June's premonition that their days on the ranch were numbered seemed bound to come true. Their life was taking an ever-more nomadic direction, particularly after they took on Temple Lodge. This restless life was fine for the children, and certainly Bert seemed to enjoy it, but she wondered how long she could keep it up. For the time being, she determined to enjoy all the falls and Christmases they would have at Millarville.

Despite help from Rita and Norm Smith, June felt they were getting overextended – at least she was. With no one to look after the home ranch year round, it seemed all she did was move from place to place, cleaning all the time. She brought the matter up with Bert who did not seem to be fazed by the added workload.

"Bert, you know this just means a lot more managing for me, and I never have any time at home for myself anymore. I seem to be just moving from place to place in one long session of cleaning. Now I have to clean Temple as well. That's too much."

"Well, look," he replied. "If we take on these other places, I'll get one of the kids to manage it. Tip and Clara have been helping look after the ranch in the summer and with putting up the hay in the fall. Clara is still young and can manage keeping the house up."

June thought about this and replied rather pessimistically, "Well, let's just hope that they're happy with this for a few years anyway."

She should have knocked on wood.

This arrangement came to an abrupt end when Tip died suddenly that fall of a heart attack. He was only sixty-four years old – far too young to die for a man who had spent his life out of doors. Nevertheless, he had always burned both ends of the candle, which probably contributed to his early demise. Clara had always been after him to stop smoking and taper off on the wine at all-night parties. He still used to smoke Bull Durham tobacco – the stuff that came in a little cotton sack, but he had certainly slowed down on the wine. In his later years he'd been happy with the occasional glass of whisky.

Still, his passing was relatively peaceful. He was snoozing on the couch when the attack came. Clara thought he was just sleeping when to her horror, she could not wake him up. A frantic call to June soon brought help, but nothing could help ease Clara's distress at her loss.

June would never forget the funeral. It was December, and on the day they held the service, winter arrived with malice. It blew in with a storm that plummeted the temperature to well below minus 50°F. No one could keep warm in the church, but the biggest concern was what to do with the body. The ground was frozen beyond the hardness of concrete, and Tip's body could not be buried. This part of the proceeding was put on hold until the next chinook lasted long enough to allow the proper hole to be dug. Considering how cold it was, Tip might have preferred to be cremated – but thoughts of courting the fate of Sam Magee may have been a deterrent. Besides, cremation was not really considered a proper burial in the traditional community of Black Diamond.

It was a great blow to all of them, but naturally Clara most of all. In her early sixties, she was still relatively young and could not believe she was so unexpectedly alone. She did not even have June around, as June and her family would now be spending most of their time at Lake Louise. Not wanting to stay on the ranch by herself, Clara moved back to Black Diamond. Even this was not much of a solution as it did not ease her loneliness, and shortly after, she moved to Kelowna where some of the Hamiltons still lived.

June took things in stride, but one of the foundations in her life was gone, and Clara was, in a sense, also gone. Sometimes June longingly thought that perhaps the day would come when they could sell the outfit and return to the ranch for good. Realistically, though, she didn't think that would happen.

Chapter X

MARRIAGES AND MOVES

June and Bert continued to get home for the fall and early winter as they stayed with the same program of opening Skoki just for spring skiing. The day would come, however, when they would be open for the majority of the winter. The 1966 season was harder for them, as they did not have Don's help. He had left for Houston early that November. Rita and Norm were still around to help out at both Temple and Skoki, though Bert was now spending a lot of his time at Temple.

By the following summer, June began to realize that running the business (plus moving and cleaning) was going to be a full-time job. They now had the ranch, the pony stand at Lake Louise, and the horse outlet at Wapta Lodge, as well as Skoki. Running the winter concession at Temple added to the ever-growing work list. (Deciding to walk away from the horse concession at Shuswap actually relieved a burden June was glad to be rid of.)

Major changes were happening to June's family as well. Don decided to take a farrier course in Texas that would take him right down to Houston. It was a great opportunity to learn the finer points of shoeing horses, though June wondered why he had to go so far away. But as always, she and Bert supported their children, and they sponsored him in this endeavor. It was essential to their work and at this point, and Don was expected to return to help run the business. It was a legacy they hoped to pass on to him and his family.

Faye's independent days in Banff also brought changes. She had met Ron Hall, a Brewster cowboy who she was now going out with on a steady basis. June thought she was too young to be serious, but she had to remind herself that Clara and Tip had encouraged her to marry at the same age as Faye was now. It was inevitable that Faye would want to marry some day and start her own family. She was too pretty and lively to not have a line-up of suitors.

Like most early settlers in the West, Ron Hall's family, now established in Cochrane, originally came from England. His grandparents had moved to Canada in 1907, initially settling in Victoria. The weather must not have agreed with them as they very shortly moved to Alberta, roaming about until finally settling in Cochrane. Ron's father, Gordon Hall (an old schoolmate of Bert's) had extensive horse experience that he passed on to his children.

The family was well known in the area, and June, though she did not know them personally, would have been familiar with the name. Ron was pleasant enough when they first met him, and he seemed to get on well with Bert. If June was concerned at this stage over what she thought was a bit of excessive drinking on Ron's part, she chalked it up to the general culture during the sixties and early seventies. Dale Portman, a young aspiring cowboy who was working in the Banff area and later worked for the Mickles, observed, "In the 1960s and 1970s there was a culture of drinking that was ingrained in our society. I know I was part of it. People often drank on the job as well as off the job. You went from your daytime job right into the next party, and if you were married, family life suffered."

At first, June tried to get along with Faye's new beau, but she was not particularly pleased when Faye announced she was getting married in the spring. The couple had not been going out that long, and June felt they did not know each other well enough for this serious move. For his part, though, Bert had no real objection, and plans went forward.

People who knew Ron as a Brewster cowboy found him to be good company, and he was popular with those he worked with or saw socially. Dale Portman remembers:

"I got to know the Hall family back when I was working for Bert and June. Ron's father was the postmaster in Cochrane, and they were a well-respected family in the community. Ron was the oldest, then Allen, Eddie, and Kenny was the youngest. I knew Eddie almost as well as I knew Ron. Eddie worked for the outfit when I was working there. He was a terrific guy, easy going and good natured and good around horses. He died too early in life from cancer. Kenny was prematurely killed as a young father when he was crushed between his parked grader and another vehicle while doing some repairs at the rear. Allen was always the snubbing post[4] of the family, rock solid, and he owned and operated a successful business in Cochrane.

"I got along fine with Ron in the years I worked for the outfit. He was good to work for, and he knew the outfitting business well. He was also the operations manager at the Lake Louise Ski Area in the winter months, while working in the family business in the summer."

June was glad when Don returned from Houston at the beginning of March. His course in Houston was only a few months long; then he was back to Skoki to help with the spring season. As June later wrote, he was there at least long enough to succumb to the charms of a Texas sweetheart. Or so he thought. Possibly he was just lonely being so far from home for the first time in his life. Either way he decided he was in love and impetuously asked the girl to marry him.

When Don met her, Mary was slim and pretty, and his stories about ranching in Canada and running Timberline Tours had her convinced he was from a family that owned a large prosperous ranch in Alberta. When he was back in Canada, he began to wonder about this decision to marry, but he did not feel that he had much choice but to stick with it.

About the same time, Faye announced that she and Ron were getting married that spring. Neither prospect pleased June, but she did not believe in interfering with her children's lives.

That spring was more hectic than usual with the growing business and two weddings to survive. Faye and Ron had a

---

4   A post around which a rope is thrown to hold something fast.

small wedding, but it was followed by a dance that kept everyone up late. The very next day Bert, June, and Don left for Houston with two pickup trucks – one with a stock rack. It turned out Mary had a horse, which partially explained Don's initial attraction to the girl. At least they had that in common. But June was concerned when she realized they had little else going for them.

Don was quite surprised as well when Mary met them at the hotel. He did not know how she'd managed to get so heavy in the few short months that he was away, but she had certainly packed on the pounds. Ruefully, he recalled that Texans always boasted that everything in Texas was big, and observed it was more than true in her case. Uneasily, he wondered if it was a trend that would continue.

With some dismay, he also realized that he was probably not in love with her, but he was essentially committed, having returned specifically to marry her. It was just too embarrassing to call the whole thing off after bringing the whole family down for the wedding. He was trapped.

Though there was little she could do, June suspected that Don was now regretting the hasty commitment. She worried for both her children, but the die was cast and all she could do was keep going and hope for the best. At least the girl wasn't pregnant. Faye's situation was more concerning as she *was* pregnant.

Don's wedding came to its logical conclusion, and with mixed relief, Bert and June flew back to Calgary, leaving the kids to drive back more leisurely with the horse and a dog to boot. She had no idea how the girl was going to fit in, and she wondered what Mary would think of Alberta, as it was nothing like Texas. Mary had never been away from home either. She would be trying to make a go of it with no friends, and quite far from her family. Outfitting was a hard way to make a living, and June knew that Don would not always be around for company. As he and Mary got closer to home, he was thinking the same thing.

It was not long before the misplaced girl was complaining that nothing in Alberta was as good as anything in Texas. In her unhappiness, she began to eat. By the end of the summer, the writing was on the wall. As the girl ballooned out of all proportion, Don found more and more reasons to be out on the trail. Certainly the initial attraction was long gone. She even lost interest in riding her horse, which would have helped keep the weight off. Her only solace was the small dog, which drove Don crazy. June was only surprised they hung on to the sham of a marriage until the following spring. With a vague hope of salvaging something from the relationship, Don asked Mary to come on the spring round-up. The experience was a disaster. Whatever illusions Mary'd had of being married to a sophisticated land baron were totally eradicated when she tried to cope with the endless riding, rain, and camp conditions.

Back in Lake Louise, the passes were opening up from winter's grip, allowing Don and Bert to reach Skoki to cut firewood. The lodge was shut down until summer, giving them ample time to prepare for the coming season. For Don, it was more than a respite from living with Mary. Before he left, he asked her to go back to Texas with or without her dog and horse. He did not want to see her when he returned.

It was probably not easy for Mary to admit that coming to Canada with Don had been a mistake. Her dreams of living in luxury off the fat of the land were long gone ... and so was she when Don returned. Her parents had sent her the plane ticket home, but made no arrangements for the horse or dog. When the divorce went through, Don had the animals shipped to Mary, though he could have used the horse. All felt it was best to make a clean break of it.

But June had much more to contend with than the fate of Don's marriage or how unsettled he seemed to have become. She was deeply concerned – in fact upset – that Faye was having a baby so quickly. It seemed to June that her daughter was too young to be shouldering the responsibility of a family. Neither Bert nor June could warm up to Ron, who was proving very hard to get along with.

Don knew Ron from crossing paths at the bar or at various parties that never seemed to end. He liked Ron well enough from these encounters and saw little hint of his complex personality. In hindsight, though, Don realized none of them really knew Ron well. In those days, Ron had rugged good looks and was popular with women – especially when he played up the cowboy persona. Don later reflected:

"Ron was a very controversial person. He was multi-talented and capable of doing any task that he put his mind to. He had top marks in his classes in the tinsmith trade. Ron had a hearty laugh and could be generous with his friends. But he was unpredictable. He could be laughing and joking one minute and fly off the handle the next. When he worked for Brewsters he respected Bill Bagley. Bill was probably the only person who could genuinely influence Ron. Bill was a highly respected cowboy/horse trainer and managed the Brewster Trail rides for years. He also looked after the extensive herd of horses at Meadow Creek near the head of the Ghost River. Ron learned a lot from Bill, including being a capable farrier. I think that Ron and I were quietly competitive in our own way sometimes. We seemed to be about the same speed shoeing horses. I am sure Dad smiled when it worked to the advantage of getting a lot of horses shod in one day! One time we had our heads down shoeing and both started shoeing the same old packhorse – one on the left front and the other on the right hind. The horse stood perfectly balanced on two legs. We both laughed and continued shoeing her."

June was willing to give Ron a chance to prove himself as a husband and father, even when any interaction with him left her cold and troubled. He had been raised by a permissive, doting mother and was not used to dealing with strong, independent women. June probably intimidated Ron, who would become defensive and ultimately aggressive when it came to making important decisions.

Ron's passive-aggressive personality left the family continually off balance, and they found themselves constantly giving into his whims or bad temper. June quickly realized he was not about to settle down, but she held her tongue, hoping to "keep peace in the family." With a baby added to the mix, June worried about Faye's future.

Ron automatically challenged anyone he perceived to be weaker than himself, but if confronted, he quickly backed down. An altercation with an old family friend left little doubt about that. Louie Kohler got into a scuffle with him over a horse. When Ron claimed the horse as his own and tried to lead it away, Louie did not hesitate to give him a swift punch. Ron scrambled out of sight and never confronted Louie again over anything. Louie, who was a great friend of both Bert and June, always wondered why Bert did not mete out the same justice. He was certainly big enough. But it was not Bert's way to engage in family fights if he could avoid it. He'd had enough of that growing up with his two brothers. Bert also knew he had to keep his temper in check, fearing he might be goaded into doing something he would later regret. Both Don and June were aware of this. Don was always a bit surprised that, though June made most of the decisions in their life, she would always capitulate to Bert when he put his foot down.

The birth of a beautiful little girl was enough to mitigate June's worries for a short while. Deborah Lynn Hall was the spitting image of Faye and won everyone's heart. She was, after all, Bert and June's first grandchild.

That spring, June came to the sad conclusion that she would have to sell her treasured log house and some of the land they owned. It was not a financial decision, but one of practicality. She was becoming exhausted with all the traveling and cleaning it entailed. She later said, "I just found my log house was another problem, and I hardly ever saw it anyway, so I sold it and twenty acres." It was a hard blow as it was the only real home she'd ever had that provided the ordinary comforts most people took for granted. She and Bert decided to buy a trailer and live in the trailer court at Lake Louise. This significantly cut down on travel and work, but now she felt she had no real roots at all. She did have more time to concentrate on the business in the mountains, though it certainly cut back on her chance to paint. There just wasn't time or room, and she did not have the opportunity to sell any of her paintings.

Though the property was sold, the Mickles held onto the house that winter, to give Faye and Debbie a place to live. Ron was not providing a home for them, so June asked Faye to act as housesitter. This way Faye could keep it in good shape before it sold the following spring.

June's prediction that Ron would not settle down proved accurate. He moved to the ranch with Faye and the baby but was rarely around. This left Faye anxious and depressed. She missed her parents badly and, by spring, convinced Ron to buy a trailer at Lake Louise as well. At least Faye was close to her family and could make adjustments to keep working for the outfit. But Ron's increased drinking put a greater and greater burden on her. As her husband, he was not likely to lose his job at Timberline Tours.

By this time, June had twenty-three employees working for her. One of them was Dale Portman, another young man who'd learned a lot about horses and backcountry travel from the Mickles. It was invaluable experience that would serve him well in the future.

Dale's initiation into the outfit did not start out that well. His friend Skip Brouche was actually the one hired, but Dale was invited to tag along that fall on a trip to the hunting camp in the Siffleur. The first day took the crew as far as Skoki lodge. Dale had spent the previous summer working as a horse guide for Brewster's stable at Lake Louise. He had a nodding acquaintance with Faye and Don but had not met Bert or June. Bert and June were always open to any young man looking for work. The lifestyle did not appeal to everyone, and they were happy when a prospective employee was able to learn and adjust to the long hours. They would have liked more of them to be experienced, but time usually weeded out those who did not fit in, or could not handle the pace.

Almost like a frat initiation rite, Dale had to prove he could drink with the best of them and still put in a hard day's work. Unfortunately, on the ride in, either Dale's stamina or his judgment left this ability in doubt. Don had his supply of whisky, and the other two were told to be likewise supplied. Don was impressed that Dale made it to Skoki at all, considering his liberal consumption of whisky. Dale has a soggy recollection of sitting around eating supper and enjoying the fun. Some of the humor was definitely at his expense. Sly references to a tolerant horse putting up with lots of rope and a sloppy load that kept falling off, largely passed him by – but he was good-natured and could take a joke.

None of this really shocked June. Neither Don nor Skip were feeling any pain, but they did manage to skid the young aspiring cowboy to an upstairs bedroom. Dale remembered none of this, but he has a clear memory of waking up in the now pitch-dark room. Not surprisingly, he also realized his bladder felt like it was about to burst. With great care he felt around the room until he found the door. This did not help much as it only led to an equally dark hall that his quivering fingers traced up and back to the same room. In desperation he finally found a jug and relieved himself into this happily found solution. He figured he could sneak out early in the morning and deposit the contents in the proper facility.

Dale did successfully empty the impromptu chamber pot, but he was caught by Bert before he could reach the kitchen to scour it out. Bert told Dale to fetch some firewood, and when Bert wasn't looking, Dale set the jug aside. Bert, for whatever reason, saw the jug and instantly commandeered it for June, who was looking for a pitcher to serve the orange juice in. In dismay, Dale soon saw the jug filled with fresh-pressed orange juice, which Bert served himself. Since Dale was the only one who knew about the jug's previous contents, his only recourse was to keep his mouth shut and hope this secret would go to the grave with him.

Dale managed to recover well enough to get a good day's work in, and he would prove to be a valuable addition to June's stable of workers. One indisputable result of his days with the Mickles was the friendship that developed between himself and Don, which has lasted to this day.

Though June found life easier living at Lake Louise, something always seemed to bring greater challenges and more heartbreak. In 1967 Clara decided to return to Alberta to be closer to June and the family. Her stay in Kelowna had not proven to be as successful as she thought it might be. Contrary to expectations, she found the life there lonely with little to do. For a woman who had lived a full life, this was very limiting. When she found a small place in Banff that suited her needs, she decided to move back to Alberta – but it was short-lived. No sooner had she settled in than she began to feel poorly.

June noticed a change shortly after Clara moved. She recalled noticing a problem when they decided to take in a movie in Calgary. This of course, was in conjunction with picking up supplies for the next trip. June had a lot to do and welcomed Clara's help. But one look at her mother made June think twice. "Mom, are you sure you're up to it? I can manage on my own, you know."

It was early summer and things were getting busy at the lake. Business was up, and June always seemed short-handed. She looked at her mother with concern because it was not like Clara to pass up the opportunity to shop – especially when entertainment was involved.

"No, I'm alright," Clara replied. "I can manage, but I will stop at home on the way back. I'm sure I'll feel better in a few days. Maybe after a rest I can come up to the lake for a few days. It would be good to see Faye and the baby. Maybe give Faye a break. She hasn't been riding for weeks now."

Clara looked at June tiredly, not wanting to reveal how bad she really felt. She knew something was wrong when the thought of visiting Faye and Debbie – who was like a ball of fire bouncing around their small trailer – made her feel exhausted.

"Sure. We'll see. I still have lots to do around here."

When June stopped in a few days later, she was truly alarmed. Clara was on the couch and the place was a mess.

"Alright, Mom, I'm making an appointment for you right now to see the doctor. Probably should have done that long ago." She immediately cleaned house and made Clara comfortable in bed then called the doctor.

June was not prepared for the doctor's news after his examination. He had further tests to do but told them he was pretty sure Clara had cancer, and it seemed fairly advanced. June and Bert sat in the doctor's office as he explained the next step.

"Well it looks like cancer, I believe a tumor in her stomach. We should operate immediately and see if we can remove it all. I've explained that to Clara, so can you bring her to Calgary? I've booked the operation for early next week. I don't want you to worry at this point. We still don't know for sure what we're dealing with. Your mother is only seventy-two, which is not that old really."

FAYE, CLARA, DEBBIE AND JUNE

June could not have agreed more. She expected to have several more good years with Clara. Up to this point, Clara had always had the energy and looks of a much younger woman.

The operation revealed the worst. The cancer was inoperable. It was so advanced the physician did not even recommend chemotherapy. In a sad interview he explained that it would only make her very sick with little chance of doing any good. Surprisingly, once Clara recovered from the operation, she felt well enough to return to her apartment. She hated being in the hospital. It was the end of August, the time of year Clara loved best, with the crisp nights and warm days brightened by slanted fall light that made the forest colors seem luminous.

The disease ran on its own agenda now, as if there was a hurry to be done and move on to some other victim. June spent all her available time with Clara, cherishing the short days left. June felt anesthetized at times, drifting through the days in semi-shock at how she could lose someone so precious that quickly. By mid-September Clara became too sick for June to care for properly, and she was taken by ambulance back to the hospital.

She died on September 21, 1967, a cold, snowy day. Though June was as prepared as she could be, it was a terrible blow. Having brought June up for many years as a single mother, Clara had formed an unusually close bond with her daughter. She had been June's mother and best friend all of her life. June had just never imagined a life without Clara in it. She never would get over the loss completely, but she still had her family and a life choked with work, giving her no time to dwell at length over her loss.

The summer concessions and fall hunting seasons were very demanding, making winter seem like a holiday even though they were still running both Temple and Skoki lodges. But June had the help of Rita and Norm Smith at Temple, and Skoki was only open for about two months after the New Year.

To supplement their income during the winter, Bert looked after a small gift shop or Derrick's grocery store in Lake Louise village, which he very much enjoyed. From October to December, Lake Louise was pretty much deserted and most businesses closed down, giving the proprietors a much-needed break. By November, the fall hunting was over, and like many others, Bert and June took the time to travel to Las Vegas and other southwest locations. June grew to love the desert scenery and was soon capturing her impressions in paintings. She and Bert also enjoyed the casinos, having grown up playing poker most of their lives. Unlike Bert, June was actually a moneymaker, as she was a skillful player and was not muddled by too many drinks. She kept a close watch on Bert and cut him off gambling if he started to make a dent in her earnings. For the most part, they came home with money in the bank.

Back at home, running Skoki was getting exciting, with many high-profile people wanting to stay at the lodge. It was gaining quite a reputation for excellent accommodations, beautiful scenery, and exciting activities. Among the better-known guests were Bobby Orr, the hockey player for the Boston Bruins, and Pierre Trudeau and his family. June especially liked Bobby Orr, finding he had an excellent sense of humor and that he readily engaged in all the activities offered. Bert managed to impress him with his skills as a hockey coach but was quite surprised (and very pleased) when Bobby asked him to coach one of their training camp games in Banff.

One mistake the Mickles made in the first year of running Skoki was to book a ski crowd simultaneously with a group of snowmobilers. It was not a good combination. The two groups had divergent interests that mixed as badly as oil and water. In 1966 Parks Canada allowed skidoo recreation in the Skoki/Red Deer area of the park; it was a poor decision that was doomed from the beginning, given Parks's mandate to preserve wilderness and wildlife. With the Mickles' ranching background, they were used to using skidoos for work and recreation and did not foresee a conflict. Naturally, the cross-country skiers valued the quiet way of traveling through the mountains and were grievously opposed to the use of skidoos in the park.

SKIDOO CLUB AT SKOKI

The skidooers set the stage when they went roaring by the skiers on the way into the lodge, wrecking the ski track. People who espoused this lifestyle of using machinery to get anywhere soon became known as "piston heads." The raucous skidooers, like their machines, were a loud, noisy crowd that liked to party. The party that evening soon got out of hand and, before Bert realized it, the skidooers took the fun outside and spent most of the night on their machines, roaring up and down the valley trying to outdo each other in stunts of bravado that surprisingly did not lead to injury.

The next morning, Bert and June had a rebellion on their hands. June was taxed just to manage any dialogue when the sleep-deprived skiers said – in no uncertain terms – that they should never book the two groups together. The conflict was just short of having an all-out war, and June was glad that the skiers did not demand a refund. The affront to the skiers was based on tradition; the lodge was originally built to be a skier's haven, and skidooing for recreation was viewed as a sacrilege. The situation was ultimately resolved when all motorized recreational vehicles were banned in the national parks.

Despite many good times spent at Skoki or on the trail, June was feeling the effects of the draining workload she had undertaken over the past five years. The workload and constant family tensions left her with little appetite, which led to her eating only irregularly. This resulted in hemorrhoids that became more and more painful. This is a common condition experienced by up to fifty percent of the population, which generally clears up with a change of diet or activity. It can also be easily treated with proper medication. In severe cases, though, surgical excision is the only remedy. It is a serious operation that is accompanied by significant postoperative pain that can take weeks to recover from, and June was not spared.

One of the events leading up to this condition was a particularly aggravating confrontation with Ron. It seemed to June that she was the only one who ever stood up to him. He had begun to insinuate himself into the business more and more, after he'd realized he held a trump card he constantly waved over Bert's head. If Ron did not get his way, he immediately threatened to take Faye away, which would effectively isolate her from the family. Like Bert, Faye hated confrontations and usually gave in to Ron's tantrums. His unpredictability left her afraid of what he might do.

A problem arose when some horses had to be replaced with fresh stock they kept at the Ya Ha Tinda. June was alone with this problem as both Faye and Bert were in the hospital. Faye was in for back problems, while Bert was in to treat an old injury to his hip. In 1967, a horse had fallen on him while he'd been crossing Porcupine Creek on the Siffleur River. This had led to sciatica.

Ron insisted on going to Ya Ha Tinda to collect the stock, but he was hung over from drinking and was in no condition to drive. June was fed up with his bullying and insisted on going herself.

"You can't truck them," he yelled. "You don't know what to take or which horses to bring back!"

June was livid. She replied quietly, but in a tone that left him blustering. "I know every one of our horses and exactly where they are going."

His reaction was not quite what she'd expected. She had called his bluff, which came as more of a surprise to him than to her. He had never encountered such a blunt confrontation from June before. For once he could not threaten to take Faye away, which gave June the confidence to stand her ground. Ron backed down and even became civil enough to help her load the horses.

The trip to the corners near the Ya Ha Tinda was terrible. She had seven horses in a six-horse trailer she was pulling with their old green truck, which did not have four-wheel drive. She was traveling alone with no help if things got dicey. And things got dicey almost as soon as she left the highway. It was late fall and the roads were in poor condition and would only get worse as she drove into the mountains. She decided to take the long route through Bearberry to avoid some of the bigger hills, but even that was not much better. As the roads worsened, she became very concerned about getting up the hills.

Finally, her worst fear became a reality when the truck powered out on a particularly slick hill. Somehow she managed to stop before slipping back into the ditch. Cautiously, she got out and put rocks behind the trailer wheels to keep it slipping farther into the ditch if the horses started jumping around. It was impossible to try to unload the horses over the yawning ditch without risking injury when they tried to slither out. If they lost footing in the wet, sloping trailer, they might even hang themselves from the halter shank that tied them to the metal hitch.

With mixed emotions, June retreated to the cab, trying not to panic while she considered the next course of action.

There was little else she could do as the day faded. In fact there was nothing she could do but wait for help.

With great relief she finally saw the dim lights of a truck looming on the horizon. She could not believe her good fortune when she realized it was a park ranger driving a much more sensible four-wheel-drive truck.

Unfortunately, the fellow did not understand why she hadn't unloaded the horses. He was not a horseman and did not see how dangerous that would be. But he was justifiably concerned about having the power to pull her out. He could do some serious damage to his truck trying to haul all that weight over the steep section, when they were already on a considerable incline.

"Do you know what you're asking, lady?" he questioned. "I don't think I can do that."

"Well, can we at least try? I'm sure we would injure the horses if we tried to unload them and then there would be a real mess. And I can't leave them here in the trailer – they could get hypothermic and start falling down."

"Okay, just pray we don't run into anyone barreling over the hill."

To his surprise he managed to skid them up the hill. He stopped at the top and came back to see how things were.

"Listen, I think I should just keep going. We'll unhook here to get down the hill, but I better take you up the next one. It's even steeper, but after that you should be okay."

June was almost sick with relief. She really wanted to get the horses back safely for the winter.

She finally reached Dave Wildman's place where the horses were unloaded and fed, but she could not stay. She wanted to get back to see how Bert and Faye were doing. Though Dave tried to convince her to stay the night, she insisted on leaving. In hindsight, she might have thought better of it.

The snow was coming down harder as she pulled out on the road home. Soon, the driving snow and descending darkness conspired to confuse her at the first intersection, and she became hopelessly lost. Fearing she would run out of gas, she finally emerged on a road she recognized, which led to Cremona. She decided then and there to drop the wretched trailer off with friends, who also had spare gas to top up the tank. Though it was dark and snowy, she would not stop. She felt an urgency to get to Banff to see Faye and Bert, and nothing her friend Jackie could say would persuade her to stay. June was very concerned that the family would worry about her if she did not show up soon.

She finally staggered into the hospital sometime before midnight. Bert's only comment was, "You look like you're the one who should be in the hospital." And at that point that was exactly how she felt. She was also relieved when a change in diet, some medicine, and a break from Ron cleared up her hemorrhoids.

June and Bert found time to get away from the business before winter set in, which was important for June, who was facing another season in Skoki without help from her two children. Faye was pregnant again and had work helping out at the ski hill, and Don had gone to Australia.

His restlessness after his split with Mary had June concerned that it might be a while before he settled down. Don was aware that he was drifting and came up with a unique solution. He had always wanted to go to New Zealand and Australia, and felt a trip abroad might be just the thing. He made arrangements, announced his plan, and left in the fall of 1969.

When Don returned that spring, he seemed like a new man. June thought that the trip to Australia was one of the best decisions he'd ever made. It had freed him from the shackles of his marriage and given him some distance from family problems. It also gave him plenty of opportunity to blow off some youthful steam without anyone looking over his shoulder. To June's delight he seemed to have matured a lot and was ready to take more responsibility in running the business. His whirlwind trip had curbed his edginess, making him much more fun to be around. He'd also made good friends while in Australia, two of whom returned with him to Canada the spring of 1970. In true Mickle tradition they were immediately adopted and put to work. Don's return lifted June's spirits, especially as he brought much-needed help, and she felt more than ready for another hectic summer.

Don even started paying particular attention to a shy but very attractive girl who worked for June at Temple Lodge. Grace MacKinnon was an art student from St. Andrews by the Sea in New Brunswick. Like many students from the East, she wanted to see the mountains and the most affordable way to do that was to get a summer job in the heart of the Rockies. Grace brought a refinement and sophistication to the relationship that Don had not experienced in previous liaisons, and he was entranced.

Though Don's presence and his growing relationship with Grace was a light on the horizon for June, the increasing family tension was not. Ron had begun convincing himself that he and Faye should be the rightful inheritors of the outfit, a stance that grew in proportion to the belligerence he developed with his drinking. No one had the energy to deflect the constant, daily hectoring. This new position may have had something to do with the changed family status of having another child. Faye was quite happy with the addition to her family, but it did little to settle Ron down. He was drinking more than ever, and most of the work of making ends meet fell to Faye. June helped by hiring Faye to bake pies for Skoki. This was very convenient for Faye, as she could stay at home to bake the pies, which earned enough for Ron and her to get by. It did not help that a lot of what she earned supported Ron's drinking.

June and Bert had always intended that Don take over the outfit, but it became increasingly clear that he could not do this if Ron stayed on. There was not room for both of them. Don loved his sister and did not want to add to her burden of dealing with her husband while trying to be a good mother for Debbie and Marty.

Like an ocean liner drifting into deadly waters, June had no idea how to change course to avert disaster. They drifted on, working just to keep things afloat. Ron was assuming more and more control, but as his addiction worsened he began to sell off assets to fund his drinking. Slowly he began to decimate the business.

Don found an escape from a worsening situation by working for the Yoho trail crew (as well as taking over the Emerald Lake horse concession with twelve horses), but he was always around to help when things got busy. He also kept his options open at Rogers Pass and had as much winter work available there as he wanted. June could find no such escape. Finally, the stress of running the business and dealing with family problems undermined her health. That fall she was diagnosed with cervical cancer.

"June, I called you in to discuss your latest physical exam."

June was a stickler for regular check-ups, something she wished she could impart to Bert and Faye. Both seemed to have a pathological aversion to seeing doctors.

"Your pap test came back positive for ovarian cancer. I know you feel fine right now – which is a good thing. It means we have probably caught it fairly early. But it does mean an operation. Since you are over your childbearing years, I recommend a full hysterectomy."

When June told Bert, he seemed almost panicky with concern. He would literally be lost without her. She managed to calm him down and even convinced him to visit her in the hospital, a place he hated.

Though the operation was a success, in that all the cancer was removed and she did not require backup chemo, it left June drained. Her nerves were shot, and the thought of going back to running Timberline Tours was something she could not face. She had run herself into the ground and wanted as little to do with it as possible.

With all that seemed to be going wrong, June was grateful when Don announced that he and Grace were getting married. They were happy together and had been going out long enough for both to know it was the right choice. Don had weathered a few wild years, but they had not taken him down a wayward path. Instead, he'd landed on his feet with his priorities intact.

Don continued to work at Emerald Lake and picked up work with the trail crew when he could. He also had the winter work in Rogers Pass to look forward to. This would be one winter he would never forget. The young couple settled on a house in Field, BC, which was close to the pony stand yet not too far from Rogers Pass to make it home on days off and holidays.

The winter in Rogers Pass was the wildest anyone had seen. It started snowing in October and did not stop until the following spring. The heavy snow year was not just confined to BC, however. The whole Lake Louise area experienced the same record snow as well as the concomitant record avalanches, which ultimately threatened the CPR rail line and the Trans-Canada Highway. Great things happened that winter. Peter Fuhrmann, the public safety and avalanche control expert for Banff and Yoho, managed to destroy the Sunshine ski area parking lot when the avalanche he released through control efforts slammed into the parked cars and the small ticket booth in the lot, reducing the booth to toothpicks. Amazingly, no one was hurt. A week before, Peter bombed Mt. Bosworth in Yoho National Park, creating a giant slide path from a previous small one. The huge slide first took out the Trans-Canada, then spilled over to destroy the CPR tracks below that. Again no one was hurt, but when he suggested bombing Mount Burgess just across from the hamlet of Field, residents rebelled and the town was left intact.

By 1972, Bert and June formally sold the outfit to Ron, but first split it up, giving Don control of Emerald Lake. It seemed fitting for Don, considering they had planned for him to run the business from the start. This way both children were provided for, and Don seemed happy with the arrangement. Grace was happy with this as well, particularly as they were expecting their first child. It was another bright light for both Bert and June, who really enjoyed their grandchildren.

Faye had hoped the added responsibility would settle Ron down, and she encouraged him in taking over the business. The couple could not pay for it outright, but Bert and June nervously agreed to terms they could handle. Despite this, it soon became apparent that the payments from Ron would not materialize. June was so glad to be out of the business, she did not let it get to her. She and Bert still had land holdings of growing value, and that fall they sold the remaining land near Millarville. The sale allowed them to purchase cheaper land near Spruce View just west of Innisfail. Things moved rapidly for them when they decided to build a house on the property that winter. The next summer they were offered an unexpected business opportunity running a small concession and gift shop at Num-Ti-Jah Lodge, just twenty minutes north of Lake Louise.

This was perfect for them. The lodge had been built by Jimmy Simpson, one of the original mountain men who made a living trapping, hunting, and guiding throughout the Rockies in the early 1900s. This early eccentric expatriate from England left a legend of his own with some people saying he had been encouraged by his wealthy, well-connected family to immigrate to Canada. The circumstances were never elaborated on.

The freedom of the West appealed to Jimmy, with its unfettered living uncharacteristic of more developed civilizations. In the mountains, no one paid too much attention to boundaries or social niceties, stopping short of lawlessness. It was Canada, after all.

When Jimmy Simpson camped at Bow Lake in 1898, he vowed that one day he would "build a shack here." Twenty-five years later he began building the first log cabin on the site and had a permanent base for his outfitting business. He called his operation Num-Ti-Jah, a Stoney word for pine marten, a small animal similar to a sable. In 1937 the Banff–Jasper highway was completed as far as Bow Lake. Jimmy, his wife, and their children Margaret, Mary, and Jimmy Jr. began expanding on the original dream of a "shack." In 1940, the Lodge had six guest rooms. By 1950, a beautiful log and stone hotel with sixteen rooms stood on the shores of Bow Lake. In the fifties and sixties, Jimmy Simpson's reputation attracted tourists keen to hear his stories. While Jimmy became a living legend, his son took charge of the Num-Ti-Jah operation. Jimmy Jr. had his own mountain stories from an outfitting career that spanned thirty-five years, ending in 1974, two years after his father died. Jimmy Jr. continued to manage the lodge until his retirement in 1996. He was also a good friend of Bert and June's, being cast from the same mold as his father.

Jimmy Jr.'s sister Mary was running a small novelty shop in the lodge to sell trinkets to the increasing swell of tourists. But this was not her bailiwick, and though the shop was a modest success, Jimmy found it a "pain in the ass." His sister did not have any real interest in it either and was not opposed to letting it die a slow death. When Bert and June stopped by for a visit, June's eye for business immediately kicked in when talk of running the store came up. She looked around and realized that, run properly, the store could be a moneymaker. Now that they were out of Timberline Tours, they needed another enterprise, and she and Bert jumped at the chance to run the store when Jimmy Jr. offered to lease it to them. June was sure her talent with painting and clothing would provide plenty of merchandise and that it would move well. But more importantly, it gave her the chance to get back to doing something she loved. Timberline Tours had drained her emotionally and physically, leaving her health in question at times. Those years had eaten up any spare time to pursue her painting, which she longed to do and now could.

June felt their life was finally on track. She was getting her health back, the new business was soon bringing in good revenue, and they had the winters to enjoy their new home at Spruce View. It also gave them a chance to travel to Las Vegas and indulge their love of gambling. The summer brought them back to Bow Lake where they were close to the family. Though they saw a lot of Don and Faye's families, taking delight in the grandchildren, they did not get involved with the outfit or how Ron was running it – other than to demur when he repeatedly failed to make payments.

Initially, Don had accepted Ron and tried to avoid any undue conflict that might arise when Ron increasingly took over the business. As time went on, though, he found Ron puzzled him.

"Ron became a prisoner of the rum bottle, but I always wondered if other troubles were underlying. I can remember being on long rides with Ron – when there was no liquor involved. He would be laughing and joking then suddenly yelling and mad at something and taking it out on his horse. He could then be sad and pensive – then thoughtful and reflective. It was like riding with three or four different people."

Despite finding life a bit easier, June found Ron's increasingly erratic behavior disconcerting and always worried about the effect it had on Faye and the children. June's anxiety over Faye's wellbeing took another hit after a close encounter Faye had with a grizzly bear.

Faye's one relief from the steady work and worries of domestic life was to go riding. If there were no clients, she would often go by herself to be immersed in the beauty of the spectacular scenery that assaulted the senses in all directions. The impartial monoliths bestowed a calm that transcended the daily grind of life. It gave her peace and a feeling there was something beyond her own worries. A favorite ride was to the Little Beehive Teahouse behind Lake Louise. The trail followed along the west shore then rose steeply to the open slopes above the Lake, revealing unparalleled vistas of Mount Temple and the Valley of the Ten Peaks in the southern distance.

She was deep in thought when she suddenly found herself on the ground. Then everything went black. She had no idea how long she was out, but when she came to all she could remember was the rotten smell of the bear's breath. Dazed, and off the trail, she had no recollection of how she'd gotten got there. She immediately climbed back up to the trail. Neither the horse nor the bear were around. She managed to reach a small bench where she was sitting, trying to clear her head, when an elderly couple approached. She was still incoherent and could only remember something about a bear. The man headed down the trail for help, leaving his wife with Faye.

Janey Pederson (a friend of Faye's) was looking after the pony stand that day and was taking a group of customers up to the lookout not far behind Faye. When she came to the trail junction that led upwards to the lookout and the teahouse, she spotted Faye's horse. Faye had been riding a new horse Ron had just acquired, and she'd been keen to get him out on the trail. Janey did not become concerned until she realized the horse's reins were still threaded through the running martingale. This meant Faye had not dismounted on her own. Janey immediately caught the horse and led him the short distance to the hitching rails below the teahouse, where she tied him up. Feeling something was not right, she told her group to stay for tea while she investigated further. She began walking back to the lookout trail when she ran into an elderly gentleman, who stopped her.

"There's a lady up there who seems hurt. She keeps talking about a bear and told us to turn back!"

Now seriously concerned, Janey followed him up the trail where she saw a wobbly Faye sitting on the bench. All Faye wanted to do was get away from everyone. She recognized Janey, but could not recall what had happened. More alarmingly, she could only vaguely remember her kids or her husband. Janey asked if she could ride, but that was out of the question. At that moment they met a Brewster horse party out for a day ride, and Janey immediately asked one of the wranglers to go back to the stand for help. The best solution was to keep walking, supporting Faye most of the way down the trail. They were almost down when Ron showed up with a horse. Janey remembers Faye's main concern on the way down was the impression she thought they were making on the hiker. "Janey, they'll think we're gay!"

Bert and June were at the stand when they got there and quickly had Faye in the car and off to the hospital in Banff. She did have a concussion, but she also had a large scratch across her belly. Though she could not remember what happened, it seemed likely that a grizzly had charged her. The horse must have spooked and dumped her over the bank. She had a welt on her head, and her confusion confirmed the concussion.

Faye recovered but realized that being knocked out had probably saved her from any further injury from the bear. She had been of no interest to it once she was no longer a threat.

GRACE MICKLE

In 1974, Don applied to work for the warden service in Yoho and was taken on that spring as a seasonal warden. He and Grace found a small white house in the town of Field where they settled in to welcome Flora, June's third grandchild. Grace was glad they'd found a place in Field that allowed them some distance from the close family living arrangement in Lake Louise. She truly liked Don's family but was never comfortable with Ron. He had an unpredictable edge that left her uneasy. Whenever Don mentioned there was a family reunion coming up, Grace would steel herself for possible conflicts that always danced around any long-term resolution to the family's problems.

Ron, who was accountable to no one but himself, began to depredate the business in earnest. As time went by, this lack of accountability took its toll. Other friends were aware of Ron's creative ways of generating revenue to support his liquor consumption. Soon, rumors filtered back to Bert and June that Ron was selling off the horses and equipment to generate the income he needed to frequent the bars. He was essentially running the business into the ground. Faye tried valiantly to allay the losses by running Skoki and the pony stand all on her own.

Eventually, the partying affected Ron's health, accelerating his mood swings. Faye was kept off balance, never knowing what to expect when his temper flared over minor aggravations. On many visits, Faye seemed subdued, almost afraid of annoying him, and Bert and June became concerned he was becoming abusive. Bert was terrified he would take Faye and the kids away if they tried to interfere.

Despite her frustration, June knew Faye would have to come to terms with the deteriorating situation.

Things came to a head when Ron sold their trailer and bought a house on a quarter-section of land east of Sundre. Bert and June co-signed for the purchase, giving the bank the collateral they needed. But there was still no way Ron could make the payments. He and Faye only had the place for a little more than a year before Ron was forced to sell to avoid a bank foreclosure.

Bert and June were seriously worried about Faye, who was herself at her wits' end. June wrote in her diary, "The stress was almost more than she could bear." Faye would take every opportunity to get away and spend weekends with her parents. During this time, she finally decided to leave Ron. This was a tremendous relief for the rest of the family, though Faye harbored residual guilt about not making a success of her marriage. But by now she realized staying with Ron would eventually become too hard on her and the children. Though they had to keep in mind that Ron still had rights as father to his children and he was undeniably a fixture in their lives, June couldn't have cared less what happened to him.

Any residual good will she might have had was totally shattered when she found evidence that he'd shot one of her favorite horses. June had found the horse's carcass at the Bow, with a hole in the skull. There was no immediate answer to how it had happened, even though June was sure Ron had had a hand in it. This was later verified when Geoff Wilson, Jim Simpson's right-hand man, confirmed that Ron had shot Mocha. Geoff said he'd been there. He felt so bad about the incident that he finally got it off his chest and told Bert about it a few years later. Bert just nodded and said, "He always was hard on horses."

The divorce opened the door to resolving the problem of Timberline Tours. With Faye no longer involved with the outfit, the Mickles were free to repossess it. They had no intention of picking up that line of work again, but they wanted to sell it before Ron could render it completely worthless. The most valuable aspect of this holding was the license to operate in the park. Only two outfitters were granted this right in Banff National Park, meaning no competitors could set up an operation in the Lake Louise district. The other outfitter was Ron Warner, who ran his horse concessions and camps out of Banff.

It was heartbreaking to inventory what was left. When they finally sold to Paul Peyto, the business was worth only what they had bought it for twelve years earlier. Twelve years with no financial gain or business growth. Ron had also alienated many of their regular guests, but they hoped that, under new management and ownership, some of these old friends would come back. Feeling somewhat guilty about turning her back on those years that had brought so much joy and heartache, June wished Paul Peyto all the best and turned to welcome a much quieter life with Bert and her family.

Chapter XI

THREE DEATHS

In the spring of 1974, when Don showed up in his warden uniform, complete with new Stetson and a badge number, June felt life was moving in the right direction. The warden service was an excellent job that presented endless possibilities. It offered security, a regular paycheck with benefits, and exciting, varied work. The first few years were not quite as secure, as it was a seasonal position with only six-months' summer work, but there was work in the winter as an avalanche observer. The government was hiring at this time, and it would not be long before Don got a full-time position.

The warden job required wearing several hats. A warden had to be proficient in law enforcement, fire management, backcountry patrols, public safety and mountain rescue, resource management, and avalanche control in the winter. Very few people joined with expertise in all these functions, so the learning curve could be steep. Don was well-grounded in avalanche work, and his horse proficiency made him a valuable asset. His outdoor skills for backcountry patrols were invaluable, and though his skiing was not at Olympic

DON IN UNIFORM

level, it was solid, and backcountry travel was not a problem. Like everyone else, he had to learn law enforcement, but in those early days, once you knew how to write up a ticket and turn on a siren and lights, you were good to go. He was also familiar with guns, another necessary requirement. His biggest challenge was learning how to climb. Both Bert and June looked askance at him when he described some of the climbs he was required to go on. Rescue skills were also mandatory, which gave him a few thrills.

One of the unexpected benefits of the job was the chance to work with many old friends. Dale Portman, who had worked for the Mickles in the mid-sixties, was also working as a warden and had just that year obtained a permanent position in Yoho. Other friends like Bob Haney and Perry Jacobson were similarly employed in Jasper and Banff respectively. John Nylund would eventually become the barn boss in Banff. To everyone's surprise, even Keith Foster, who would eventually become Chief Park Warden of Grasslands National Park, was now working as a full-time warden in Jasper.

What Don did not expect was to be working for Hal Shepherd, who had recently qualified as Chief Park Warden in Yoho – the same Hal Shepherd who'd so vigorously chased Faye around the kitchen, after he'd gotten into the whisky at the Windy warden station.

Hal had a fearsome reputation due to his drinking and the fact that he looked like a one-eyed eagle kicked out of the Green Berets. He had lost his eye as a child and often wore a black eye patch. He actually had a glass eye, which had an eerie effect, as it was difficult to tell where he was looking. He also insisted on wearing a peaked military hat, and on occasion packed a handgun in a shoulder holster hidden beneath a military jacket. The military look was honestly won as he had fought in World War Two and had been a Japanese prisoner of war. In fact, most of his war years were spent surviving that ordeal. As a sergeant major, he'd been responsible for the men under his command. His care for them had resulted in him being bayoneted by a guard when he refused to let sick men be forced to work in the mines. For this action, Hal received the George Cross Medal and an MBE in the British Empire.

Don was much relieved when he learned that Hal had quit drinking (a stipulation for his promotion to CPW), as some of Hal's exploits during the earlier part of his career were scary just to listen to.

Now that she was free of Ron and the pressure of trying to make ends meet, Faye was also settling into a rewarding time in her life. Bert and June had bought her a small trailer to live in at Lake Louise, which meant she could support her children and stay close to the family. She did not even pretend that Ron would provide child support, let alone alimony. It wasn't worth the stress to even ask for anything. This way, she did not feel she had to give him visitation rights, unless the children really wanted to see him. By now, Debbie was eight years old and Marty was two years younger. More importantly, June was pleased to see that Faye was meeting new friends and starting to go out again. Soon the family settled into a routine of working at the Bow in the summer and moving back to Spruce View for the fall and winter. When Faye sold the trailer and moved in with her parents on the farm, the children had a real home. They attended school near Innisfail, where Faye found work at the local restaurant.

June was now able to get back to her painting in earnest. But for two to three months of the winter, she and Bert traveled to Arizona. They also found time in the next few years to add on to the little house to make room for the kids and a sewing room for June. After the hectic years of running Timberline Tours, June was amazed at how normal life could be.

Faye was still a young, attractive girl, and it was not long before she began dating again. But she decided she needed a place of her own when a relationship with close neighbor Lyle Pedersen turned serious. Before long she purchased another trailer that she kept on the property. It gave the couple the privacy they needed as the kids still had their bedrooms in the main house. It was a cozy arrangement since Lyle spent most of his time there. June could see that Faye was really happy for the first time in many years. Only the restaurant job was not Faye's first choice, and she was quite happy when she found better work at the local co-op.

The next three years were precious for June. Don was doing well in Yoho, learning all aspects of the job and working with close friends in the service. Both he and Grace liked Field where they were raising their daughters, Flora and Johanna. Bert and June were doing well at the Bow thanks to June's skills as an artist and her business acumen. She did not rely totally on her own creations – making enough to sell would have taken all her time – and out-sourced a lot of the work to other people, who brought different craftwork with a distinctly Canadian theme. June was fairly discriminating about acquiring new products, and most things sold well. In the evening she would paint an animal or scenery on a leather hanging and sell it as soon as the paint dried.

She still had to put up with keeping Bert in line from time to time. Don laughingly recalls a minor incident with a purloined picnic table. One of the maintenance workers in Lake Louise told Bert they were replacing some of the older picnic tables, and that he should grab one of the discarded relics before the tables were gone. No one saw any advantage in letting perfectly good tables go to waste. Bert agreed; they could always use it in the yard at home. He merrily loaded the picnic table in the back of his truck and off he went home with the prize, via Rocky Mountain House. An over-zealous tourist saw the park table in an unmarked truck and reported it stolen to the Rocky Mountain House RCMP detachment. They passed the information on to Ted Loblaw, the ranger in the district and Bert's nephew. Ted lay in wait and soon saw the offender driving slowly down the highway. (Bert never did drive fast.) When Ted pulled Bert over, both men were surprised.

"Bert. What have you got there? You poaching picnic tables now?" Ted was laughing.

"Well, these young guys in maintenance said I could have it. Why are you here?" Though he was laughing, Bert was annoyed that such a small thing as taking a picnic table was an offence.

Ted wasn't worried. "Tell you what. Just have me over for a beer some day when you're set up. Better use for it any way than keeping it for a bear-feeding station."

Don chuckles when he recalls, "June didn't see the humor in it either when she heard the story."

The summer of 1979 began promisingly, with unusually good weather at the Bow. The season started out busy and just got busier. The endless tour groups rolled in, and June had record sales pushing Canadiana at Americans, Germans, Japanese, and of course, Canadians. The now-familiar large tour buses seemed to dominate the highways. They had days that never seemed to end, but as the sun sank below the bluing mountain peaks, June's ledger showed clear profits.

The only thing that nagged at June was Bert's surprising lack of energy. She did what she could for him but was too distracted by work to worry much over it. On occasional breaks, she would let her mind wander back to the previous spring when they had had such a good time in Las Vegas, despite some occasional bad luck at the Keno tables. These were good days that held promise for the hard-won golden years ahead.

But by July, Bert was uncharacteristically listless. She had actually noticed him slowing down that spring but hoped it would pass. It didn't, however, and June began to worry. Getting Bert to a doctor was harder than pulling molars from a horse. She decided to enlist Faye's help in getting him in for a check-up, but even Faye had no success. When September rolled around, June had made up her mind. Bert was doing no better, so she booked an appointment with their doctor in Banff.

Perhaps Bert knew intuitively that life often takes an unexpected channel. The night before going to Banff he woke up with a pain in his chest and complained of indigestion. But some Rolaids seemed to calm him a bit, and he was able to get a few hours sleep.

June was now really concerned, and at first light she went to the shop to see if anyone could cover for them. She was still looking for a replacement when Bert appeared at the door. He just stared at her with a queer expression. Suddenly his eyes glazed over and he sank slowly to the floor with a small moan. Desperate to get him on his feet, June almost screamed when she yelled for help. With dismay, she realized he was unconscious and barely breathing. She knew immediately that it was a heart attack.

Her cries finally yielded results when one of the staff rounded up a doctor from England who was staying at the lodge. Things moved quickly. They soon had a helicopter dispatched from Banff, which arrived in minutes. Meanwhile, the doctor administered oxygen while he performed chest compressions to try to restart Bert's heart. The look on the doctor's face was careful, giving no indication of what he suspected. The helicopter seemed to arrive immediately, and soon they were loading Bert into the helicopter for a quick flight to the Banff hospital. It was the last time June was to see him alive.

Numbly, June accepted a ride to Banff with one of the staff boys, her mind going in all directions. Her scattered thoughts left little memory of that ride, except to think how to contact her children, hoping against hope the news would not be as devastating as she feared.

The look the doctors gave her at the hospital did not surprise her. Their soft words brought home indisputably that Bert had died. A grey chasm yawned ahead with no signposts to follow. Deep in grief, June's dazed mind tried to absorb what they were saying. Quietly, with compassion, the man in the white coat explained that it would not have mattered if Bert had been in the hospital when the attack occurred; nothing could have saved him from the massive collapse of his heart. A fleeting thought passed through June's mind: Bert had the greatest heart she had ever known. It was bigger than the whole world, so how could it have failed? But she knew he had not lived the healthiest of lifestyles. Though not a big eater, he certainly was rarely without a cigarette, and God knew he liked his rye whisky. His physical exercise, though considerable when he was young, had all but subsided to late nights and a good game of cribbage.

By the time June was able to speak to Don, she was exhausted. He had been informed by staff at Bow Lodge and had subsequently talked to Faye. He, too, was numb with shock and made his way to the hospital as soon as he heard. With Faye and Don present, June could let go for a few moments, but nothing eased the pain that would take years to cope with.

She had loved him completely from the moment they met, and that had never diminished in all their years together.

Bert had been a well-loved man who was a fixture in the mountain community for decades, and the outpouring of support seemed unlimited. At first, June wondered how she would cope with all that needed to be done, but soon found the work helped by being a diversion from grief. She had no lack of help either.

BERT SMOKING AT POINT CAMP

It was a large funeral with so many old friends and family wanting to take leave of Bert that June could hardly keep track of who attended. She also had her hands full consoling Faye, who had relied so heavily on Bert over the years. Don was just as heartsick, but had his family to help with his loss – and he also took on much of the burden of making all the arrangements. June had always been on top of things financially, which meant all the paperwork was in order. After the reception at Lenny's farm, June went back to the Bow. As she later said, "What good could I do moping around?" She had spent a lifetime working hard and found this discipline kept her going. But this kind of fortitude had barely been tested.

June doggedly went to work in the shop, to cope with a brief spurt of activity in mid-fall when people came out to enjoy the last fine days of the year. Finally, she kept busy closing the shop for another year. She enlisted Faye's help when she could, not just for the help but to distract her from missing Bert too much. Though she kept it to herself, June's daily diary entries indicate she was not that successful at this.

Faye found her father's death difficult to accept. His loss only added to the stress and anxiety she had been struggling with after living with Ron. One day in early November, she showed up for the weekend complaining of feeling tired, with a nagging pain in her stomach that rebelled against even the blandest food. This time June would brook no stalling and insisted Faye see a doctor as soon as she returned to Spruce View.

Faye hated doctors and had never cultivated a reliable family physician. The local doctor in Innisfail, used to the stoic residents of small town Alberta, dismissed her complaint as nothing more than a passing stomach ache and prescribed Diaval (used primarily to help regulate glucose levels in the blood), then sent her home. When that did not help, it only served to reinforce Faye's distrust in doctors. She knew her trouble was not sugar levels in her blood. Three weeks later, she was lifting some heavy cans from a shelf at the Co-op when she felt something "break" in her stomach. It terrified her. She knew instinctively that it was life-threatening – a thought she quickly suppressed, keeping it to herself. This time June took her to a highly recommended doctor in Red Deer.

With only a brief exam after listening to her story, this doctor sent her to an oncologist in Calgary. It took little time to diagnose cancer and have Faye booked immediately for an operation in Edmonton. She was in so fast she had no chance to object to the operation.

A week later, when Faye was recovering in the hospital still weak and groggy from the anesthetic, the oncologist took some quiet time to let her know what they'd found. They had successfully removed a tumor (which was very large), but further exploration indicated that the cancer had spread. They would be much clearer after the lab results came back from the tissue samples they took from other parts of her intestinal cavity, but he wanted her to start chemotherapy immediately. He also told her the cancer was terminal, and he went on to say that chemo could give her five years of life or possibly more, depending on how she responded – and they would not be bad years.

Faye said nothing except to ask the doctor not to tell her family. She could not bear burdening June with such news so close to Bert's death. Besides, she had faith in other cures and thought there might be a way to over-come this disease outside of the hospital, which terrified her. She did not tell June or Don of the fatal diagnosis, but did say she would not undergo chemotherapy. No one else in her family was happy with this decision, but they managed to live with it because they didn't know the cancer had spread.

While Faye was recovering in Edmonton, June and Rita took a short trip to Las Vegas. Over the years, working together had led to a friendship that had deepened, particularly after Bert's death. June found Rita to be a good traveling companion and felt, with all that had happened, that they both needed a vacation.

The first few days were a welcome change, but by the fourth day, with poor luck at the tables, June found herself longing to get home. Rita agreed and they left soon after. June was relieved to be on the plane but could not relax, plagued by a foreboding premonition that led her to comment to Rita, "Everything runs in threes. I wonder what will happen next?"

Rita replied, "A person never knows." But she too was glad to be heading home. Three days later, as June was leaving for Innisfail, the phone rang. It was Don with the shocking news that Rita was dead. She'd had a massive heart attack and died in her sleep during the night. June could barely sit down. Rita had died on the twelfth of December, and the funeral was held on the fourteenth. Even this was plagued with disappointment, as the weather was so bad June could not get to the service. She was beginning to feel singled out for tragedy, never getting a break from misfortune.

Things never let up. Faye got a call from Edmonton to come in for more tests. But Faye did not believe in western doctors; she was deeply spiritual, and that led her to put trust in faith healers. She had heard about such psychic healers in the Philippines and decided that she would try their alternative cure.

These healers in the Philippines had come to the attention of the North American public in 1959 after the publication of *Into the Strange Unknown*[5]. The book's authors called the healing practice "fourth dimensional surgery," and wrote, "We still don't know what to think, but we have motion pictures to show it wasn't the work of any normal magician, and could very well be just what the Filipinos said it was – a miracle of God performed by a fourth dimensional surgeon."

This was a scary road to take, as many physicians and spokespersons for the American Cancer Society denounced the practice as fraudulent sleight of hand which, though not dangerous in itself, posed a serious threat to recovery because the patient usually chose this method of healing over the more proven benefits of Western medicine. The healers were essentially doing nothing to slow or halt the progression of the illness.

But certainly the videos of the process looked convincing. Faye's mistrust of doctors and hospitals was very real, as was her faith that a spiritual healer could accomplish what Western medicine could not.

Her faith was so deep she convinced everyone around her that it would work. It certainly was not something June could deny her, and by mid-December both she and Faye were in Edmonton to obtain Faye's travel visa for the Philippines.

Faye was not scheduled to leave until the twelfth of January, giving them time to enjoy the Christmas holidays together. June recorded in her diary a happy Christmas

---

5   Ron Ormond and Ormond McGill, *Into the Strange Unknown*, Hollywood, Calif.: Esoteric Foundation, 1959.

with all the family and felt, for a brief time, a relief from the grief and anxiety that had dominated her life since Bert's death. It would not last for long. One of the harder things she decided to do was commission a plaque for Bert and have it placed on a small hill that overlooked their land and the faint trails that led to the beautiful pastures of the Ya Ha Tinda. Here they spread his ashes, some to the land that was his last home, and some to the sky to travel to the places he loved.

Despite a pleasant family Christmas, New Year's Eve brought a bleak observation. June reflected on the past year, recording in her diary: "Good for business but unforgettable tragedy. Bert and Rita died. Faye got sick. Feel like things will never be normal again." June found she often had to leave the farm and go on short trips to Innisfail, ostensibly to shop, but mostly because looking at Bert's plaque made her too sad to stay.

Faye came home on the twenty-ninth of January. June could barely conceal her anticipation, but it was mingled with the recurring anxiety of what she would find. She prayed that Faye had made the right decision and had to accept her daughter's belief in a spiritual healing.

The plane seemed to take forever to dock and allow the passengers to disembark. Tears sprang to June's eyes when she saw Faye. Her daughter looked radiant. Faye was relaxed and tanned and happy. It was hard to believe she had been on a trip to save her life instead of just a relaxing holiday in the tropics. June could hardly wait to hear what they had done.

Faye was eager to relate her experiences in the Philippines and describe the 'psychic healing.' Sure enough, her album was full of pictures of her tumor being removed by a white-coated doctor lifting out a bloody mass from her stomach. She soon had her family convinced that these doctors had cured her, although June still had personal reservations.

Faye and Lyle decided to take a trip to Las Vegas to be married, and June later wrote, "She and Lyle decided to get married even though we didn't know how permanent her cure was. Of course, Lyle and I didn't know her condition was terminal."

During those months, Faye was as happy as she could be. She and Lyle were married as planned and had a real break, enjoying all the shows and glitter of Las Vegas. They were actually married along with another couple who were good friends and helped to make the holiday seem special. It was wonderful and carefree, and the joy Faye felt was conveyed to June when she called home to check on the kids. In all honesty, June could tell Debbie and Marty that their mother was doing fine.

When Faye returned she was even more revitalized and ready to get back to work. She wanted to pay off the rest of her loan from June for her trailer and decided to work on a share basis at the Bow. She planned to sew clothing to sell and spend time in the shop looking after sales. This arrangement made June very happy as it meant she had her family back, with the kids joining them in the summer months. Lyle still had work at Spruce View but took as much time as possible to be in the mountains with his newly acquired family.

They were busy as usual, which made the next three months seem to fly by, but June cherished every minute, refusing to think of the future. She just concentrated on living in the present, treating every day as a special gift. Though Faye still had not mentioned anything about the true nature of her illness (refusing steadfastly to believe it herself), June's intuition, which she desperately suppressed, made her fear that this short, happy interlude would not last long.

By July her fears were realized. Faye's old complaint of stomach problems returned, as did her listlessness. At June's insistence Faye saw the doctor, who confirmed her tumor had returned. To no one's surprise, all Faye wanted to do was go back to the Philippines. Despite the obvious fact that the spiritual healers had done little good, her faith in them never wavered. She stayed on at the Bow for a few weeks until she could get a flight in August. If anything, this trip, with the stress and anxiety of travel, made her even sicker. She was much deteriorated when she got home.

Faye was well enough to help out for a few more weeks, but by September she could not manage that either. June recalled, "By then, I guess we were all desperate and found out she didn't have a chance." This time there was no hiding what the doctor had told Faye from the beginning. Both June and Lyle now knew the doctor considered the condition terminal. Lyle was so sad that June thought it best to tell Debbie; he had no way of concealing how he felt, and Debbie was old enough to know something was very wrong.

Don accepted this news without much surprise, though having it spelled out meant there was no more comfort in hoping for a miracle. It was a miracle the spiritual healers could not ever deliver. Faye was the only one who could not accept this. Once again she insisted on returning to the

Philippines, and once again June sent her off, terrified she would never see her little girl again.

Tragically, the only miracle was that Faye actually did make it home one last time. Lyle had gone with her to the Philippines this time, but he barely got her back before she died.

It was a terrible ordeal. Faye experienced some physical relief once she checked into the hospital to have her stomach drained. The build-up of fluids caused by the tumor was giving her severe discomfort, but once the pressure was relieved, she felt well enough to go home. Her fear and mistrust of doctors was unabated and she could not stand to remain in the hospital any longer than necessary.

June was so overcome with grief, she agreed to take on the care of her daughter despite the objections of hospital staff. Faye required twenty-four-hour care, but June was just happy to have the remaining time with her. It was hard for her, though. She wrote, "I nursed her for the two to three weeks that she lasted, and it was such a heartbreaking thing to watch my daughter fade and die, and feel so helpless." Her only consolation was in knowing that Faye was as happy as she could be, surrounded by those she loved. On good days, Faye was able to watch her beloved horses grazing in the pasture close by where Bert lay. Even the dogs and cats cheered her up.

Finally, on a quiet Sunday morning on the ninth of November, Faye turned to Lyle and said, "I have no more pain … " June had seen, early in the morning, that there was a change in Faye's condition. She seemed to be fading as she gave in to a body that could no longer sustain her.

June had no idea that death could come so fast after such a struggle to live. She thought she had time to get to the phone to call Don, hoping he could be there to say goodbye to his sister, with whom he had shared so many vital years. She could scarcely believe that Faye slipped away in that short interlude and felt cheated of sharing her final moments. But it was a blessing that Faye no longer had to fight the crippling pain that is cancer's legacy. It was over.

June fought the bitterness that threatened to swamp her when she wrote, "She died as bravely as she lived. I guess those years of stress before, brought this on. It just wasn't for her to have lasting happiness."

In June's heart, she blamed Faye's illness on the years of misery that her first marriage brought her. At least Faye had escaped that situation soon enough to have a few years of happiness with Lyle and the children.

Faye had been worried about leaving the children, but aside from having to live with losing their mother, their future was in good hands. The first year after Faye died, Debbie and Marty lived with Lyle, and June shared the responsibility of looking after them. This was no burden, but a source of joy for June. Debbie in particular was a huge consolation as she grew uncannily into the spitting image of her mother. Everything about Debbie, from looks to mannerisms, embodied Faye. She had, in addition, a peace and confidence that reassured June her life would be long and happy. Marty was as steady as anyone could wish in a boy in his early teens. Of course there was no lack of family support coming from Don and his family.

The funeral was held on the farm at Spruce View. It was difficult for all those in attendance because Faye was so young when she died. With some comfort, June had a headstone placed next to Bert's, taking solace in the idea that they were together on the land they both loved. She strongly felt their presence on quiet evenings, feeling they had never really left. After all, she needed their united strength to help her with the years ahead, which she was determined would not to be wasted in unending sorrow. She was left to live for them and the family she still had, and the living would be as complete as she could manage.

Chapter XII

JUNE'S STRENGTH

At sixty-one, June was not old when she faced her remaining years without Bert or Faye. Nonetheless, as winter claimed the country, she seemed to descend into a hibernation of loss, dealing with life as the hours turned to days. The thought of facing the long span of coming years devoid of the people who had charted her happiness was beyond her. But the demands of daily life still bound her to the present.

Death brings its own obligations, with unavoidable burdens of estate settlements and extended family entanglements. In Faye's case, neither was protracted, though the situation was somewhat onerous with regard to Ron Hall. He had insisted on coming to the funeral, and he was still the father of Faye's children. Despite that, he was in no shape to provide a home for them (even if he had wished to), and both Debbie and Marty continued to live with Lyle. The children were the closest ties June had to Faye, and they were incredibly dear to her. Giving them up to Ron or his family would have been impossible.

JUNE AT 61

While Faye was in the Philippines, June had kept busy with her painting and sewing, preparing for the coming summer at the Bow. She was also keeping company with a local rancher. Charlie Byre did not live very far away, and Bert used to visit him a lot when he was alive. Charlie always showed up for dinner or parties on special occasions, and Faye saw no reason for this to stop with Bert's death. She felt a special tie to Charlie, whom she viewed as a surrogate father to Faye, and that attachment had deepened when she'd realized that Faye was dying. June soon found her time increasingly taken up with shopping for him or going to local bingo tournaments. It eased the loneliness they both were burdened with. Charlie was also handy around the property, and was there to help her run the place. Her days of "being blue" began to diminish – something she only became aware of after looking back on what she had accomplished.

Before she died, Faye had quietly encouraged June to deepen her friendship with Charlie. When Charlie had to have a minor operation, Faye stepped in and insisted they take him to the hospital. She and June also kept the house clean and the animals fed during his absence. But the health issue had prompted Charlie to try sell his place. He eventually sold it to a young couple who agreed let him stay on while he convalesced. Unfortunately, to young people, time runs at a different pace from that of the elderly, and they quickly grew impatient with the arrangement. By degrees they put pressure on Charlie to move on – a situation he was not prepared for.

With Faye's encouragement (probably suggestion), June began to contemplate both Charlie's and her future. She decided that it might be best for all if Charlie moved in with them. In many ways this made a great deal of sense. It seemed to her that Charlie was "always there to lean on," and she and he were good friends by then. The arrangement meant they could share the cost and care of the cattle and hay, which could be stored in the sixty by eighty-foot shed on June's property. It also seemed to bring a little hope for the future, and everyone's spirit lifted as an energized Charlie launched into building a round corral for Faye, hoping she would be well enough to use it.

Faye, of course, did not get well. By the end of summer, Charlie had to get his crops off before the new owners could move in (they rented in the interim) while June faced the increasing burden of caring for a now visibly failing Faye.

After Faye's death, June gave considerable thought to her relationship with Charlie and how she felt about her future.

She reflected on her diary's summation of her life at that point. In her "memorandum" of 1979 she wrote:

"Good for business but unforgettable tragedies. Bert and Rita died. Faye got sick. Feel like things will never be normal again."

At the end of 1980 the entry read:

"Good year again for business but tragedy struck again, as my dear Faye died November 9 of cancer. I know life will never be the same again. Can't seem to think of the future but live for the day."

June did not feel particularly old at sixty-one, and she knew she had many years ahead of her. Reluctantly, she started to give serious thought to how she would spend it. Most of her life had been tied up with care for others and the daily obligations that faced her. She had never truly sat and considered just herself, or even felt she had time to ponder any long-term strategy with regard to her future. She was also tired and incredibly sad. One thing she did know: she was not ready for any romantic involvement that might lead to marriage or any other commitment. She made that abundantly clear when she installed a single bed in the basement for any overnight gentlemen callers.

Within a short time after losing Bert, she realized she liked her independence. Charlie remained a friend who helped around the place and provided companionship and an anchor for the kids. They shared many things in common, and June even introduced him to the delights of travel – something totally new to him that he enjoyed immensely.

After Faye died, the New Year seemed to signify it was time to get back to the hard work of living. With determination,

June turned to the one love that gave her pleasure. She painted every day through most of January. It was during this time she did a lot of her best work. She also sought escape through travel and hauled Charlie on his first trip beyond the comforting borders of Alberta to the bright lights of Nevada.

Nevada and Las Vegas were much bigger and glitzier than anything at home but still had the cowboy culture that made Charlie feel at ease. It was also warm, a treat Charlie had not anticipated but thoroughly enjoyed. Though they were only gone for a week, it opened Charlie's eyes, and he was happy to continue broadening his horizons.

When they returned, life took on a more normal pace with looking after the kids, visiting friends, and undertaking small household projects. June was even up to going to local dances about which she would report faithfully to her diary that she "had fun."

The kids were growing up fast, which helped them deal with their own grief. Marty immersed himself in school and hockey, while Debbie fulfilled the promise of becoming as beautiful as her mother when she was crowned Snow Queen for the Innisfail School District. She was the spitting image of Faye, and June often looked up, momentarily confused, thinking her daughter was standing before her. Memories would instantly flood her until, with an effort, she would return to her work.

By April, she felt it was time to introduce the kids to the world as well, and she towed them off to Hawaii. She did this despite the fact that Marty was in a cast with a broken leg (hockey). This limited his ocean activities, but

DEBBIE (AND MARTY) WITH HER
SNOW QUEEN CROWN

not so for Debbie. It was a short trip that they all enjoyed, and it left them ready for their first summer without Faye. With unexpected enthusiasm, the family launched into spring, June's favorite time of year, planting, cleaning, and rounding up the stock. It was time to think about the mountains again and what that would bring.

June still ran the store at Bow Lake and was very busy that spring with collecting, marking, and moving the inventory for the summer season. Debbie, now almost sixteen, started helping her out at the Bow. With the additional help, June was free to run back and forth between the shop and Spruce View, recording, "busy all day, tired," in her diary once again. Marty spent the holidays at the farm, helping Lyle, his adopted father, and Charlie with summer chores. Lyle had grown close to the kids over the years and took his role as stepfather seriously.

June's life with the kids and Charlie took on a rhythm she had not expected, simply because she did not expect anything after the shock of her devastating losses. At the time, it was enough just to get through the days, let alone plan a future. She did not really think about it too much until a year had passed and she was able to write, "Have got through another year. Been very busy but have not forgotten Bert or Faye." She ends with a positive note: "Charlie and I bought ½ van ea. Hope to go to New Zealand in Feb. 1982 with Don."

She kept her promise and did go to New Zealand. Don and June left on February 12, for Los Angeles. It was a long flight with a further stop at Hawaii and then Manila. They stayed there for a few days before going on to New Zealand. One of the highlights of this trip was to meet up with Laurie McConachy, who had worked for them long ago in Skoki. It was a nostalgic reunion as it sparked memories of better days when both Bert and Faye were alive and all the heartache and worry were yet in the future. After spending another two weeks touring and visiting, they departed for Calgary and home.

Life carried on with ups and downs as the kids worked their way through the remaining years of high school. In 1984, June had been talked into opening a shop in Innisfail – possibly thinking it would be a good venture for Faye and the kids. Her heart was never in it, though – and less so after Faye was gone. The kids were too young to be involved with anything requiring that level of commitment; they were still not settled on what career choices they were interested in. The store never did do well, so by the end of 1984, June closed it up, happy to be rid of the added work that went nowhere.

In the spring of 1984, Debbie graduated from high school and decided to go on to collage to take a Teacher's Aide course. That same year Charlie died. He had shown signs of ill health off and on, but June thought it had to do with his heart. They took several more trips to Las Vegas and other desert locations, which were great for both of them. This time it wasn't his heart, it was cancer. By the time they found it, Charley had only a month to live. One thing that brought June consolation was his reassurance that the last years of his life were some of the best he'd ever had. She wrote, "I hope he enjoyed his last few years and that I helped him when he needed it as he helped me."

November was never a good month as someone always seemed to be dying. June was happy to welcome in the New Year, which had always had her looking to the future. Between Charlie's death and closing the shop in Innisfail, she could not report too favorably on that year. It was not a success, either personally or financially. For the first time in many years, she had not come out ahead. Also, she was on her own again.

When Bert and Faye had died, June still had the kids and Charlie to look after, but now the empty nest really was empty. Marty was going into grade eleven and would soon be looking for a career away from home, just as Debbie was now doing. Though both kids still formally lived with her, it seemed they were away more often than at home. They were young, attractive, and motivated. June needed others her age and background to provide companionship for a woman soon about to turn sixty-five. But as usual, work kept her busy.

June came from an era when people made lasting friendships not dependent upon a network of computers or cell phones, and she still had plenty of friends. Initially she traveled with other couples who invited her along on various trips, but she was never comfortable with this. Understandably, she always felt like a third wheel no matter how good the friends were. She preferred to travel with other women in the same circumstance as her – not an uncommon situation. Though she felt it likely she would meet another man to be a companion and possibly share living arrangements with, she was quite certain she did not want to lose her independence. Cohabitation was fine, but she had absolutely no interest in remarrying.

June's house was not totally empty, since Marty was still going to school and Debbie was finishing her training course. Though June's life was much less hectic, she still spent the winters painting and working on other products to sell in the shop during the summer. Priding herself on finding unique items that were of good quality, she had expanded a bit and went to various craft shows looking for more material that others could sell on consignment. She also kept up her traveling, going regularly to Nevada or other places in the American Southwest during the winter. Bingo and dances remained a staple for getting her out on long winter nights.

By the winter of 1986, June actually had time to spare for herself, but she was too healthy and active to consider actual retirement. When Patty Loewen suggested they open a novelty shop in Lake Louise, she found it was just the antidote to fill those extra hours. Patty had no experience in this field, but she made up for that with enthusiasm and hard work. Lake Louise, despite being in a national park, was expanding its tourist facilities to accommodate rapidly increasing visitor use.

That spring, June got a call from a man she'd met in Nevada earlier that year. He was attentive and, at the time, June had enjoyed his company. Still, she was surprised when he phoned later that spring, saying he was in the area and wondered if he could visit. She saw him briefly, but summer kept her busy, and she did not hear from him again until that fall. Gene, however, was determined to inveigle himself into her life and saw her on a fairly regular basis throughout the fall. They even decided to take a trip to Las Vegas before it got too busy at Christmas. On the odd occasion, though, the diary entry cryptically indicates there was some tension between them. Just before they left for Las Vegas, June wrote, "Gene and I are not on good terms." It was a rare deviation for her to record any personal conflicts, especially with reference to another individual.

It was with some misgivings that June went to Las Vegas with Gene and another couple, but June was an optimist and felt it was worth giving the relationship a chance. The warm, exciting atmosphere of Vegas might be just the place to overcome any difficulties or conflicts.

But things did not go so well. June had only moderate luck gambling, which did not improve her equanimity. By the second day, she lost track of Gene and had to go to the rodeo with friends. Two days later she reports that Gene "got ornery" and stormed out. She smoothed things over so they could at least get home together, but she now had some serious reservations about their relationship. She did not get any encouragement from the family, either, in pursuing this involvement. If anything, they encouraged her to send Gene back to Nevada. Don felt that Gene was a "fortune hunter," an impression he got after Gene tried to "borrow" some money off June. June was not overly wealthy, but she had worked hard and done well in business, leaving her moderately comfortable. She also had significant assets which Don suspected looked good to the old reprobate. Don also did not think Gene was much of a cowboy – deducing it was an image he had projected to gain favor. On top of this, Don found him to be downright boring. Some faults could be overlooked in the Mickle family, but boring was not one of them.

Gene hung around for about a day after returning to Spruce View, but another disagreement left June and him fed up with each other. That day, "Gene packed up and left." He darkened her diary no longer. By the first of January 1987, June summed up the year, writing, "Not a bad year. Started new shop at LL with Pat. Deb is there, Marty living with me. Traveled some. Episode with Gene, but feel free again. Nothing bad happened."

Her year-end summaries reveal how she felt both personally and financially, but leave a wistful impression, implying that there are no guarantees of a future that is free from loss or tragedy. But knowing there is satisfaction in a life well-lived, she always had hope for a measure of happiness. There is a definite sense she was not finished with life when she wrote, " ... feel free again." To a large extent, June continued to live in the present, with fingers crossed against the unforeseen.

That summer, Marty graduated from high school, leaving him pondering the logical next step. His upbringing had exposed him to an eclectic array of skills he'd mastered in the daily demands of keeping the farm at Spruce View going. He had handled the trauma of adapting to a broken home and losing his mother early on with a resilience and strength that surprised many people (other than June). He was maturing rapidly and, before June was sure he was ready, insisted on moving out. When he developed a steady relationship with a girl he met at school, he decided it was time to move out and live on his own.

June did not think Marty was old enough for this at seventeen but realized she could not hang on to him forever. She instinctively knew when to let go and allow her children to follow their own lives, even if she did not agree with their choices. They happily came to a compromise when June suggested Marty and his girlfriend take over Faye's trailer. It was just sitting there empty, and it certainly fit the young couple's budget. Marty had also decided to pursue welding as a trade, for several reasons: welders were in high demand in the province's rapidly developing oil patch, it paid well, he enjoyed it, and he could train from home. June was not sure if his relationship would lead to marriage, and she did not really encourage it, but for the time being she was happy to have him close at hand until he finished his training.

With Gene out of the picture, June was once again a lone wheel, which she felt acutely when visiting or traveling with happily married friends. She got around this by renewing her riding in earnest. She had been at Spruce View long enough to become good friends with her neighbors. They had always had a common interest in riding, but June had been too busy or up to her neck with the latest crisis to have much time to go out with them. But with both shops running smoothly and no pressing personal commitments, she felt free to take friends up on a long-standing invitation to go on riding excursions in the foothills. They focused on an area west of Bragg Creek, where they staged daily rides from a well-established horse camp.

There were a number of people from various horse clubs, which made gender or marital status a non-issue. June enjoyed these excursions immensely and soon found another companion. Ed unfortunately had a heart condition, and when she met him he was recovering from a heart attack. But he was undaunted. He was determined to enjoy the time left to him and was soon escorting June to local dances around the country. For the next two years, they rode extensively together, even buying a stock trailer to haul the horses to areas she had not seen in years. One memorable trip was to Skoki where she showed him all the trails she used to guide on. They were content in this relationship (though he did not live with her) and covered many miles before he died of a heart attack in 1989.

The previous summer, she had quit the concessions at Lake Louise and the Bow, leaving her free to enjoy the last winter with Ed. Just a few years earlier, she would have been surprised at how much enjoyment she was getting out of life.

She did not give up entirely on her connection to the mountains and the pull they had on her. Don and family were now living in Banff National Park, and she visited frequently. She was active and fit for her age, and Don did not

JUNE ON DECEPTION PASS

hesitate to take her on backcountry trips where they had the use of warden cabins. It was sheer luxury to travel like this after years of setting up camp with cold, wet tents.

Another watershed for June was in 1989, when Debbie married a boy she had been seeing since she started nurse's aide training. Wade Smith had grown up around Spruce View, and his family had been neighbors for years. When Marty moved to Slave Lake for work, shortly after finishing his welding apprenticeship, June began to feel rudderless. Though it signaled the beginning of a lonelier period for her, she was relieved that both children were maturing without significant teenage angst or rebellion. She was also glad that Debbie seemed to have found a solid match with a local boy from a good family.

Still, life had a way of throwing a curve ball when least expected. Ron Hall had not abandoned his children completely, and had been making overtures to be involved in their life. Perhaps he saw them as individuals who would care for him in the future as his own ability to look after himself spiraled downward. Marty, in particular, wanted to establish a connection with his father and help him get on his feet.

Debbie was not sure she wanted Ron back in her life, but could not say no when he requested an invitation to her wedding. She approached June about him attending and they both agreed to "bury the hatchet" for the day.

This did not sit well with Lyle, who saw himself as the children's real father, having invested more in their well-being than Ron ever had. Despite the tension caused from this conflict, the wedding came off beautifully. Don and Grace's two teenage girls, Johanna and Flora, were the bridesmaids and Marty gave Debbie away.

With Marty working up north most of the year, Debbie and Wade moved into the trailer. It was comforting for June to have them close at hand, but the relationship had changed. June had been through this with her own children and knew how to adapt. Debbie was not a little girl any more, but a young woman starting her own family, and June was more than happy for her. She fervently hoped Debbie would be spared some of the hard things both she and Faye had had to cope with.

With things rolling smoothly, June could relax and live the rest of her life doing what she enjoyed most. She was still not, nor ever would be, looking for a new husband, but she enjoyed the company of men and was not prepared to live entirely alone. On reflection, she had to admit that the ones she did form a relationship with usually seemed to die. She had certainly been racking up the men.

Undeterred, she soon found a new companion. This was not surprising, for June was full of fun and possessed with a zest for life few women her age had. She was soon riding with Laurence, another local cowboy who liked to ride and dance. He was a good traveler and enjoyed making trips south in the winter. He was also younger than she was.

June was riding a horse Don had given her from his own string. It was not a young mare, but it had picked up the bad habit of pulling back when June approached with the saddle. The mare was also a tall horse, and at June's age this made it difficult to mount. She still got out riding but was never really comfortable with the horse and the saddle seemed to get heavier every year.

To her delight, Laurence found another horse for her. It was a little pinto just retired from the pony chuck wagon races. With this background, the horse had speed and could be a handful, but he was a perfect match for her. His name was Comet, and she had never loved a horse as much as him. To pay for him, she sold the mare to an old family friend and embarked on more years than she had anticipated riding in the foothills of the Rockies.

The same could not be said for Laurence. Though she enjoyed his company for the most part, she found him overbearing at times. He evinced a sense of proprietorship she did not appreciate – especially when it led to unwarranted criticism. When he started criticizing how she dressed or what she ate, she knew it was not what she was looking for in a relationship. She had grown too independent and had survived too much trauma to put up with this unnecessary strife.

The final straw came at the rodeo finals in Las Vegas. She and Laurence had gone down with another friend, whose husband had recently died and who wanted to get away from home for a while. Perhaps it was the presence of a third party, but whatever the reason, June finally had enough of Laurence's harping. She continued to go riding with him after they got back, but made it clear she wanted to see less of him. She was quite happy to continue their association but just as distant friends.

The position of being on her own again did not last long. The family friend who'd bought her horse was someone she had known most of her life. Louie Kohler was from a ranching family the Mickles had known while living in Black Diamond so may years ago. He had been a close friend of Bert's, and they had much in common. Being with Louie brought back fond memories of more carefree days when death and worry were on a distant horizon. June was comfortable with him and was glad when the acquaintance was renewed with the sale of her horse. But Louie was a very shy man. He had an eye defect that made it hard for him to make friends. Unexpectedly, he came into some money when he won a lottery, and it opened up several doors for him. He could now afford an eye operation that he had always put off, and June was happy to see him through this. In fact, she encouraged him to take this step.

He was grateful for this support and soon revealed that another ambition he harbored was to travel. His eye impediment had always held him back, and no one had ever

JUNE AND LOUIE (2001)

volunteered to go with him. With his new looks, he was ready to tackle the world.

The lottery ticket went a long way. Once Louie had recovered, he and June took a cruise to the Caribbean for ten days. Louie had never experienced a culture as foreign to him as those exotic islands, but to his surprise he enjoyed the novelty and June's company – as well as the warm weather. June considered it a success and was happy to have found another traveling companion.

Louie was six years younger than she was and a person she had known most of her adult life. But though he eventually moved in with her, she continued to regard him as just an old friend and not a romantic involvement. None of her family would have cared if she did. They all knew Louie and were essentially glad June had someone other than herself around the place to help out. Her home at Spruce View was still well out in the country and not close to any immediate services. Maintenance was always a problem even with help from Debbie and Wade and from Marty when he was at home.

Though June was okay with Louis living in the house as a companion, she was not about to put up with any unwanted problems. As Don writes, "Louis had been married to a Scottish woman and had traveled to Scotland with her a few times. It was not a happy union. She (Margaret) died of cancer in the late 1980s. Lou was on all sorts of addictive pain medication for his bad back. He smoked a lot and was drinking too much when he started visiting Mom. She got him to see a different doctor, and he managed to quit the addictive drugs, quit smoking and curbed his drinking – with a lot of coaching from Mom. She made it quite plain to him that she didn't want a man hanging around that had a drinking problem!"

Shortly after he moved up north, Marty broke up with his first girlfriend, and he was enjoying the freedom of a good-looking young man out on his own. He did not say much, but it was not hard to see he was not about to settle down with any one girl for a while. In fact, the family could not keep track of all the different girls that showed up on his arm when he was in town. June could see he was just enjoying those carefree times when the next day, week, or month brought no worries or obligations. There would be plenty of time to be serious later. Marty had no real wild streak in him like some of the Mickles or his father Ron, for which she was very thankful.

Her confidence in him was not misplaced. After a few years of knocking around the north, he returned to Cochrane. He was looking for work other than welding, and June decided to send him on a computer course. The training was geared toward running gas plants and turned out to be his future vocation. About this time he married and settled down.

Before Louie moved in, he and June took another trip together, this time to England. June wanted to meet some of her English cousins on her father's side, and Louie had relations in Scotland. It was a bit arduous with all the traveling, but it was a trip she looked back on with fondness. Though it was pleasant, it left June in no doubt where her heart lay. England was quaint and had its cottage charm, but the weather was oppressive, and she could not escape the feeling she was confined to a small, sea-bound island. The ocean had its appeal, but she was land-oriented and missed the vast emptiness of the Canadian West. She was always happiest when she got back to the freedom and solitude of the mountains.

She was now approaching seventy and was glad to learn that Debbie was pregnant with her first child. Great-grandchildren had never been on the horizon when she was younger, but she was deeply pleased to see her family growing and prospering. She reflected that seventy seemed old to her in years, but not in how she felt. She was still very active with her riding, traveling, and painting. Her paintings were more popular than ever, and she continued to add to her income from numerous sales. She also took up playing horseshoes in a local tournament and was soon the regional champion and steadily adding trophies to her shelf.

When Louie moved in, she had a room built for him, giving them both the privacy they needed. Other than that, they acted like an old couple who had been together most of their lives. In a sense they were. As she wound her path through the nineties, she and Louie settled into routine, little marred by catastrophe or tragic upsets. The peace those years brought, though, never kept the sadness out of her voice when she spoke wistfully of Bert. Beneath the laughter they shared when bringing up old memories, there remained the underlying wonder: why could she not have had those years with Bert?

June and Louie soon got into a routine of spending the summer on the farm, then moving for six months of the winter to the Mesa area, in Arizona. They bought a trailer that they left there all year round, which became a second home as they nestled into their quiet lifestyle. June, though young for her age, had had enough of living on the edge of an adventurous life.

June and Louie stayed at Spruce View longer than she might have if left on her own. Just before Louie moved in, she'd had several painful bouts with a troublesome gall bladder. She finally had an operation to remove it, but stomach problems would continue to plague her off and on for the rest of her life.

During this period, Don's daughter Flora married and was starting to raise her own family. More great-grandchildren were on the way. Marty, to no one's surprise, also began contributing to the growing number of great-grandchildren.

The last of the grandchildren to marry was Johanna. If any of June's grandchildren exhibited some of the unsettled traits of the Mickle family it was she. Johanna, however, directed her energy into physical pursuits, which led to work in the outdoors. Her greatest interest and work came from catering to camps as a cook and as a professional hiking guide.

June and Louie varied their routine little through the nineties, but by 1999 her eyesight began to fail. She had been diagnosed in 1998 with the onset of macular degeneration, which arose from untreated glaucoma. She'd had this condition in a minor form through most of her adult years, but it had not interfered with her eyesight and had gone undiagnosed well past the time she should have been receiving treatment for it. The macular degeneration was catching up rapidly, and she and Louie both knew they could not live on the farm when it got worse.

For the first time in her life, June would live permanently in a town. She decided on Cochrane as it was close to Spruce View, and she would not lose touch with her friends. It was also a good location to be near her family. She and Louie found a condominium in a seniors' facility close to the Bow River where they could take daily walks along the local paths that hardly seemed to be in a town. She loved it. In fact, they both liked it so much they decided to sell their trailer in Mesa and spend most of the year at home. Despite June's failing eyesight, she could still paint, using a large magnifying set-up that could handle smaller canvases.

Louie was happy, having a reason to get a much bigger television set.

June also still had Comet, now residing not far from Cochrane on a small acreage owned by her old friend, Billy Monroe. Throughout these years, June never failed to ride in the Cochrane rodeo parade, dressed as always in the cowboy hat and buckskin jacket she had made years before as a gift to herself.

Her last entry in the handwritten story she started years ago sums up the wealth in friends and family that she deservedly earned. "I had a lovely 80th birthday party at the Legion. All my friends and family were there. We had a lovely turkey and ham dinner with all the trimmings. Later a bunch came to see our new condominium."

JUNE AND COMET IN THE COCHRANE PARADE

Epilogue

June Mickle's long life spanned almost a century, during which time unprecedented leaps in technology led to a global culture that bears little resemblance to the simple life she was born to. The wild country that she explored as a child is now largely parceled up into small, expensive acreages owned by people who earn their living in an urban environment rather than from the land. Because she witnessed these changes in her lifetime, she adapted and accepted the new world that her grandchildren helped create. Her last home in Cochrane, with all its up-scale amenities, was a haven she truly enjoyed. The electric-powered dishwasher, TV, vacuum cleaner, and washer/drier were luxuries she never dreamed of throughout most of her adult life, and she had no problem accepting the ease they brought to her life.

She also kept up a regime of regular exercise that included daily walks along the river, ending with a heart-pumping climb up a flight of boardwalk stairs. On her eightieth birthday, she was fit enough to ride Comet in the Cochrane parade. Riding was her passion, and she did not stop until she could not get in the saddle unassisted. When Don had to help her mount Comet and showed worried concern, she knew it was probably her last ride. As it was, she only sat in the saddle long enough to get her picture taken.

During the last ten years that she and Louie lived in Cochrane, she was content to see that, for the most part, her offspring were thriving happily in their family lives and chosen careers. Don had forged a successful and rewarding career in the warden service, and both Debbie and Marty were happily married and had families of their own. Flora and Johanna also married and were adding to the extended family with more great-grandchildren. Family celebrations were busy, crowded, and loud.

June remained close to Debbie and Marty. As Debbie put it, "We were always very close, and she treated Marty and I more like her kids than her grandchildren." Debbie and her husband Wade Smith have two daughters. They live on a quarter-section in the Glendale Hall area, not far from Innisfail where they both work.

Marty's roving eye finally settled on Sue, whom he married, and they had three sons. He quit working up north when an opportunity arose to work with computers in the oil industry, and it proved to be quite lucrative. He and his family now live near Sylvan Lake on a small acreage with an impressive house and several horses. His sons are skilled riders, but most of their riding is done in local arenas. Bert's impressive backcountry skills never got passed on much beyond Don.

Marty had conflicted feelings about his father, Ron Hall. He felt that if Ron were given a chance to play an active role as grandfather to his and Sue's sons, he might turn his life around. He tried to get Ron interested in his children by taking him on fishing outings and other events he thought would pull him in. None of this worked. Marty tried valiantly for a few years, hoping when they arrived for a visit they would not find Ron drunk. Finally, in frustration, he made his visits fewer and fewer, and eventually stopped altogether. It was too discouraging for his young boys to witness this final decline.

Ron died alone in a small shack he had been renting off an old friend. The Halls looked after the funeral, but it was a small affair that only Marty attended on behalf of the Mickles. June was quietly relieved that Ron was gone and would no longer be a drain on her family.

During the last years of her life, June faced the daunting task of dealing with the loss of her eyesight from the macular degeneration. This was a great loss for her as it meant she could no longer paint. She tried to cope with this handicap by using very large lenses for small works of art, but eventually even that did not help. Her condition also put an end to the winter trips to Mesa. She missed the relief of the warm weather during the cold Canadian winters, but did not miss the ordeal of travelling that far from home. Despite this setback, June continued to enjoy the company of friends and family, knowing she was lucky to have a good supply of both.

Before June died, Don brought Comet to town, giving her a chance to say a final farewell to the little horse that, comparatively speaking, was even older than she was. Comet did not outlive her for long. He died a year later at the age of thirty-one.

June often wondered if her story would ever be told. I, as the author, had known June for several years and thought her life a remarkable one. The decision to pursue this story cemented itself after I was privileged to sit in on an interview June was giving to a young woman from Edmonton, who was collecting stories on people growing up in the Rockies in the 1920s.

I was sitting on June's soft pink couch that seemed to have no bottom. Across the room, the grey winter light filtered in from the front window, softly lighting June's elderly face. I was half listening to the many stories I had heard before when my attention was caught by a simple but revealing insight into her life.

June smiled shyly, wistfully describing to the young woman what it was like to live "at the tail end of nowhere."

"It was wonderful to sit with a sketchbook inside a warm cabin as a winter blizzard pushed snow against the door. I could watch a deer run across the far horizon on a summer night. I could ride as far as any horse would take me. I could sketch and paint the story of my own free life: horses, foothills, mountains, snow."

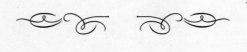